The Essential
PETRARCH

The Essential
PETRARCH

Edited and Translated,
with an Introduction, by

Peter Hainsworth

Hackett Publishing Company, Inc.
Indianapolis/Cambridge

Printed in the United States of America

15 14 13 12 11 10 1 2 3 4 5 6 7

For further information, please address:

Hackett Publishing Company, Inc.
P.O. Box 44937
Indianapolis, IN 46244-0937

www.hackettpublishing.com

Cover design by Abigail Coyle
Text design by Meera Dash
Composition by Agnew's, Inc.
Printed at Versa Press, Inc.

Library of Congress Cataloging-in-Publication Data

Petrarca, Francesco, 1304–1374.
[Selections. English. 2010]
The essential Petrarch / edited and translated, with an introduction, by Peter Hainsworth.
p. cm.
Includes bibliographical references and index.
ISBN 978-1-60384-289-1 (cloth) — ISBN 978-1-60384-288-4 (pbk.)
1. Petrarca, Francesco, 1304–1374—Translations into English.
I. Hainsworth, Peter. II. Title.
PQ4496.E21 2010
851′.1—dc22 2010026425

The paper used in this publication meets the minimum requirements of American National Standard for Information Sciences—Permanence of Paper for Printed Library Materials, ANSI Z39.48–1984
∞

Contents

Preface

Petrarch is one of the reference points of European lyric poetry, a figure who determined for centuries the paradigm of what poetry could and should be, or in the mind of his detractors, what it should not be. The core of this anthology is formed by a selection of about a third of the poems in his *Canzoniere* and includes famous poems, representative ones, and personal favorites, three categories that to a very large extent coincide. The other work in Italian that is included is *The Triumph of Eternity,* the last and most affecting poem in the sequence of six allegorical *Triumphs,* which were never quite finished but were immensely influential for two centuries after Petrarch's death.

Petrarch himself would have been surprised and probably disappointed to discover that his Italian poetry has generally been more highly valued since the Renaissance than his vast and varied production in Latin, the language that he and his friends saw as the natural medium for serious literature of any kind. Over the last hundred or so years scholars, critics, and educators have reassessed the significance and importance of his Latin work. There is now general agreement that it has to be taken into account in any overall interpretation of Petrarch as a man and a writer. The Latin writings are represented here by the third book of the *Secretum,* the imagined dialogue with Saint Augustine in which Petrarch makes the reader privy to a remarkable review of his own personal failings, and by five of his most important letters. These offer further perspectives on some of his major emotional and existential concerns and also respond to obvious questions, such as whether the woman he calls Laura actually existed, and how he himself saw the poetry in Italian for which he would eventually be best known. The reader may feel that the answers suggested by these texts are qualified and ambiguous, but an enduring part of Petrarch's fascination lies in his multifaceted ability to be both remarkably oblique and remarkably clear at the same time. It is no accident that his beloved Laura is a figure of light, and, as he himself observes, excessive light dazzles.

My warmest thanks go to various friends and colleagues who have helped me with their comments and corrections, especially Richard Cooper, the late James Council, Christopher Faram, Martin McLaughlin, Alexander Murray, William Mills, Simon Price, David Robey, and Michael Sheringham. I also wish to thank Rick Todhunter and Meera Dash at Hackett Publishing and Harbour Fraser Hodder for their transatlantic efficiency and friendliness. Jane Hainsworth has given me constant, much needed love and support throughout this book's absurdly long gestation, and I cannot thank her enough. I am responsible of course for the many imperfections that remain.

Peter Hainsworth, Oxford, February 2010

Introduction

1. Petrarch's Life and Career

Petrarch was born in 1304 in Arezzo. His father, Ser Pietro di Parenzo or Ser Petracco, was a notary from the small town of Incisa in the Arno valley, who had lived and worked in Florence where he was a member of the White Guelph party. Like Dante and many others, Ser Petracco was exiled in 1302 when the Black Guelphs took complete control of the city. Dante found refuge in the courts of northern Italy; Ser Petracco stayed with his family in rural Tuscany for a while and then moved to Avignon, which had become the seat of the papacy in 1305, and which offered the prospect of both refuge and employment. His family joined him in 1312, making a home in the small town of Carpentras. Petrarch thus grew up in Provence in fairly close proximity to the French-controlled papal court. Provence remained his base until 1353, though with frequent, lengthy absences.

His early schooling took place at home. He was then sent with his brother Gherardo to study law, first at Montpellier and then at Bologna, where he spent most of the years between 1321 and 1326. But Petrarch was unenthusiastic about law and gave more time and energy to Cicero, Virgil, and classical studies in general. On his father's death in 1326 he returned to Avignon, where he entered the service of the Colonna, a noble Roman family that under the headship of Stefano Colonna had kept its power and influence at the papal court in spite of the move to Avignon. Petrarch prided himself on winning the friendship of Stefano's sons: Giovanni, who became a cardinal and a figure of considerable power, and Giacomo, who became Bishop of Lombez in southwest France. He felt particularly close to the latter and spent the summer of 1330 in Lombez with him and some other friends. All three are notable presences in his writings.[1] There were also other lengthy journeys away from Avignon, which, as he claims in some poems, were dictated by the need to put as much distance as possible between himself and Laura (whom he had first seen in 1327).[2]

Petrarch was now a cleric, having taken minor orders in 1328–1329, purely for reasons of convenience, it would seem. He was granted a canonry in his diocese by Giacomo Colonna in 1335, which brought in a certain

[1] For more on the Colonna family, see the discussion of Letter 1 in section 5 of this Introduction.

[2] See Poem 360 of the *Canzoniere* and Letter 1.

amount of money but required neither his presence nor any other commitment. Similar canonries would follow in Italy as gifts from various patrons. The income they generated would make Petrarch moderately well-off in material terms, but being a clergyman would not play a significant part in his emotional life or his writings. So far as we can tell, it was never a consideration in his complex moral assessments of his feelings and behavior, nor did it stop him from having children by two unidentified women, a son Giovanni and a daughter Francesca, who were born in 1337 and 1343, respectively.

Petrarch had a difficult relationship with his son and an affectionate one with his daughter. But neither are mentioned much in his work and their mothers not at all. The female figure who dominates his Italian poetry and some parts of his Latin work (notably Book 3 of the *Secretum*) is the woman he calls Laura. Petrarch himself gives very little concrete information about her, and scholars have added nothing certain to what he says.[3] A personal note that he wrote on the flyleaf of the Latin manuscript of Virgil's works, which was one of his dearest possessions, soon after Laura's death in 1348 states that he first saw her on April 6, 1327, at matins in the church of St. Clare in Avignon, which the poems also say was Good Friday. There are hints elsewhere that Laura was married and had children. Otherwise, all that Petrarch's many eulogies of her reveal is that she was beautiful, virtuous, and intelligent, with blond ringlets, dark eyes, and a pleasing speaking and singing voice. She always rejected Petrarch's advances, though some poems suggest that she reciprocated his feelings. There are references to the two of them meeting and talking at times, as well as to Laura crying, or having an eye infection, or going away from Avignon for a while. But these ostensibly realistic incidents and everything else about her might, in fact, be literary invention, even down to her name. The dates, for example, look particularly suspicious. Not only does Petrarch first see Laura on April 6, but she dies at the same hour of the same day in 1348. What is more, April 6 in 1327 was not actually Good Friday. But Petrarch never allows Laura to dissolve completely into fiction. Writing in the later 1330s to Giacomo Colonna, who seems to have thought she was a purely allegorical figure,[4] he insists that both Laura and his passion are all too real. In spite of the omissions and contradictions (there are evident ambiguities even in this letter), and in spite of her absence from large areas of his work, it would be a cynical or unsympathetic reader who wants to delete Laura from Petrarch's lived experience. However much transformed in the processes of literary expression and elaboration, she remains a founding aspect of his Italian poetry and his work as a whole.

[3] There is no convincing evidence that she was Laure de Sade, the wife of Hugh de Sade (an ancestor of the famous Marquis), as was claimed by the Abbé de Sade in the 18th century, almost certainly in order to add to the family's prestige.

[4] See Letter 1.

This does not mean, however, that writing poetry for or about Laura was immediately important for Petrarch. He claimed later that he and his brother had written vernacular love poems and songs in the wilder days of their youth in Avignon but had given up such things as they matured. In fact, Petrarch was writing Italian poems at least occasionally, and perhaps quite frequently, during the 1320s and 1330s. Some of these survive, and a few (Poems 23 and 35 are the outstanding examples) eventually found their way into the *Canzoniere*. Much later he writes to Boccaccio that when he was young he did think of starting a large-scale project in the vernacular but then abandoned the idea.[5] In all probability, if he was writing about Laura at this time, it was mostly in his Latin poems.[6]

Latin love poems might be excusable in so far as important ancient poets had also written love poetry. But poetry in the vernaculars of Provence and Italy posed serious moral and linguistic problems. It was conventionally associated with youthful folly and predicated upon adultery and sensual desire, while the language of Tuscan poetry was still a provincial idiom, with no recognized grammar. It had made some impact outside Tuscany but was certainly not recognized as the national literary language. As such it was felt to be far inferior to Latin, which was understood throughout Christendom, was historically consistent, and brought writer and reader into contact with traditions stretching back directly to the Bible, the fathers of the Church, and the great culture and figures of antiquity. Petrarch and his contemporaries reveled in the exclusiveness of Latin, which preserved the secret treasures of learning for those who could appreciate them, and deplored the way in which vernacular writing was available to women and the uneducated. The vernacular was the *volgare*, the language of the *vulgus*, whose interests Petrarch always dismissed as primarily material and practical.

We might think that the main problems regarding the power and status of the vernacular had been triumphantly overcome by Dante. He finished the *Divine Comedy* not long before his death in 1321, when Petrarch was seventeen. As well as having popular appeal in and around Florence, the *Divine Comedy* had been quickly recognized as a masterpiece by Tuscan and northern Italian intellectuals. Commentaries were already appearing in the early 1330s, which treated it as a poem deserving the same sort of elucidation and study as, say, the *Aeneid*. For the young writer Petrarch, Dante seems to have been more like a threatening father than an inspiration. He pretends not to have read the *Comedy* until Boccaccio sent him a copy in 1359, and manages only grudging recognition of Dante's achievement in his letter of reply.[7] In the later letter to Boccaccio included here (Letter 4), he has become much more positive about Dante but still chooses to deprecate vernacular

5 See Letter 4.

6 Such as Letter 2, to Giacomo Colonna.

7 *Familiares* (*Letters on Familiar Matters*) 21.15.

poetry as a whole, largely on the grounds of the way it is mangled by uneducated performers. In reality, by the time this letter was written, Petrarch was working steadily on his own vernacular poetry, revising old poems, adding new ones, and gradually putting together what would become the *Canzoniere.* The problem seems to have been that, like other educated writers of the time, he could not, or would not, articulate serious arguments for the value of vernacular writing.

There were no such doubts about writing in Latin. In the vernacular, Petrarch wrote only poetry.[8] Everything else, whether in prose or verse, down to the marginal notes he made on drafts of his vernacular poems, is in Latin. We might find that surprising, but for Petrarch and his friends, Latin was the obvious choice. It was the intellectual and literary language of Europe, past and present, as well as the language of law, medicine, and philosophy; of the Vulgate Bible and the Church Fathers; and of Virgil, Cicero, and all the other ancient Roman writers that Petrarch and his contemporaries admired. But Petrarch's choice of Latin was not just a matter of convention and convenience. There was also a polemical edge to it with far-reaching implications that are bound up with his whole literary and intellectual stance.

Contemporary Latin usage had developed considerably over the nine hundred or so years since the fall of the Roman Empire. It was still recognizably the same language that the Romans had used, but it had grammatical constructions, stylistic conventions, and a range of vocabulary that were all new or different. In other words, it was no longer classical Latin but what would soon come to be disparaged as medieval Latin. Petrarch makes a sustained and in many ways successful attempt to discard nonclassical features and to recover and reenact the linguistic and stylistic practices of the great ancient authors. At the same time he programmatically avoids imitating any specific authors, such as Virgil and Cicero, who would regularly be cited in subsequent centuries as models for verse and prose, respectively. Instead he aims to configure a style that is founded on detailed knowledge of ancient literature but is unique to himself.

The rejection of contemporary practice, the recovery of the ancient past, and an emphasis on the self are hallmarks of Petrarch's work overall—recast, revised, defended, proclaimed in endlessly different ways, sometimes doubted, but never abandoned. Where his position shows itself at its firmest is in his dismissal of scholastic thought and writing, that is, the Aristotelianism of universities such as Paris and Padua, associated with the disciplines of law and medicine as well as theology and philosophy. In their place Petrarch sets the *studia humaniora,* the study of language, poetry, history, rhetoric, and moral philosophy, ideally in Greek as well as in Latin. Though his own efforts to learn Greek came to nothing, and he read what Greek literature he could in Latin translations, he proclaimed (citing Saint Augustine) that Plato was close to being a Christian, whereas contemporary Aristotelianism was

[8] One short letter in vernacular prose has survived.

fundamentally irreligious. In reality, he found it hard to be sure about the positive contribution of the *studia humaniora* to living a proper Christian life, as the texts in this book repeatedly demonstrate, and on the face of it he was hesitant even about the literary quality of what he wrote. It was only with the 15th-century humanists (Petrarch himself does not use the term) that the difficulties were surmounted. A fully classical Latin became normal, Greek texts were read again in depth in the original, and, for many humanists, the issue of Christian belief receded into irrelevance.

Until well into the 1340s Petrarch's literary activities were as much scholarly as creative. He reassembled and edited Livy's history of Rome, the surviving books of which had been separated from each other since the fall of the Roman Empire. He began building up the largest private library in Europe, which eventually contained more than two hundred volumes. He sought out manuscripts of works that had been lost for centuries and made them available once again, either copying them out himself or having them copied by friends or scribes. He made his first significant discovery in 1333: Cicero's oration defending the poet Archias (*Pro Archia poeta*), which he found in Liège in the course of a journey to Paris, Flanders, and Germany. More important for him was the discovery in Verona in 1345 of the sixteen books of Cicero's letters to Atticus, which gave him the idea of making a collection of his own letters.

As throughout his life, he was traveling a great deal in these years, driven, he says, by his own restlessness and the need to distance himself from Laura, and also acting at times on behalf of his patrons. But he also acquired a base. In 1337 he obtained a house in Provence near the Fontaine de Vaucluse, "the closed valley," to which he retreated as much as possible to read, think, and write, as he describes in Letter 2. He considered this form of *otium* (leisure) anything but inactive, and later celebrated and defended it in his treatise on the life of solitude, *De vita solitaria*. It was a difficult classical ideal, a middle path between the business of the *vulgus* and the Christian contemplative life, which he celebrated not quite wholeheartedly in *De otio religioso,* a treatise addressed to the monks of the Abbey of Montrieux, which his brother joined in 1343. In 1338–1339, in Vaucluse, he embarked on two major Latin works, *On Famous Men* (*De viris illustribus*), a series of biographies originally limited to prominent ancient Romans, and an epic poem, the *Africa,* on the struggle between the Romans and the Carthaginians in the Second Punic War and the eventual defeat of Hannibal by Scipio Africanus. The poem was never finished, and only brief passages were ever released during Petrarch's lifetime.

All the same, coupled with his scholarship and learning, the *Africa* was enough to establish his reputation as a poet. By the early 1340s he had transformed himself from humble Francesco Petracchi (or Francisco Petrachi) into the more euphonious and classically resonant Franciscus Petrarca. He was now a public figure, and in 1341 he enjoyed what he saw as his greatest public triumph. After a three-day examination in Naples of his worthiness as a scholar and author by the king, Robert of Anjou, he received a crown of laurel leaves on the Capitoline Hill in Rome, probably on April 8. He felt that an ancient tradition had been restored, and that his own link with the great Roman poets had been duly recognized. As the years passed, he would keep on telling himself and his readers that the triumph was in fact a hollow one; poetry and poetic immortality meant nothing in the face of death, damnation, and eternity. All the same, he was never able to renounce the laurel completely, any more than he was able to renounce his love for Laura. Partly thanks to the verbal connections between "laurel" and the name "Laura," which work in both Latin (*laurus*) and Italian (*lauro*), writing about Laura and writing about the laurel would constantly merge. In the *Canzoniere* in particular, their attractions and the problems associated with each of them become almost inseparable (see section 2 below).

Though Petrarch's admiration for Robert of Anjou may have been genuine, it was characteristic of him to adapt to the political realities of the time, consorting with figures his friends in Florence (which was a republic) saw as tyrants, while managing to keep his dignity and continuing with his own work untroubled.[9] He spent 1343–1345, for instance, in Italy, under the patronage of Azzo da Correggio, the tyrant of Parma, living mostly in Parma and Verona, and working on the *Africa* and the biographies of famous men, as well as on a collection of exemplary anecdotes from ancient history and literature, the *Rerum memorandarum libri* (literally, *Books of Things to Be Remembered*), which he abandoned after finishing the first book in 1345.

His celebrations of ancient Roman power and prestige are mostly nostalgic or abstract, especially in the 1330s and 1340s when he is writing about the Roman Republic. But there are moments when he seems to think that political renewal is a possibility in the present.[10] At one time he even became politically active, with consequences that probably affected the rest of his life.

Like Dante before him, Petrarch consistently and repeatedly denounced the Avignonese court as corrupt and offensive, and pressed for a return of the papacy to its proper seat in Rome. This hostility to the "second Babylon," as he called it, was probably always hazardous for someone in Petrarch's position. It became positively dangerous when he gave his qualified support to the quixotic attempt by Cola di Rienzo to reestablish the ancient republic in contemporary Rome. Cola inevitably came into conflict with the interests of the Colonna and other powerful Roman families. He managed to negotiate his way out of trouble in the first instance (though in the end he was lynched by a Roman mob in 1352), but Petrarch had seriously compromised himself. He backpedaled and, with some difficulty, kept his balance, though there followed a serious split with Cardinal Giovanni Colonna. He gives his version of the events and issues mostly in the letters he collected

[9] See Letter 5.

[10] See, for example, Poem 53 of the *Canzoniere*.

and edited around 1360 as the *Sine nomine* (*Letters without a Name*), which manage to be simultaneously highly polemical and ambiguously allusive regarding the actual events. Whatever the details, his ties to the Colonna and to Avignon were seriously weakened. They may then have been further undermined when both Giovanni Colonna and Laura died in the plague of 1348, and were given an additional blow when a new pope, Innocent VI, who had little time for Petrarch, was elected in 1353.

He was already spending more and more time in Italy (he learned of the deaths of Giovanni Colonna and Laura while in Verona), and decided to establish himself there permanently. He spent the rest of his life under the patronage of various northern Italian princes and, for a while, of the Venetian Republic. He visited Florence in 1350, from which stemmed a personal friendship with the other major Italian writer of the time, Giovanni Boccaccio (1313–1375), most famous now as the author of the *Decameron* and other works in the vernacular, but as eager an enthusiast for ancient culture as Petrarch himself. Though they would meet only infrequently, the friendship lasted and gave rise to an important series of letters, with Boccaccio playing the role of the admiring disciple and Petrarch the indulgent teacher and adviser. Somewhat to the dismay of his Florentine friends, Petrarch opted first of all to live in Milan, which was ruled by the Visconti family and was Florence's archenemy, though he also spent time in Venice and Padua and other northern cities. He finally left Milan for Venice in 1361, and then, a few years later, established himself more firmly in Padua. He became particularly close to Francesco da Carrara, the ruler of Padua,[11] who, in 1369, gave him the land in the village of Arquà in the Euganean Hills on which he built the house where he spent most of his last four years. But he was constantly on the move, within Italy and beyond, in part at least driven by his own restlessness. He was also a useful member of diplomatic missions on behalf of his patrons. He was received by Emperor Charles IV in Mantua in 1352, and went on a mission to the French court in Paris in 1362. Even in 1373, about six months before his death, he took part in the negotiations to end a messy war that had broken out between Venice and Padua. In spite of his traveling and the complex business of maintaining his position and his reputation, he seems to have been able to continue writing and studying much as he had done in Provence.

The years from 1350 onward were immensely productive for Petrarch, though with certain changes of emphasis. There are signs that the political crisis of the 1340s overlapped with a spiritual crisis, one of the main outcomes of which has often been thought to be the *Secretum*, the remarkable imaginary dialogue in which Petrarch represents himself being interrogated by Saint Augustine about his moral failings. In any event, during the 1350s he began to project an image of himself as a Christian scholar and moral philosopher rather than a poet. He wrote a series of polemical treatises

[11] See Letter 5.

defending himself and the culture he represented against real or imagined slurs from the ignorant, that is, in reality, doctors, lawyers, and university intellectuals working within an Aristotelian and scholastic framework, all of whom he included among the *vulgus*.[12] But he was losing confidence in the *Africa;* apart from moral and religious doubts about a notionally pagan epic, after the Cola experience he was less enthusiastic about the Roman republic than he had been. He gradually stopped working on the poem during the 1350s. When younger admirers read it after his death, they were somewhat disappointed. *On Famous Men,* on the other hand, continued to grow, though it was never finished, acquiring a more Christian coloring with the addition of lives of biblical and contemporary personages. His shift away from republicanism seems to be reflected in the fact that the biography of Julius Caesar was noticeably expanded.

Other important works that explored new literary territory were embarked on and uncharacteristically completed. One, which fitted well with Petrarch's new image of himself, was *De remediis utriusque fortune* (*On the Remedies for Both Kinds of Fortune*), two books of allegorical dialogues: the first on the dangers of bad fortune, the second on the equally serious dangers that good fortune brings. Another, which fitted less well, though Petrarch might have pointed out that it mostly contained material going back to the 1340s, was the *Bucolicum carmen* (*Bucolic Poetry*). This was in fact a collection of pastoral poems on the Virgilian model, with a strongly allegorical twist. That meant that the poems could give complex treatment to a range of personal and public issues (including, once again, the depravity of the Avignonese Court), though the intended sense often only becomes fully intelligible with the help of a detailed commentary. Petrarch himself provided one for the first poem in the sequence.

One other reason why Petrarch abandoned the *Africa* was probably that he felt uncomfortable with large-scale unitary narrative. In purely literary terms, he achieved the most when he worked in a broadly autobiographical vein with short or shortish units that he revised and supplemented over the years, gradually building up structures that seem to move between apparently casual variety and complex detailed patterning. The genre that particularly suited him in Latin was the letter; in Italian it was the short lyric. He seems to have begun serious work on collections of both in 1349 or 1350. He worked on his Italian poems and his Latin letters at intervals for the rest of his life, adding new texts as they were written. These included some that were ostensibly written years earlier but were now often completely recast or totally invented to suit the aesthetic, moral, and autobiographical requirements of the work in question. In any event, the great advantage of this

[12] Notably the three books of the *Invectives against a Doctor* (*Invective contra medicum*), *On His Own Ignorance and That of Many Others* (*De sui ipsius et multorum ignorantia*), and *Against the Man Who Cursed Italy* (*Contra eum qui maledixit Italie*).

kind of composition for a writer who revised as obsessively as Petrarch did was that it left room for further additions or modifications, and at the same time it was possible at any stage for individual parts, and up to a point the overall structures, to have an air of completion.

His collections of letters begin, in the early 1350s, with the three books of *Verse Letters* (*Epistole metrice*). Most of these were even more retrospective than the *Bucolic Poetry* and fitted well enough with his version of his progress from poetry to philosophy. They include his earliest datable poem to have survived, a lament on the death of his mother written in 1318–1319. But without a doubt the most important and interesting collections contain the letters in prose—the twenty-four books of the *Familiares,* the letters on "familiar," or personal, matters, and the seventeen books of the *Seniles,* letters written in old age.[13] The two collections in fact overlap in time and are not substantially different from each other. The topics range over all Petrarch's interests, the addressees run from close personal friends to kings and popes, and the manner and style are appropriately varied to suit both the topic and addressee. The art is evident. Both collections are grounded in personal experience, but a good deal of that experience is literary, and the shadow under which the letters are composed comes from the moralizing essays of Seneca's letters to Lucilius, rather than the more directly personal and impromptu letters of Cicero. Perhaps surprisingly, it is the *Verse Letters* that are particularly revealing of the details of Petrarch's personal life. With all the collections the implicit readership is not limited to the named addressees. But the public Petrarch is writing for is self-selecting and numerically restricted; it is a group of friends who share his literary interests, empathize with the feelings he expresses, and bring to bear similar aesthetic and moral attitudes. Its ideal limits are transhistorical: the *Familiares* end with a book of letters addressed to Petrarch's favorite classical authors. The *Seniles* should have ended with the letter To Posterity (Letter 5), which was left incomplete and became detached from the collection.

Though Petrarch may have made some sort of a collection in the early 1340s, he was probably writing Italian poems mostly in an occasional way. But northern Italian princes and their courts had appreciated lyric poetry in the Tuscan manner at least since Dante's time and wanted something more from the greatest writer of the age. The first version of what would become the *Canzoniere* may have been composed for Azzo da Correggio in 1356–1358.[14] Versions for other patrons would follow in the last years of Petrarch's

13 These are the customary shorthand substitutes for *Familiarium rerum libri* (literally, "Books of Personal Matters") and *Senilium rerum libri* (literally, "Books of Matters of Later Years"). The English translations cited in the Further Reading use the titles *Letters on Familiar Matters* and *Letters of Old Age.*

14 The accepted account of the history of the *Canzoniere* is Ernest H. Wilkins, *The Making of the Canzoniere and Other Petrarchan Studies* (Rome: Edizioni di Storia e Letteratura, 1951). This account has been severely questioned recently. See Teodolinda

life. Whatever he said about merely responding to pressures from others, he was clearly working on his Italian poems with increasing intensity in the 1360s. The first surviving version of the *Canzoniere,* normally referred to as the Chigi version after one of the Renaissance owners of the manuscript, is in the hand of Boccaccio, who copied it from a text that Petrarch let him have in 1362–1363. By this point Part I contained most of what would become Poems 1 to 189, and Part II what would become Poems 264 to 304. Petrarch's working method in subsequent versions was to continue adding poems to the ends of the two parts, usually with some revisions of the order of the previous batch. Many individual poems were written or thoroughly revised in the 1360s, or even later, including some that were ostensibly written during Laura's lifetime. The final version of the *Canzoniere,* now in the Vatican Library,[15] is partly in his own hand and partly in that of his scribe, Giovanni Malpaghini. It was not produced at anyone else's request and only finished (if it was definitively finished) months before his death. Finished or not, it is the first major work of European poetry for which we have a text produced and edited by the author himself.

The *Canzoniere* was not the sole major vernacular work on which Petrarch was engaged in the last two decades or so of his life. Over the same period he worked on the series of six allegorical *Triumphs,* which are also centered on Laura but display Petrarch's classical learning a good deal more openly. The *Triumphs* have a more obvious overall architecture than the *Canzoniere,* though one that is unevenly realized. Perhaps Petrarch was once again defeated by the grand design. (See also section 3 below.)

He continued writing until the very end of his life. He knew that study of the kind he practiced was endless, and he seems to have treated the final revisions and refinements to his own texts in the same spirit. He died, probably of a stroke, during the night of July 18, 1374.

2. The *Canzoniere*

The term *Canzoniere* historically just means a collection of songs or poems. The title, which appears at the beginning of the manuscript that Petrarch and Giovanni Malpaghini spent perhaps a decade working on, was *Rerum vulgarium fragmenta Francisci Petrarce laureati poete,* literally, "The fragments of vernacular matters of Francesco Petrarca laureate poet." Reduced to its first three words, that title has enjoyed a revival in Italy in recent years. It is not only what Petrarch himself intended but a good deal more precise and revealing than the alternatives. It indicates that the author saw himself as a Latin poet who chooses to write here in the vernacular, and that

Barolini and H. Wayne Storey, eds., *Petrarch and the Textual Origins of Interpretation* (Leiden and Boston: Brill, 2007).

15 MS Vat. lat. 3195.

the text consists of discontinuous pieces. "Fragments" also suggests the idea of a lost whole—perhaps the fragmented self that modern readers usually feel is a core issue in the collection, perhaps the idea of a lost wholeness to poetry, which would reflect Petrarch's ambiguous feelings about the status of vernacular verse. However, for obvious reasons of convenience and familiarity, I have followed general Italian practice and retained the title *Canzoniere* here.

In its final version the collection consists of 366 poems, a figure that has led some critics to find a key to the whole in the days of a leap year or those of a normal year plus one. Petrarch himself gives no indication that he thought in numerological terms, and his piecemeal method of composition argues against the presence of a complex hidden architecture of this sort. That does not mean that there is not a complex patterning at work. Petrarch arranged the poems in a real or invented chronological sequence, marking the passage of time with a number of anniversary poems (not all quite in order) that refer to the number of years that have gone by since he first saw Laura in 1327 or, after 1348, since her death. That event is of course tremendously important, but it does not affect the order in quite the way we might expect, at least in Petrarch's original manuscript. He divided the collection into two unequal parts, Poems 1–263 and Poems 264–366. This division does not quite fit with the titles that have been regularly used for the two parts since sometime in the 15th century: "Poems Written during the Lifetime of Madonna Laura," and "Poems Written after the Death of Madonna Laura." In the original manuscript, the death has been anticipated in the sonnets leading up to Poem 263, but it is only registered as having occurred in Poem 267. The real contrast at this point is between the major self-assessment carried out in the weighty *canzone,* Poem 264, that opens the second part, and the string of sonnets celebrating Laura that conclude the first part. The death of Laura and Petrarch's deepening awareness of the need for spiritual change are made almost to coincide, but not quite.

The contrasts in poetic form are also important. Petrarch is most famous for his sonnets, and 317 of the poems in the *Canzoniere* are in sonnet form. Almost all of these have a rhyme scheme of ABBA ABBA in the quatrains, and a majority use CDE CDE or CDC DCD in the tercets. The sonnets, with some variation in rhyme patterning and an infinite variety in the internal organization of their material, furnish the collection with a basic formal constant, which sets off the fifty-one poems in other forms. The most important of these is the *canzone.* This is the word for a song of any kind in modern Italian, but in medieval and Renaissance literary usage it designated the most prestigious and complex form of vernacular lyric poem. *Canzoni* are far weightier than sonnets. They are commonly between fifty and eighty lines in length (though some are much longer) and divided into a number of stanzas (commonly five or six), usually with a short *congedo* (*envoi* or leave-taking) at the end; each stanza in a given poem has the same rhyme scheme and the same metrical scheme, which the poet constructs according to a fixed set of rules, with the result that the structure of each *canzone* is normally an individual creation. All of Petrarch's *canzoni* are metrically distinct from each other, except for the sequence on the beauties of Laura's eyes (Poems 71–73), which use the same stanza form, though their total lengths are different. This is then the form in which he particularly demonstrates his prowess (as his contemporaries would have seen it) and in which he explores issues that concern him in most depth and at greatest length.[16]

As well as the *canzone,* Petrarch also gives a new importance to the *sestina* or *canzone–sestina,* of which there had only been two examples that we know of before him, one by the Provençal poet Arnaut Daniel, the other by Dante.[17] The *sestina* is a particularly rigid form of *canzone* that responds perfectly to Petrarch's propensity to use recurrent issues and images in novel ways and which he manipulates brilliantly. It consists of six stanzas plus an *envoi* or *congedo;* the stanzas all have six lines with the same six words in rhyme position. These repeating words do not rhyme with each other and are permuted according to a fixed pattern moving inward from the outer words of the preceding stanza (ABCDEF, FAEBDC, CFDABE, and so forth) until all permutations are exhausted in the last stanza. All six words are then repeated in a three-line *congedo*—in Petrarch, normally in the order in which they first appeared. The *Canzoniere* also includes a small number of poems in other minor forms—*madrigali* and *ballate*[18]—that are perhaps indebted to contemporary musical practice.

Petrarch mixes together poems in different metrical forms in a way that has no real precedent in earlier manuscript collections of poems that have survived. One of his aims was certainly to create a variety that was both pleasing because of its unpredictability and disturbing because it ran against established ideas of order. At the same time he introduced elements of patterning, grouping *canzoni* together, or contrasting them with groups of sonnets. The most interesting pattern is the contrast between the overall structures of the two parts of the collection. The first begins and ends with strings of sonnets and has a major sequence of *canzoni* very close to its center (Poems 125 to 129). The second also has *canzoni* close to its center, but also begins and ends with *canzoni.* Though it would be easy to overstate, the relationship between the two uneven parts of the whole collection is comparable to the relationship between the two uneven parts of a sonnet. Petrarch seems to

16 The first and canonical discussion of the *canzone* is by Dante in his *De vulgari eloqentia.* For a fuller introduction to Petrarch's use of different metrical forms, see Peter Hainsworth, *Petrarch the Poet* (London and New York: Routledge, 1988), 210–20.

17 Arnaut Daniel's *Lo ferm voler qu'el cor m'intra* ("The firm desire that enters my heart") and Dante's *Al poco giorno e al gran cerchio d'ombra* ("To the short day and the great circle of shadow").

18 Fourteenth-century Italian *madrigali* are short, freely organized poems, usually intended to be set to music and sung; *ballate* are dance songs with a refrain.

seek out formal divergences as well as conceptual and emotional ones, and to find intricate ways of balancing them against each other, on a large scale as well as on a small one.

The great majority of the poems are concerned with his love for Laura, the obsessional fascination that remains fundamentally unchanged for more than thirty years. It is unaffected by the fact that Laura refuses to give herself to him physically and at times may seem not to respond to him at all, and it keeps its force for at least ten years after her death. Time goes by, as marked by the anniversary poems. There are incidents, particularly visits and absences, but there are no significant external events beyond her first overwhelming appearance in his life and her death. Whether there are significant internal developments is something for the individual reader to decide. Petrarch does not so much give us a story of his spiritual, psychological, and literary progress over the years as present us with a series of complex snapshots that we may decode and connect together in various ways. Individual poems give different perspectives, and sometimes combine several in one poem, shifting between memories, reflections on the present, and fears and hopes for the future, and between different images and interpretations of what Laura is, was, or may be. At different times she is cast as a courtly lady, a goddess, a nymph, a shepherdess, a force for Petrarch's ultimate good, a friendly presence, an image of the divine, or a phantasm of his own creation that is distracting him from thinking about the salvation of his soul. And what does he want? Physical union, companionship, to be with her in heaven, to get rid of her? And what do any of these things mean? Petrarch often voices a definite view as if he had resolved the issue, but taken together the poems seem to be trying out all the possibilities available to him, though many of them turn out to be recurrent, much as the basic situation is on the face of it also static. Some modern critics have seen a subtle story of how a soul may progress from the toils of sinfulness to a due repentance and reorientation toward God. Renaissance readers were more inclined to emphasize Neoplatonic ascent from the beauties of this world to the realm of ultimate truths. Both approaches may be overmoralistic. Even the concluding poems addressing God and the Virgin may be voicing a desire to abandon the obsession rather than success in doing so.

The *Canzoniere* is such a classic of Western European literature and has been so influential that it is easy to forget how odd its basic story, or nonstory, is. Lyric poetry in Provençal and Italian usually had no story at all beyond the before and after presumed by enamorment, or rejection, or, less frequently, the death of the beloved. The poet who does invent a story, and whose shadow Petrarch seems constantly to be struggling with, is Dante. Beatrice, alive and dead, has a similar role to Laura, spread over a comparable period of the poet's life. But Beatrice is unquestionably a force for good in Dante's life and poetry, eventually leading him to the Godhead and being herself happily transcended at the end of the *Divine Comedy.* Petrarch fragments and questions the Dantean story. For Petrarch the body of the dead beloved, which Dante had never quite eliminated, keeps coming back as something needed and unforgettable, and her heavenly form tends to take the place of God, who is remote and unknowable. Ultimately, since that heavenly form may be imaginary, both Laura and the poetry she calls into being may lack any substantial foundation.

The *Canzoniere* is a rewriting of Dante in a more human vein. Petrarch retains the desire for the absolute, but he has lost the confidence that love and poetry stem from the divine, or are a means to reach it. With that loss comes also a loss of confidence in the authority of the poetic voice and its power to articulate important truths. Yet new positives emerge. Petrarch creates a kind of self-portraiture, or perhaps a theater of the self, which had not appeared in European poetry before, though the elements from which he makes it certainly had. The reader is caught in a fascinating game that moves between identification, spectating, enjoyment, and admiration. The figure of the poet, whose ultimate justification Petrarch seems explicitly to undermine, simultaneously reappears in a new light, and with it a different kind of poetry emerges.

One of the ways in which Petrarch gives this reframing of poetry force and conviction is by injecting into it some of the classicism of his work in Latin. However elaborate it might be, lyric poetry in Provençal and Italian had taken very little directly from ancient authors. Poets were in dialogue with each other or their immediate predecessors, rather than with Virgil or Horace. Dante opened up the field with the *Comedy*. Thereafter, throughout the 14th century, poet after poet exults in incorporating Graeco-Roman history and myth into their verse. What distinguishes Petrarch, the major Latin scholar and writer of his time, is that he classicizes better than any of his contemporaries. He draws on classical myth and history in relative moderation, and with a deep sense of the poetic power of the names and stories evoked. He takes lines from classical poets (and also from the Church fathers and the Bible), but only to rework them and make them his own.[19] Most importantly, his style seamlessly integrates classicizing and vernacular features. This will become the epitome of the high lyric style in the Renaissance. In its own time, it was more like a middle style, a remarkable combination of conversational turns of phrase and more formal rhetoric. The antitheses for which Petrarch will become famous (or notorious), for instance, come principally from classical love poetry and had barely figured in his predecessors, but they are deployed with virtuoso ease, almost as if they were already a standard resource of Italian poetry. No one before Petrarch had managed, or perhaps wanted to manage, his mixture of fluency and complexity, which, in complete contrast to the disordered flux of his thoughts and feelings, has a literary order and clarity such as might be found in Horace or Ovid.

[19] For two striking examples among many, see Poems 159 (lines 13–14) and 264 (line 136), where Petrarch reworks Horace and Ovid, respectively.

One myth in particular is recurrent. It is the story of Daphne, the nymph pursued in Thessaly by the god Apollo; she asks her father, the river Peneus, for help and, just as Apollo reaches her, is turned into a laurel or bay. Apollo then makes the laurel his favorite tree. Petrarch knew the story principally from Ovid's account in the *Metamorphoses* (1.452–567). With the help of allusions in other ancient authors, he chooses to emphasize the symbolic rather than dramatic aspects of the story. Apollo is the god of poetry and glory, and the laurel furnishes the crowns for poets laureate and for victorious generals and emperors. As such it comes to represent poetry itself and the "immortal" fame that Petrarch's own coronation in Rome in 1341 (see section 1 above) theoretically conferred on him, but which his Christian conscience tells him is valueless.

In the original Italian the symbolic resonances can be concentrated around the talismanic name. With a very few exceptions (none of them certain), the name Laura does not appear in the *Canzoniere* as such, but as *l'aura,* "the breeze, wind, air." Petrarch comes back again and again to that pun, but also to another; with a change of vowel Laura is also *lauro,* "laurel." The dramatic Ovidian transformation becomes a linguistic switch from feminine to masculine, which, in Petrarch's imagination, carries connotations of the change from something mobile, elusive, and impermanent to something stable and lasting. The two forms move between each other in either direction: Laura is, or becomes, the laurel, and vice versa. It is a remarkably rich nexus, although it used to be dismissed as a rather tired play on words, in contrast, say, with the wit of John Donne and the English Metaphysical poets. In fact, the verbal play encapsulates Petrarch's preoccupation with fame and poetry, about which he has doubts and questions that are ultimately very similar to those he has concerning his love for Laura the woman. The links may reach out in other directions: *lauro* is also *l'auro* ("gold"), the color of her hair, or with a slight addition, *l'aurora* ("dawn"). Ultimately, it is possible to feel that the sounds and meanings hovering around the name Laura set or embody a musical and thematic tone that is one of the distinctive features of Petrarch's poetry.

He himself never acknowledges that this Italian verse is anything more than *rime* ("rhymes") and, unlike Dante, does not present himself as an Italian *poeta*. There is a clear implication that a real *poeta* would be a poet of the laurel, one who has transcended the sensual and speaks on grand and public themes in the Virgilian manner, as he himself attempted to do in the *Africa*. In Italian he either fails to make that transition or refuses to do so. There are a few poems included in the collection that are addressed to friends and veer away from the issue of love, but the only poems that adopt a definite public stance are three *canzoni* on political themes (Poems 27, 53, and 128) and three sonnets denouncing the papal court at Avignon (Poems 136–38).[20] All these poems are in the first third or so of the collection. It

[20] Of the poems mentioned here, this selection includes 53, 128, and 136.

may be that there is a hidden narrative here, of an attempt in the first part of Petrarch's career to adopt the role of public poet, with then a subsequent renunciation that leaves Laura, or Laura–*lauro*, supreme, and an implicit recognition that vernacular lyric poetry must be primarily personal. Most subsequent European lyric poetry would follow in the direction that Petrarch pointed, gravitating away from the overtly public to the endless fascination with the personal and the individual. Petrarch makes a particular success of including in the personal the failure to go beyond it.

However ambiguous or defensive he is in his statements about Italian poetry, in practice he is completely assured. There is a submerged polemical and normative intent in the *Canzoniere,* as there is also in the *Triumphs.* Both are exercises in limitation, which implicitly declare the importance of depth over range, in part, again, as a way of overcoming or sidelining the specter of Dante. The *Divine Comedy,* following up the dynamics of diversity evident in Dante's work as a whole, had brought together in one single artifact a host of different discourses, ranging from low comedy to the higher forms of theology. Dante's immense achievement had, however, negative effects; much Italian poetry that followed in his wake in the 14th century ranges far and wide thematically and stylistically but lacks the control or vision traditionally associated with great poetry. Petrarch finds ways forward, not by dictate or through explicit literary programs (which are hard to find in his work, either in Latin or in Italian), but through the sheer aesthetic power and example of the poems he writes. He declares implicitly that the central and dominant subject for poetry in the vernacular of any literary quality is indeed love, whatever other facets of the self it may talk about indirectly. The political *canzoni,* the sonnets denouncing the Avignonese court, and the few other poems on nonamatory themes mark out the limited extent to which those bounds may be exceeded. In a similar way he effectively asserts the primacy of the sonnet as a metrical form, though the *canzone* may be used to move into a higher register, and other forms may move in to a slightly lower one. In all these areas he curtails what Dante had done inside and outside the *Comedy.* To keep to hierarchic metaphors, he imposes a consistent stylistic, thematic, and formal mean, which is below Dante's heights but above his depths. In Italian, Petrarch seems to achieve the blend of ease and order that his contemporaries were implicitly aiming at, and that he himself cultivated in Latin, perhaps not always successfully.

Petrarch writes constantly about conflicting desires and emotions, and often claims to be doing little more than expressing his feelings. In fact he is the most self-aware of poets, which means also that he is immensely conscious of how other writers have articulated similar feelings in the past. It is as if any self-projection of his own is simultaneously a form of dialogue with tradition. This means that any poem is a remarkably self-conscious literary artifact. The miracle is that in the originals there is no sense of strain or contradiction between artifice and self-expression. The two are interdependent, and together they give rise to poetry that combines classic beauty (symmetry, musicality, lucidity, harmony, repose) and romantic disquiet (solitude, loss, fragmentariness, obscurity, incompletion). These features are apparent in all of Petrarch's work, prose and verse, Latin and Italian, but it is in the *Canzoniere* that their synthesis is most consistently and completely realized.

My selection here contains around a third of the poems, sufficient, I hope, to convey an idea of the temporal aspect of the whole, even though its patterning and architecture have necessarily been lost. I include Petrarch's greatest and historically most read poems, but have aimed also to give the reader a sense of the endless variety of his work within the apparently narrow confines that he set himself.

3. The *Triumphs*

Petrarch's second major work in Italian is his not quite finished sequence of six allegorical poems. As in the *Canzoniere,* the dominant theme of the *Triumphs* is Petrarch's love for Laura and the moral and intellectual issues connected with it. Each poem represents a vision. In the first and longest poem, Love defeats Petrarch and forces him to join the thousands of others following behind in a procession that recreates the idea of the "triumph" of a Roman general. But Love is defeated by Chastity, and then come the triumphs of Death, Fame, and Time, each overcoming the power that preceded it, with Eternity achieving final victory. In clear contradiction with the last poems of the *Canzoniere, The Triumph of Eternity* imagines a beatific reunion with Laura in heaven that seems quite untroubled by doubt and guilt.

Petrarch seems to have made no effort to resolve the contradiction and may have thought of the *Triumphs* and the *Canzoniere* as exercises in different genres with different requirements. The *Triumphs* delineate a more exemplary and clearer spiritual itinerary than the *Canzoniere,* and appear much closer to the *Divine Comedy* in manner and metrical form (*terza rima,* which never appears in the *Canzoniere*). In fact Petrarch was probably stimulated to begin writing the *Triumphs* by Boccaccio's *Amorosa visione,* an allegorical vision in *terza rima* that is heavily indebted to the *Comedy* but celebrates a much more earthly form of love.

Petrarch began the sequence in the 1340s and was still working on it in the last few years of his life. Unconnected fragments and different versions of some parts survive. The repetitions and abrupt transitions in *The Triumph of Eternity* might indicate that what we have is a provisional form of the poem, but both sets of features also reinforce and complicate the sense that the aspiration to a happily unchanging state is not one Petrarch pacifically and wholeheartedly embraces.

The *Triumphs* as a whole make a much greater display of Petrarch's learning than the *Canzoniere,* especially in lists of names, mostly from antiquity, with minimal efforts to give character or vitality to the figures they designate.

The sequence was studied enthusiastically in the 15th and 16th centuries, but it does not win favor with nonspecialist modern readers, except for the more obviously personal and lyrical parts. Finished or not, *The Triumph of Eternity* is the most striking and affecting part of all.

4. The *Secretum*

The *Secretum* is an imaginary dialogue in three books between Franciscus, representing Petrarch's human, earthly side, and one of his favorite authors, Saint Augustine, who is the voice of his more ascetic, self-critical side. The dialogue takes place in the presence of an allegorical female figure who is named Truth and who, significantly, does not speak at all, but apparently listens to everything that is said.

The full title is *De secreto conflictu curarum mearum* (literally, "On the secret conflict of my cares"). It may have been first drafted in the mid-1340s, and then revised at least once some years later. Petrarch claimed in his Preface that it was a private work, as its title indicates, intended solely to aid his meditations in times of spiritual need. But we need not take him at his word; one of his ways of engaging the reader is to suggest that he or she is being granted access to a private realm, with the accompanying privilege of being able to make a personal assessment of what goes on there. What the reader is not told (and this is one of the *Secretum*'s fascinations) is exactly what lessons to draw.

In the first two books Augustine lays bare a string of failings in Franciscus' character and manages to elicit admissions of guilt and promises to reform. I have translated Book 3, which is taken up entirely with what Augustine considers the two most serious problems—Franciscus' love for Laura and his passionate desire to win immortal fame as a writer. These are of course the two central issues in the *Canzoniere*. Here they are articulated in discursive form and with more dramatic force. Franciscus seems fundamentally an unconvinced penitent, who accepts some of Augustine's points but resists others, and Augustine, however convinced of being in the right, has to keep on recognizing that his powers of persuasion have only limited success. In the end Franciscus seems to postpone any final decision, while expressing the hope that he will do better in the future. This is an unsatisfactorily ambiguous conclusion from a religious perspective, but perhaps the only appropriate one in literary and personal terms. For all its medieval coloring the *Secretum*, like the *Canzoniere*, voices a new sensibility, which intimately rejects or eludes the dogmatic certainties it is drawn to, and dares to embrace its own uncertainty about what to put in their place.

5. The Letters

As I discussed in section 1 above, Petrarch gathered his letters together in three main collections, the *Verse Letters* (*Epistole metrice*), the *Familiares,* and the *Seniles*. They range over a host of topics in politics, literature, history, travel, moral philosophy, and much more. The five letters I have selected are ones in which he discusses matters of central concern to himself, and all, directly or indirectly, have a bearing on the *Canzoniere* and on his love for Laura. The first of two letters from the *Familiares* (Letter 1) included here contains the strongest assertion he makes anywhere outside the *Canzoniere* of the reality of his passion, although in a context that might still leave room for doubt as to how truthful he is being. The verse letter (Letter 2), which is from the same year and to the same addressee, Giacomo Colonna, gives one of Petrarch's most dramatic representations of his passion's effects on him, before proceeding to a description of his life at his rural retreat in the Vaucluse. The second letter from the *Familiares* (Letter 3) is perhaps the most famous one he wrote. It describes Petrarch's ascent of Mont Ventoux with his brother, which also becomes a moral ascent, or at least an attempt at one. The later letter from the *Seniles* (Letter 4) includes some of Petrarch's most important statements on vernacular poets and poetry, and also encapsulates the polemical stance he adopts in much of his later writing toward contemporary scholastic orthodoxy. In the last, never completed letter To Posterity (Letter 5), he attempts to summarize his life and work for a readership of the future that might have heard of him and might want to know more.

As is usually the case with a writer's correspondence, it is helpful to have some background information regarding the addressees and the composition of each letter. In the paragraphs that follow I also include comments on content and tone, which often pose problems for the modern reader.

Letter 1 (*Familiares* 2.9) is addressed to Giacomo Colonna (1300/1–1341), the son of the tough, long-lived leader of the Colonna family, Stefano Colonna (1265–1348/9), and brother of Cardinal Giovanni Colonna (d. 1348). All three were Petrarch's patrons, and he was proud to think of the two brothers as his friends. Giacomo was Bishop of Lombez, a small town south of Toulouse that is now a village. Petrarch had spent a happy summer there with Giacomo and two other friends in 1333. There was a plan for him to go with Giacomo to Rome that autumn. Instead he stayed in Avignon, probably detained by Giovanni Colonna to help in his efforts to outmaneuver the rival Orsini family at the papal court in Avignon, while Giacomo and Stefano confronted them more directly in Rome. Letter 1 was probably written in late 1336, though Petrarch himself specifies only the day and month (XII Kalends of January, that is, December 21), not long before his first visit to Rome in early 1337. Like many other letters, it may well have been refined at a later date.

The letter claims to be a reply to a letter from Giacomo that jokingly chastises Petrarch for pretending to emotions and ideas that he does not really feel, and for inventing the figure of Laura simply as a way of talking about his desire to be crowned poet laureate. In the course of his reply Petrarch goes over ideas and concerns that are central to his work as a whole, above all how to reconcile the study of the ancient classics with Christian belief. He also asserts in the strongest terms the reality of Laura as a woman and the reality of his passion for her. But a good deal of the letter is jocular, or aims to be, and the literariness is evident. It may be that the question of Laura's existence, tucked away in the middle of the letter, is actually the real point and a serious one, but she also becomes an excuse to discuss general questions of invention, fabrication, and irony, and the protestations of passion are strikingly conventional in spite of their vehemence. In the end we may feel that we as readers are actually caught up in a multilayered literary game, rather than having the ambiguities resolved for us once and for all.

Letter 2 (*Verse Letters* 1.6), also addressed to Giacomo Colonna, dates itself to 1338, since Petrarch says that he has been in Vaucluse for a year and he acquired his house there in 1337. This letter deals directly with Petrarch's feelings for Laura, and in rather more violent terms than does Letter 1 or poems in the *Canzoniere* (notably 129 and 360), which take up some of the same material. Unlike the poems, Letter 2 sets his passion in relation to his day-to-day life in his retreat at the Fontaine de Vaucluse, and presents a carefully wrought, polemically charged picture of how, in contrast to friends seduced by the pleasures of Avignon, he spends his time there reading his favorite classical authors and working on his own literary projects.

In my translation I have used unrhymed iambic pentameters for Petrarch's hexameters. The result is an increase in length of some twenty lines and a lack of exact correspondence in line numbers between the translation and the original.

Letter 3 (*Familiares* 4.1) is addressed to Dionigi da Borgo San Sepolcro, an Augustinian friar and a theologian and philosopher of some repute. Petrarch probably got to know him in Paris in 1333 when Dionigi was teaching at the university. He was appointed bishop of Monopoli in southern Italy in 1339, but stopped off in Avignon, where he and Petrarch presumably saw each other again. He then went on to Italy, eventually joining the court of Robert of Anjou in Naples, where he died in 1342. Petrarch always addresses him and writes about him with affection and respect.

Petrarch notes in the course of the letter that ten years have gone by since he abandoned his legal studies at Bologna University. Since that was in 1326, the letter was apparently drafted in 1336, and Petrarch claims, in fact, to be writing it on April 26 immediately after coming down Mont Ventoux. But there is at least some element of fiction here. The letter is certainly much more artful than Petrarch pretends in his conclusion, and the references to his brother Gherardo climbing on ahead may refer allegorically to his becoming a Carthusian monk, which probably occurred in 1342. If so, the letter may have been composed in the 1340s or even later.

Mont Ventoux is in the Rhône valley about forty kilometers northeast of Avignon. There is debate over whether Petrarch actually climbed it. Some scholars see all the elements in the letter as allegorical. For instance, the old shepherd that Gherardo and Petrarch encounter when they first set out could represent Virgil. On this interpretation Petrarch would be representing himself as replicating Virgil's poetry and outlook but then hoping to surpass his paganism by becoming a modern Christian poet, which in the letter is represented by the ascent of the mountain. There is some straining in such an approach. The letter seems characteristic of Petrarch's procedures in much of his writing, particularly his Italian poetry. It offers an autobiographical account that has an air of being grounded in reality, but which prefers to accentuate literary resonances and references rather than provide circumstantial details. The allegorical dimension becomes explicit at certain moments but seems never to take over completely; for the most part, the physical climb is contrasted with spiritual ascent, though it parallels it in some ways. Characteristically, the conclusion is left open. In spite of believing he has made some progress, Petrarch continues to the end to foreground his weaknesses and uncertainties, leaving the reader free to interpret and judge as he or she thinks fit. Or rather, his concluding paragraph tacitly encourages the reader to identify and puzzle out the issues independently, using that freedom of the will that he identifies as the crux of his own problems, and which, as he is subtly aware, is a problem for the rest of us too.

Letter 4 (*Seniles* 5.2) is addressed to a much more famous figure, Giovanni Boccaccio. As mentioned in section 1 above, Petrarch met Boccaccio for the first time in 1350 and the two became personal and literary friends who met infrequently but exchanged a considerable number of letters, all in Latin, of course. Of these letters seventeen by Petrarch survive against only three by Boccaccio. Most of Petrarch's letters focus on literary and moral issues, are carefully wrought, and have a strong public element to them. As mentioned already in section 1, throughout the correspondence as we have it, Petrarch plays the affectionate master, who may be self-deprecating but is basically sure of his position, whereas Boccaccio is generally glad to be the willing and admiring pupil.

This important letter of 1364–1365 was written when Petrarch was living in Venice and is one of the few in which he raises the question of vernacular poetry. Like Boccaccio, he found it difficult to acknowledge its real importance, in spite of all the time and effort he gave to it. In particular there was the problem of Dante, who had shown quite clearly in the *Divine Comedy* that a major work of literature could be produced in the vernacular that bore comparison with the ancient classics or even perhaps surpassed them. In an earlier letter to Boccaccio,[21] who was a passionate admirer of Dante, Petrarch had forced himself to acknowledge Dante's stature, and defended himself somewhat unconvincingly against charges of being envious of him. This later letter, which like the one just mentioned never refers to Dante by

[21] *Familiares* (*Letters on Familiar Matters*) 21.15, written in 1359.

name, recognizes his primacy as a vernacular poet in a much more straightforward manner. The subject under debate is now primarily the relative merits of Petrarch and Boccaccio as vernacular poets, with Petrarch acknowledging with assumed modesty that he probably is second only to Dante and reassuring Boccaccio that third place in this context is no mean achievement. We cannot be sure whether Boccaccio did in fact burn his youthful poems when he saw what Petrarch had achieved, as Petrarch says has been reported to him, but readers of the 120 or so lyric poems by Boccaccio that have survived have generally thought that Petrarch's verdict was, if anything, a generous one, and that Boccaccio's real talents lay in prose narrative (the *Decameron* in particular), about which Petrarch here says nothing.[22] In the course of his reassurances, however, he makes some unusually positive statements about the potential of the vernacular, while insisting, as he generally does, that his own vernacular poems belong to his youth and that he had done with them years ago. The problems that he now stresses have to do with professional entertainers, who perform his poems for profit in princely courts and mangle them in the process. It may be that one important reason that Petrarch put together a collection of his poems himself was to protect them against such treatment.

Petrarch is reticent on this score. He is much more explicit and much more comfortable in the later stages of the letter, in which he denounces contemporary scholasticism with a savage caricature of an atheistic devotee of Aristotle, and vigorously defends his own integration of ancient thought and culture with Christianity. These pages summarize fundamental aspects of Petrarch's thought in his later work, in which he consistently projects an image of himself as having developed from a poet into a moral philosopher. Interestingly, however, this letter propounds such ideas in a context in which he is discussing not just poetry but the vernacular poetry that he finds so hard to justify.

As noted in section 1, Petrarch had ended the *Familiares* with a book of letters addressed to ancient authors, and intended that the *Seniles* should end with the letter To Posterity (Letter 5). But he continued adding to the *Seniles* until very near the end of his life and never completed a final version of this letter. He probably made a first draft in the early 1350s, with perhaps the aim of justifying his acceptance of Visconti hospitality in Milan to his republican Florentine friends. He then made extensive additions in 1370–1371, but still broke off the narrative abruptly at the point of his return from Padua to Vaucluse in 1351. The various patchy drafts were then stitched together by friends not long after his death, and the makeshift result released as an independent work.

[22] Petrarch did acknowledge the worth of the story of Griselda, which concludes the *Decameron*. The Latin translation of this story in *Seniles* (*Letters of Old Age*) 17.3, which he made very near the end of his life, became the form in which the story was known throughout Europe.

In spite of its incompleteness, the letter To Posterity tells us a great deal about how Petrarch saw himself and how he wanted to be seen by his future readers. As always, he projects a complex personality, showing himself by turns to be defensive, vulnerable, questioning, assertive, and complacent. Modern readers may be particularly surprised by his curt dismissal of Laura and his feelings for her. In fact, the really surprising thing is that his love for her should be mentioned at all, and in by no means negative terms. What should have been a straightforward moral progression away from sensuality (and from poetry) becomes complicated, even debatable, and the person who claims to have made the transition becomes all the more interesting for not quite allowing us to take him at his word. As so often, Petrarch leaves us with the sense that there is something more to be said, which we can only guess at.

6. Translating Petrarch

One possible strategy for an English translator of Petrarch's Italian poetry is to opt for a more or less modern version of the Petrarchist manner as it was first developed by Sir Thomas Wyatt and then taken up by Sir Philip Sidney, Edmund Spenser, and other Elizabethan poets. This has all sorts of advantages, but it runs the risk of presenting Petrarch in the perspective of later generations, who in reality knew a very limited amount of his work directly and who rapidly reduced him to a byword for conventionality. I have always been unhappy with this longstanding image of Petrarch as a purveyor of "long-deceasèd woes," as Sidney calls them.[23] Since first considering translating a selection of his poetry, I have wanted to bring out some of the richness and complexity that the English Petrarchan tradition, such as it is, has tended to play down or cover over. The prime way in which I decided this might be possible was to give priority to the sense of what Petrarch is saying in his poems, yet without discounting how he says it. For the Petrarch I knew and loved in the original Italian did anything but mouth conventionalities. This decision had immediate consequences; however difficult to accept, certain things had to go, first and foremost the music, or the polyphonic texture created by diction, rhythm, and rhyme, which is overwhelmingly beautiful in the original, but which proves inert in English imitations. I opted for unrhymed iambic pentameters for his rhyming hendecasyllables (and for six- or eight-syllable lines where he has *settenari* or seven-syllable lines). These were obviously much easier to manipulate than rhymed verse, but they were also, I thought, a justifiable choice. Iambic pentameter lines are relatively unobtrusive but they satisfy the primary function of indicating that these are verse texts, not prose ones. They also allowed me to concentrate on bringing out more strongly the connections, contrasts, transitions—in short,

[23] *Astrophel and Stella* 15, "You that do search for every purling spring," line 7.

the discursive complexities of Petrarch—as well as such features as antitheses, lists, balancing words and phrases, all of which are both stylistic tics and core elements in his thinking and feeling.

As I implicitly suggested in section 2 above, Petrarch himself does not generally try to amaze with verbal pyrotechnics, nor to construct amusing word games. In the few isolated instances where something of the sort occurs, there is also something more interesting going on. The carefully easy, middle style, which makes its first, deeply impressive appearance in the sonnet opening the *Canzoniere,* is maintained throughout the collection, with subtle but perceptible variations: contrary to first impressions, Petrarch never repeats himself as a poet within the ostensibly narrow limits in which he chooses to work. The best strategy I could devise for finding an English analogue was to take the syntax and idiom of essays and narrative in standard contemporary English prose as the base template, allowing for some variations; so, for example, I edge toward a debating manner in *canzoni* such as Poems 264 and 360, but also now and then introduce fairly colloquial phrases, as Petrarch does. I decided to run the risk of blandness, hoping to compensate for it by allowing a little more energizing concreteness to come in than Petrarch likes, but which English expectations treat as a sine qua non of any kind of poetry.

An intelligent, self-aware Petrarch is historically justified, but the strategy I adopted might also run the risk of making him too much our contemporary. Some of his uncertainties and ways of dealing with them do seem very modern (even postmodern), but he is of course a 14th-century poet working with and renewing the poetic and amatory conventions of his time. Adoration of unattainable objects is by no means dead, and modern discourses of desire can often be surprisingly rich in medieval and Renaissance residues. But the idiom of Petrarch and the situations he represents gave their last gasps in high poetry in English in the late 19th century. To love a woman for twenty-one years without ever touching her, and then to continue with the devotion for ten or more years after her death, was exceptional even in the 14th century, but given the general character of medieval love literature in prose and verse it was not unbelievable at least as literature. Certainly it seemed as natural then as the conventions of soap opera seem now, for the beloved woman to be treated as a superior being who can bring happiness or despair by granting or withholding a look, who can be compared to goddesses, whose hair is gold, whose eyes shoot fire, and who otherwise does almost nothing but be beautiful. I thought I could rely for the most part on the apparent strangeness of all this to maintain the sense of the historical distance of the poetry as a whole, in preference to giving the language an antiquated patina.

That proved a fairly practical approach overall, but from the beginning I kept running up against significant terms with which I had to compromise, since they often refused to pass comfortably into English. In early Italian poetry *donna* retained much of the sense of Latin *domina,* a superior lady (comparable to "mistress" in the English Renaissance sense), to be contrasted with *femina,* an inferior Eve-like woman. On the whole I opted for "lady," hoping that irrelevant associations would be repressed by the context. Then there are terms such as *virtù* ("virtue"), *umiltà* ("humility"), and *valore* ("worth" and also "power"). A literal translation might pass in certain contexts, but it often seemed better to find a paraphrase. The nuances in the original often vary, depending on the context, and these are certainly not technically precise terms in Petrarch, who has no sympathy with scholastic attempts to find objective definitions for abstractions.

Another set of headaches stemmed from some of Petrarch's favorite adjectives, words with imprecise meanings whose function may at times be as much musical as semantic, though that is certainly not always the case. *Bello,* which occurs in one form or another more than three hundred times (in a total of 366 poems), may give the lightest additional touch to what it qualifies. Sometimes I have omitted it altogether; once or twice I have risked the older English "fair"; and at those moments when it is emphasized I have resorted to "lovely" or "beautiful," ponderous though both are in comparison. For *dolce* I have regularly settled for "sweet," though it is more saccharine in both its sound and associations than is the Italian. For *soave* ("soothingly pleasing," particularly used of sound), *leggiadro* ("pretty," with suggestions of delicacy, almost insubstantiality), *vago* ("attractive but insubstantial," with connotations of the Latin *vagus,* "wandering, unstable, errant"), I have tried various solutions depending on the context.

The puns on Laura's name (discussed in section 2) pose a particular problem, given their thematic and musical importance. Something of the basic Laura–laurel connection may remain in English, but the play on *l'aura* ("breeze, air") is inevitably lost, as are the connections with *l'auro* ("gold," the color of her hair), or *l'aurora* ("dawn"). Perhaps an alert and sympathetic reader may be able to call some of these lost connections to mind when, say, winds or trees appear in the English. Much else is lost too. I try to console myself with the thought that Petrarch's poetry is predicated on distance, loss, and frustration. But Petrarch managed to transform those negatives, even if he was never certain about the status of the poetry that resulted. As translator, I feel even worse than Petrarch claimed to feel at the end of Poem 308, when he attempted to do justice to the dead Laura:

> but when I reach that part which is divine,
> that was a bright and brief sun to this world,
> at that point daring, wits, and art all fail.

Petrarch's Latin prose demands almost as much from the translator as his Italian poetry. His efforts to recover a lost classicism do not always seem to be directed toward clarity of expression. Though the general sense is usually graspable, the detailed progression of an argument can be elusive. It is also by no means easy to gauge the tone of many passages, let alone find English equivalents. Overall I have aimed at moderate formality and sobriety, though with some variation to reflect modulations in the original. The dialogue between Franciscus and Augustine in the *Secretum,* for instance, includes conversational exchanges with moments of ironic humor, elaborate addresses in which Augustine tries to persuade Franciscus to change his life, and other passages that fall somewhere between these two. I tried to convey these changes of tone while always steering a middle course between pomposity and contemporary chattiness. The sense of the *Secretum* is, however, reasonably clear, as is that of the letter To Posterity (Letter 5). But the letter to Giacomo Colonna on the reality of Laura (Letter 1), and even more the one to Boccaccio on vernacular Italian poetry (Letter 4), have a disorienting allusiveness and ambiguity that are no doubt deliberate. In both cases I have aimed to provide a serviceable version, while remaining very much aware that Petrarch is holding back perhaps as much as he is apparently revealing.

All translations of Petrarch's quotations from other Latin authors are my own. The main reason for this is that Petrarch's versions often include slight adaptations, or are based on texts that differ from standard modern editions. Quotations from the Bible follow the text of the Revised Standard Version. The notes cite the English titles of the source texts and give the relevant books, lines, and (where appropriate) paragraphs, according to standard modern numeration.

Editions Used and Further Reading

Editions Used

Canzoniere

Canzoniere, edited by Gianfranco Contini. Turin: Einaudi, 1968.

Canzoniere, edited by Mario Santagata. Milan: Mondadori, 1996.

The *Triumphs*

Trionfi, Rime estravaganti, Codice degli abbozzi, edited by Vinicio Pacca and Laura Paolino. Milan: Mondadori, 1996.

The *Secretum, Familiares* 2.9 and 4.1, and the Letter to Posterity

Prose, edited by Guido Martellotti, Pier Giorgio Ricci, Enrico Carrara, and Enrico Bianchi. Milan and Naples: Ricciardi, 1955.

***Verse Letter* 1.6**

Rime, Trionfi e poesie latine, edited by Guido Martellotti and Enrico Bianchi. Milan and Naples: Ricciardi, 1951.

***Seniles* 5.2**

Senile V.2, edited by Monica Berté. Florence: Casa Editrice Le Lettere, 1998.

Further Reading

Complete Translations of the *Canzoniere*

Petrarch's Lyric Poems, translated by Robert Durling. Cambridge, Mass.: Harvard University Press, 1976.

The Poetry of Petrarch, translated by David Young. New York: Farrar, Straus & Giroux, 2004.

Historical Anthology of Translations of the Italian Poems

Petrarch in English, edited by Thomas P. Roche. London: Penguin, 2003.

Translations of Other Works of Petrarch

Invectives, edited and translated by David Marsh, I Tatti Renaissance Library, vol. 11. Cambridge, Mass., and London: Harvard University Press, 2003.

Letters of Old Age [Seniles], 2 vols., translated by Aldo S. Bernardo, Saul Levin, and Reta R. Bernardo. Baltimore: Johns Hopkins University Press, 1992.

Letters on Familiar Matters [Familiares], 3 vols., translated by Aldo S. Bernardo. Baltimore: Johns Hopkins University Press, 1976–1985.

On His Own Ignorance, translated by Hans Nachod, in *The Renaissance Philosophy of Man*, edited by Ernst Cassirer, Paul Oskar Kristeller, and John Herman Randall Jr., Chicago and London: University of Chicago Press, 1948, pp. 49–133.

Petrarch's Africa, translated by Thomas G. Bergin and Alice S. Wilson. New Haven: Yale University Press, 1977.

Petrarch's Bucolicum Carmen, translated by Thomas G. Bergin. New Haven: Yale University Press, 1974.

Petrarch's Remedies for Fortune Fair and Foul, translated by Conrad H. Rawski. Bloomington: Indiana University Press, 1991.

The Triumphs of Petrarch, translated by Ernest Hatch Wilkins. Chicago: University of Chicago Press, 1962.

Studies of Petrarch

Barolini, Teodolinda, and H. Wayne Storey, eds. *Petrarch and the Textual Origins of Interpretation.* Leiden and Boston: Brill, 2007.

Foster, Kenelm. *Petrarch, Poet and Humanist.* Edinburgh: Edinburgh University Press, 1984.

Hainsworth, Peter. *Petrarch the Poet.* London: Routledge, 1988.

Kennedy, William J. *Authorizing Petrarch.* Ithaca, N.Y., and London: Cornell University Press, 1994.

Kirkham, Victoria, and Armando Maggi, eds. *Petrarch: A Critical Guide to the Complete Works.* Chicago and London: University of Chicago Press, 2009.

Mann, Nicholas. *Petrarch.* Oxford: Oxford University Press, 1984.

Mazzotta, Guido. *The Worlds of Petrarch.* Durham, N.C., and London: Duke University Press, 1993.

McLaughlin, Martin, and Letizia Panizza, with Peter Hainsworth, eds. *Petrarch in Britain: Interpreters, Imitators, and Translators over 700 Years.* Oxford: Oxford University Press, 2007.

Mortimer, Anthony, ed. *Petrarch's Canzoniere in the English Renaissance.* Milan and Bergamo: Minerva Italica, 1975.

Roche Jr., Thomas P. *Petrarch and the English Sonnet Sequences.* New York: AMR Press, 1989.

Biography

Wilkins, Ernest H. *Life of Petrarch.* Chicago: University of Chicago Press, 1961.

Poems from the *Canzoniere*

Part I

1

Voi ch'ascoltate in rime sparse il suono

You who hear sounding in my scattered verse
those sighs on which I used to feed my heart
during the time of my first youthful error,
when part of me was different from today,

for all the varied ways I weep and argue,
veering from vacuous hope to vacuous pain,
from any who know love through having lived it,
I hope I may win pity, not just pardon.

But now I can well see how everyone
has long thought me a scandal. Hence I often
will only share the shame with my own self,

and shame's the fruit of my vacuity,
and repenting, and knowing clearly that
whatever this world loves is a brief dream.

1: "scattered verse"—not brought together in one long unified poem.

3

Era il giorno ch'al sol si scoloraro

It was the day on which the sun's rays lost
all color at their Maker's suffering,
when I was captured, being quite off-guard,
and your fair eyes, my lady, bound me tight.

I did not think that it might be a time
to fight off blows from Love, and went along
carefree and unsuspecting. Hence my woes
started amid our common human grief.

Love found me totally devoid of arms,
and the road clear to the heart through the eyes
that are now tears' passage and exit route.

And yet in my view it did him no honor
to wound me with an arrow in that state,
and to you (armed) not even show his bow.

1: Good Friday. According to Poem 211, Petrarch saw Laura for the first time on April 6, 1327, though historically this was not in fact Good Friday.

4

Que' ch'infinita providentia et arte

He who displayed infinite providence
and art in His amazing masterwork,
who made this and the other hemisphere
and Jupiter a kinder force than Mars,

coming to earth to bring light to the pages
that had for many years concealed the truth,
took John and Peter from their fishing nets,
and had them share with Him the heavenly kingdom.

He did not grant grace of His birth to Rome,
but to Judaea, so pleased He always was
to raise humility above all other states.

From a small town He's given us now a sun,
one that makes us thank nature and the place
where such a lovely being had her birth.

1–4: The lines refer to the creation of the earth and the planets.

5–6: The coming of Christ clarified the previously obscure prophecies of the Old Testament.

7: The Apostles John and Peter were fishermen (see Matt. 4:18).

12–14: The sun is Laura, who may have been born at Caumont near Avignon.

5

Quando io movo i sospiri a chiamar voi

When I release my sighs to call on you
and speak the name that Love wrote in my heart,
LAUding begins the first sound to be heard
of the sweet syllables from which it's formed.

Your REgal state that I encounter next
doubles my courage for the high endeavor.
But "TAlk not" cries the end, for honoring her
needs stronger mettle than you'll ever have.

And so the name itself teaches to LAUd
and to REvere, just through addressing you
who merit every reverence and honor—

except Apollo's anger might be stirred
to hear a mortal tongue presume to speak
about his branches of unfailing green.

This is the first poem in the *Canzoniere* in which the name of Laura (here in the unusual form *Laureta*) is equated with *lauro,* the laurel (see Introduction, section 2). The poem breaks down the constituent syllables of this word and plays on them, first in their entirety (2–7) and then incompletely (9–10).

12–14: Here as elsewhere Petrarch takes up the myth of the laurel being sacred to Apollo, the god of poetry and fame.

6

Sí travïato è 'l folle mi' desio

My crazed desire has gone so far astray
pursuing one who turns in flight from me,
who, lightly stepping past the snares of Love,
flies off before my lumbering pursuit,

that now the more I call it back and point
it down the safe, sure track, the less it listens.
Spurring is useless, pulling the reins too,
for Love makes it unruly naturally.

And once it takes the bridle to itself,
I am left helpless in the power of one
who carries me to death against my will:

all this to reach the laurel and to pick
its bitter fruit, the taste of which makes wounds
worse than they were, rather than brings relief.

This poem is an allusive retelling of the story of Apollo's pursuit of Daphne, with Petrarch substituting himself for the god. See Introduction, section 2.

7

La gola e 'l somno et l'otïose piume

Gluttony, sloth, and vapid luxury
have banished any virtue from the world;
and hence our nature, overwhelmed by habit,
has almost lost sight of its proper path.

All light that shines benignly from the heavens
to shape our human life is now so dimmed
that people point out as a thing of wonder
one who would tap a stream from Helicon.

What wish is there for laurels or for myrtle?
"You go by poor and naked, love of wisdom,"
so say the crowd, intent on sordid profit.

You will have few companions on the other road.
Thus all the more I beg you, noble soul,
don't break off from your generous enterprise.

8: Helicon is the range of mountains in ancient Boeotia sacred to Apollo and the Muses, where the springs of poetry were supposed to rise.

9: The laurel crown was notionally for epic poetry, the myrtle for lyric.

12–14: A friend, who may be Giovanni Colonna, is being urged not to abandon a major poetic project he has embarked on.

10

Gloriosa columna in cui s'appoggia

Colonna, glorious column on whom rest
our hopes and the great name we Latins bear,
whom angry fits from Jove have never turned
from the true path for all his wind and rain,

here are no palaces, theaters, or arcades,
but there's instead a fir, a beech, a pine
among green grass, and the fine mountain near,
to come down lost in poetry, or to climb—

these lift our minds up high from earth to heaven:
and there's the nightingale that every night
sweetly laments and moans out in the shadows,

entrammeling our hearts in thoughts of love:
but you leave all these good things spoiled and stunted,
by keeping from us, sir, your company.

1: The opening puns on the name of the Colonna family, Petrarch's patrons in Provence. The addressee may be either Stefano, the patriarch of the family, or Giacomo, to whom Petrarch addressed the letter proclaiming Laura's existence as a real person (see Letter 1).

2–4: Petrarch is probably saying that Colonna has kept faith with the destiny of Rome, no matter what trials have been inflicted on him.

12

Se la mia vita da l'aspro tormento

If, in the face of torment and fatigue,
my life can shield itself for long enough
for me to witness how your later years
have rubbed the sparkle, lady, from your eyes,

and see the fine gold of your hair turned silver,
the garlands and the green garb put aside,
and that face bleakened which, for all my troubles,
makes me too slow and timid to complain,

Love finally will make me bold enough
to stop concealing what a martyrdom
I've lived through every year and day and hour,

and if the time has turned against desire,
at least my pains must finally be granted
some succor from your all too tardy sighs.

16

Movesi il vecchierel canuto et biancho

The little, pale-faced, hoary-locked old man,
quits the sweet home where he has lived his days,
quits his astounded relatives and friends,
who see the father they have loved now fail them;

and dragging off his antiquated frame
through the concluding days of his life's course,
he wills himself along as best he can,
broken by age and wearied by the road,

and comes to Rome, pursuing his desire,
to look upon the likeness of the one
whom he hopes yet to see above in heaven.

So I, alas, so far as can be done,
seek out at times in other women,
lady, the much-desired, true form of you.

11–12: Probably a venerated image of Christ represented in a Byzantine icon preserved in St. Peter's in Rome, rather than the Veronica, the shroud reputedly imprinted with the "true image" of Christ.

22

A qualunque animal alberga in terra

For every living being that dwells on earth,
leaving aside the ones that hate the sun,
the time for toil lasts only through the day.
And then, when heaven illuminates its stars,
some come back home, others nest in the wood,
to rest at least until the following dawn.

And I, from the first moment that the dawn
starts to shake darkness from around the earth,
awakening living beings in every wood,
have no respite from sighing with the sun.
Then when I see the flickering of the stars,
I weep and weep, just longing for the day.

When evening chases off the light of day
and darkness here makes other people's dawn,
brooding, I gaze upon the cruel stars
whose power has made me out of sentient earth,
and curse the day when I first saw the sun
that makes me seem a wild man of the wood.

I do not think that ever in a wood
there fed so wild a beast, by night or day,
as that for which I weep in shade and sun,
not being tired by sleep-time or by dawn,
for though a mortal body made of earth,
I got my fixed obsession from the stars.

Before I come again to you, bright stars,
or tumble down into the lovers' wood,

17: The sun here is Laura. She is also the beast of line 20.

25: The line may refer to an ascent to a Christian heaven, but the image draws on the Platonic belief that after death the soul returns to the particular star that was its home before birth.

26: Virgil speaks of a special wood in his underworld where the souls of unhappy lovers are confined (*Aeneid* 6.442).

leaving my body to be dusty earth,
would I saw pity in her, which in one day
can compensate for years, and before dawn
can make me rich right from the setting sun.

To be with her when there's no longer sun
and no one sees us other than the stars,
just for one night, and never there be dawn!
And she not change herself to green-tree wood
to go free from my arms, as on that day
Apollo chased her here below on earth!

But I'll be under earth in sapless wood
and day will go by thick with myriad stars
before so sweet a dawn receives the sun.

36: For Petrarch's use of the myth of Apollo and Daphne, see Introduction, section 2.

37: "in sapless wood"—perhaps Petrarch is simply saying that he will be dead and buried in a wooden coffin.

23

Nel dolce tempo della prima etade

There was a sweet time in my earlier years,
which saw the birth and then the seedling form
of wild desire that grew to do me ill.
Since singing soothes the bitterness of pain,
I'll sing of how I lived in liberty
so long as Love disdained to lodge with me.
Then I'll go on to tell how deeply he
felt mortified, and what ensued for me,
so that I'm now a general object lesson,
though I've already written
so much on my disaster I've worn out
a thousand pens, and almost every valley
throbs with the echoes of the heavy sighs
that prove how painful is the life I live.
And if here memory fails to give the help
it used to give, let the torments excuse it,
and an obsession that just causes hurt,
turning all thoughts away from other things
and with such force that I forget myself.
It owns the inner me, and I the shell.

To tell the story, many years had passed
since the day Love attacked me the first time,
and I looked less the young man I had been.
Around my heart a habit of cold thought
had made an almost adamantine cast
that kept my firm resolve as strong as ever.
As yet there were no tears to bathe my breast
or break my sleep. And what was not in me

Early drafts of parts of this poem date to the 1320s, though it was not finished until much later. It is Petrarch's longest and most elaborate *canzone* (for more on this form, see Introduction, section 2) and the first instance of the form in the *Canzoniere*. In it Petrarch presents himself as undergoing a series of transformations inflicted by Love and Laura. His source throughout is Ovid's *Metamorphoses*.

astounded me when it appeared in others.
What am I now! what then!
Life's luster is its end, as day's is sunset.
The sadist god of whom I speak, apprised
that hitherto the impact of his arrow
had not passed further than my outer coat,
recruited to his ranks a powerful lady
on whom force, cleverness, or begging pardon
had never an effect, and still have none.
Those two transformed me into what I am,
making the living man a verdant laurel
that loses not one leaf in the cold season.

What a state I fell into when I first
became aware of my transfigured person,
and saw my hair made foliage of that tree
with which I once had hoped it would be crowned,
the feet on which I stood and moved and ran
(the body's parts take from the soul their cue)
become two roots beside the flowing waters
not of Peneus, but of a prouder river,
and my two arms mutate into two branches!
And I freeze still with terror
to think how next white feathers coated me,
after my hope that mounted up too high,
was struck by a lightning bolt and fell dead.
And since I had no notion where or when
I might recover it, alone and tearful,
I walked on day and night where I had lost it,
searching beside the waters and beneath them.
And then my tongue, as long as it was able,
was never still about that dismal fall.
So I took on a swan's voice and its color.

31: I.e., it is the end that counts.

40: For the story of Daphne, see Introduction, section 2. Here, unusually in the *Canzoniere,* Petrarch himself, not Laura, is the one who is changed.

48: The Rhône, the river near which Laura lived, is seen here as superior to the Peneus, along whose banks Daphne was pursued by Apollo.

50–60: Petrarch combines the myths of Cygnus (*Met.* 2.367–80) and Phaethon (*Met.* 2.304–39). Cygnus was transformed into a swan, which released him from the desperate grief he felt at the death of his nephew Phaethon, who had lost control of the sun's chariot and been killed by Jove. The white feathers may also be an allusion to Petrarch's hair turning white prematurely.

I went like this along the banks I loved,
for, though I wished to speak, I always sang,
calling for pity in an alien voice,
but never once did I make music of
the pains of love in such sweet or soft tones
that her harsh, savage heart would stoop to me.
How did it feel then, if mere recall scalds me?
But there is much more than has yet been said
about my bitterly sweet enemy
that I still need to say,
although what she is must surpass all speech.
This thief who steals the spirit with a look,
opened my breast, and with her hand removed
my heart, admonishing, "No word of this."
I next saw her alone, so changed in manner
I did not recognize her (oh human sense!)
and fearfully went on to voice the truth.
At which she quickly reassumed
her usual guise and turned me, oh alas,
into a half-alive, dumbfounded stone.

She spoke with such displeasure in her face
she made me tremble there inside the stone,
hearing, "Perhaps I'm not what you believe."
And I said to myself, "If she unlocks me,
no life will be so harmful or so bleak.
Come back again, lord Love, and let me weep."
I don't know how, and yet I moved from there,
putting the blame on no one but myself,
for that whole day half-living and half-dead.
But since time is so short,
the pen falls short of what the will desires,
and most things that are written in my mind
I leave aside and speak just of a few
that cause astonishment in any hearers.

72–80: Petrarch here draws on the story of Battus, who promised Mercury not to reveal a certain secret to anyone but then told it to Mercury himself when he appeared to him in disguise. He was punished by being turned into a touchstone (*Met.* 2.676–707). Laura's disguise is to appear unusually receptive.

75–77: He thinks she has become better disposed to him and mistakenly dares to tell her of his desires.

Death now had wrapped itself around my heart;
I could not prize his grip free while not speaking,
or give aid to my battered vital powers,
since all live speeches were forbidden me.
So I gave out an ink-and-paper cry,
"I'm not mine, no. If I die, it's your loss."

I really thought to change thus in her eyes
from an unworthy to a deserving case,
and hoping this had given me fresh daring.
But sometimes humbleness quenches disdain,
at others fires it. And I learned this next,
when for a long time I was cloaked in darkness,
for she, my light, had vanished at those pleas.
Finding no shadow of her anywhere,
no trace of her feet, like someone traveling
who sleeps along the road,
I wearily flopped on the grass one day,
blaming the sunray that had run from me
and miserably giving in to tears,
which I let indiscriminately fall.
Snow never disappeared beneath the sun
the way I felt all of my being melt,
and make a fountain at a beech tree's foot.
I stayed a long time with that watery flow.
Who's heard of springs being really born from men?
But what I say is a plain, well-known fact.

That soul which has nobility from God alone,
(for from no other source may such grace come)
retains a similarity with its maker:
so never is it sated with forgiving
those who with humble heart and countenance,
no matter what their sins, come to ask mercy.
And if it, out of character, demands
to be much begged, it still mirrors our Lord,
and so acts to deter the more from sinning.
For it's not true repentance

95–120: Petrarch has in mind here the story of Byblis, who wrote a letter to her brother Caunus, telling him of her illicit love for him. Distraught at her rejection, she was transformed by sympathetic water-nymphs into an ever-flowing spring of tears. (*Met.* 9.460–665).

for one sin if another is prospected.
So when my lady, feeling pity stirring,
deigned to regard me, recognized me, saw
the penalty was equal to the sin,
she kindly brought me back to my first state.
But there's nought in the world a wise man trusts.
At further pleas from me she turned my bones
and sinews into flint, and I was left
as a mere voice, wrenched from my former form,
calling for death, and just for her by name.

A suffering spirit, wandering, I recall,
through empty caverns deep in distant lands,
I wept for years over my unchecked rashness.
And then I found that that pain ended too,
and came back once more to my earthly limbs,
so as to feel, I think, still greater pain.
I followed then so hard on my desire
that I became habitually a hunter
and one day found my lovely, heartless quarry
bathing in a spring pool
quite naked, when the sun was blazing strongest.
No other sight could give me such a pleasure;
I stopped and watched, at which she became modest.
To punish me, or to conceal herself,
with both hands she splashed water in my eyes.
I'll tell the truth, though it may seem a lie:
I felt myself drawn from my normal image,
and suddenly transformed into a stag
that roams alone from one wood to the next.
Still now I'm running from my pack of hounds.

My song, I never was that cloud of gold
that once descended as a precious rain

136–40: Echo unwisely allowed herself to speak of her unhappy love for Narcissus and was changed to rock by Juno, with only her human voice surviving (*Met.* 2.339–510).

148–60: Actaeon, out hunting, came across Diana bathing. She was horrified to have been seen naked and changed Actaeon into a stag. He was then hunted and torn apart by his own hounds (*Met.* 3.138–252).

161–68: Jove came to Danae in a shower of gold (*Met.* 4.610–11). He changed into fire for love of Aegina (*Met.* 7.615–18) and became an eagle to carry off Ganymede (*Met.* 10.155–61).

and for a while dampened the fire of Jove.
But, yes, I was the flame that one look lit,
and was the bird that soars most through the air,
uplifting her I honor in my poems.
But I could not abandon the first laurel
for any novel shape. Its sweet shade still
clears any lesser beauty from my heart.

30

Giovene donna sotto un verde lauro

I saw beneath a green-leafed laurel tree
a young woman more white and cold than snow
that sunlight has not struck for years and years.
I loved her voice and lovely face and hair
so much I see her still before my eyes
and always shall, whether on hill or shore.

My fantasies will finally reach shore
when no green leaf rests on the laurel tree.
When I've a heart at rest, eyes that are dry,
we'll see fire freezing cold and snow ablaze.
I've not upon my head as many hairs
as all the years I'd wait to see that day.

But since time's on the wing and years flee by,
with death's shore being in an instant reached,
whether with dark hair or with hair that's white,
I shall pursue the shade of the sweet laurel
under the hottest sun and through the snow,
until my last day closes up these eyes.

Never were seen such lovely eyes as hers,
either in our time or in ancient years.
They melt my being as the sun melts snow
and from my melting flows a stream of tears
that Love guides to the foot of the hard laurel,
with diamond branches and with leaves of gold.

This sestina (for the form, see Introduction, section 2) represents Laura and the laurel tree into which she changes in startlingly brilliant stylized metaphors. The translation retains some repetitions of the six key words but not all.

1–3: Laura, untouched by the heat of passion, is spectrally pure, as is the poetry she inspires.

24: In human terms, the branches are her arms, the leaves her hair. The images of diamonds and gold suggest both preciousness and a hard resistance to love.

I fear my hair and face will change before
my idol, carved in a live laurel tree,
shows any real compassion in her eyes.
If I count right, it is seven years today
that I have sighed my way from shore to shore,
by night and day, through summer heat and snow.

All fire within, the whitest snow without,
with these same thoughts, although my hair will change,
I'll always walk in tears by any stream,
perhaps to bring compassion to the eyes
of someone born a thousand years from now,
if well-grown laurel can survive so long.

Topaz and gold displayed on sunlit snow
shine less than does blond hair above the eyes
leading my years so quickly to their end.

28: Since Petrarch saw Laura first on Good Friday in 1327, this line dates this poem to Good Friday of 1334. As with other so-called "anniversary" poems, it is advisable not to treat the dating too literally.

31: The snow probably refers to his pallor.

36: His weeping may result in poetry (the laurel), which may perhaps move readers a thousand years later.

32

Quanto più m'avicino al giorno estremo

The nearer that I come to that last day
which must curtail our human misery,
the more I see Time speeding lightly by,
and hopes I placed in him fail and fall short.

I tell my thoughts, "Not for long now shall we
go on speaking of love, for the hard, heavy
weight of earthliness, like snow freshly fallen,
is now dissolving. So we shall have peace.

For with the flesh the hope will crumble
that for so long deprived us of our wits;
so too will tears and laughter, fear and rage.

Thus we shall clearly see how frequently
a benefit may come from fearful things,
and how so often sighs are all in vain."

14: The line leaves ambiguous whether it is the sighs of love that are vain, or sighs of concern about death.

33

Già fiammeggiava l'amorosa stella

The star of love already was aflame
toward the east, and the other star that still
makes Juno jealous in the northern sky
was wheeling her rays round in shining beauty;

the aged crone was up to start her spinning,
half-dressed and shoeless, and had stirred the embers,
and lovers were being needled by that hour
which has a way of summoning their tears,

when my sole hope, ravaged before her time,
entered my heart, not by her usual path,
which sleep kept closed and suffering drenched in tears.

How changed, alas, from what she was before!
And yet she seemed to say, "Why lose heart now?
You are not yet denied sight of these eyes."

1: "The star of love"—Venus.

2–4: The nymph Callisto was changed into a she-bear by Jupiter in order to save her from the jealousy of Juno. When Callisto was eventually hunted down, she became the constellation of the Great Bear.

7–8: The hour is dawn, at which time lovers have to separate.

9–11: He has a vision of Laura in a state near to death. It comes to him by some other route than via his eyes (the "usual path").

34

Apollo, s'anchor vive il bel desio

Apollo, if that fine desire still lives
that fired you once by the Thessalian waters,
and if you have not, with the passing years,
forgotten now the blond hair that you loved,

from numbing frost and harsh inclemency
that lasts as long as your face hides away,
guard now the sacred, honored laurel leaves
in which you first were trapped, and later I:

and through the power of the hope of love,
which helped you bear a bitter human life,
expel these exhalations from the air.

So then in wonder both of us shall see
our lady take her seat upon the grass
and make shade for herself with her own arms.

Apollo as the sun-god is asked to dispel noxious mists and clouds so that Laura will appear. But she is also identified here with both Daphne, the nymph loved by Apollo in his human form, and with the laurel tree she became (see Introduction, section 2). Since Apollo is the god of poetry, the poem is partly an allegory of the desire to recover the art of poetry as practiced by the ancients. More simply, like the preceding sonnet, this poem may also refer to the illness of Laura.

2: "the Thessalian waters"—the river Peneus in Thessaly.

10: Apollo was exiled from Olympus for a time and lived as a Thessalian shepherd.

35

Solo et pensoso i più deserti campi

Alone and brooding I go pacing out
the emptiest fields with slow and sluggish steps,
and watch intently so as to avoid
places where human footsteps print the ground.

I find no other screen to shelter me
from plain exposure to the public gaze,
since one can read in every joyless move
an outer sign of how I burn within.

By now I think that mountains and hillsides
and woods and rivers know the tenor of
my life, which is concealed from everyone.

But I cannot explore such rugged paths,
and such wild ones, if Love does not always
come talking with me as I do with him.

50

Ne la stagion che 'l ciel rapido inchina

At that time when the sun sinks rapidly
toward the west, and our day flies to people
awaiting it perhaps somewhere beyond,
finding herself alone and far from home
the tired old woman on a pilgrimage
doubles her pace and hurries more and more.
And then, all by herself,
with her day's journey done,
perhaps she finds relief
in some short rest, through which she can forget
the aches and troubles of the road she's traveled.
But, oh, each pain that daylight brings to me
grows when the eternal light
sets out upon its parting journey from us.

As the sun turns away his flaming wheels
to give space to the night, and ever longer
the shadows spread down from the topmost peaks,
the skinflint peasant gathers up his tools,
and, with the music of his mountain songs,
empties his heart of all its heaviness,
and then loads up his table
with miserable victuals—
food like those acorns that
the whole world honors and keeps well away from.
Let anyone who has the chance be happy:
for I as yet have never had one hour
of rest, let alone joy,
through any movement of a heaven or planet.

24: According to classical poets, men lived happily on acorns in the Golden Age, though no one would really like to go back to such a diet.

28: In the Ptolemaic universe the various "heavens" in which the planets were located circled around the earth.

When the shepherd sees the great planet's rays
plummet toward the refuge where he lodges,
and darkness seep over the eastern lands,
he ups himself, and, with his usual stick,
leaving the pastures, springs, and beeches,
quietly moves his troop along its way.
Then far from other people
he spreads green rushes out
in some cavern or shack,
and, free from care, settles himself and sleeps.
Ah, cruel Love, you drive me then the most:
and have me chase the call and steps and tracks
of the beast wasting me,
and leave her free to lie low and escape.

And there are sheltered bays where sailors stop
and, when the sun hides, throw their bodies down
on the hard timbers under rough cloaks.
But I? The sun may plunge into the waves,
may leave Spain at his back, and leave Granada,
Morocco, the Pillars of Hercules,
and men and women and
the world and all live things
may feel their troubles eased,
but I can't end my obdurate distress,
and grieve that every day adds to the damage.
For this obsession now has grown in me
almost for ten years now,
and I've no notion who might set me free.

And—since I find some small relief in words—
I see each evening oxen coming back,
unyoked from fields and hills that they have furrowed.
Why is the weight of sighs not taken from me
at any time? Why not the heavy yoke?
Why, day and night, are my eyes wet with tears?
Poor fool, what did I want
when I first gazed so hard

41: The beast is Laura.

48: "the Pillars of Hercules"—the Rock of Gibraltar, which Hercules was supposed to have set up to mark the limit beyond which men should not go.

55: Since Petrarch says that he first saw Laura in 1327, the line seems to date this poem to 1336–1337, though how reliably one cannot say.

into the lovely face
and carved its mental image in a place
from which no strength or stratagem will ever
move it, not till all-dissipating death
has got me for its prey.
Though I'm not sure I can believe that either.

My song, if being with me
from morning until evening
has banded us together,
there's nowhere that you'll want to show yourself.
You'll care so little about public praise
you'll be content to go from hill to hill,
thinking how I've been treated
by fire from this live flint on which I rest.

78: Laura is represented as a flintstone, cold and hard in itself, but able to ignite passionate love.

52

Non al suo amante più Diana piacque

Diana's lover felt no greater thrill
when—likewise by some chance—he saw her bathing
totally naked in the chilling waters,

than I felt when the rough alpine sheep-girl
was crouched down rinsing out a bit of veil
to hold her loose blond hair back in the wind,

so that she made me, now when heaven is blazing,
shiver all over with a chill of love.

This is the first of only four *madrigali* (a short form with variable rhyme scheme favored by contemporary musicians) that Petrarch included in the *Canzoniere*.

1: To emphasize the parallel with himself, Petrarch here makes Actaeon, who had the misfortune to see Diana bathing (see note to Poem 23, line 148), into her lover.

2: Actaeon happens to see Diana, as Petrarch happens to see the sheep-girl.

4–6: Since Petrarch does not usually cast Laura as a shepherdess, it may be that he did not write the poem for her, though in the original he appears to use his standard pun on her name with the wind in line 6 (*l'aura*).

53

Spirto gentil che quelle membra reggi

Noble spirit, regulating that body
in which a brave, sharp-witted, and wise lord
is hosted on his earthly pilgrimage,
you've risen now to hold the honored rod,
with which you scourge Rome and its miscreants
and redirect it to its ancient ways.
I address you, for nowhere else I see
a ray of virtue, which is spent worldwide,
and find no one ashamed of doing wrong.
What Italy, which seems not to feel her troubles,
is waiting for, or wants, I do not know.
She's old, inactive, slow.
Will she sleep always and will no one wake her?
Would I could get my hands around her hair!

I have no hope of her head stirring ever
from her dull sleep, however loudly called,
so heavily does such a weight oppress her.
But destiny's at work, if to your arms,
which have the power to shake her hard and raise her,
our capital, our Rome is now committed.
Lay hands upon the venerable locks
with confidence, and sieze the unkempt tresses,
and get the sluggard free from all the slime.
I weep over her outrage day and night
and place the great part of my hopes on you.
If the people of Mars
will ever raise their eyes to their own honor,
that grace I can see happening in your time.

Written at some point during the turmoils afflicting Rome in the 1330s and 1340s, this *canzone* addresses a recently elevated Roman senator. He has often been identified as Cola di Rienzo, though he was never a senator. But the addressee may be the much more obscure Bosone da Gubbio, elected senator in October 1337.

4: "the honored rod"—almost certainly the scepter of a Roman senator.

26: The Romans were considered special favorites of Mars.

The ancient walls that still today the world
fears, loves, and trembles at, when it recalls
the times gone by and once again looks back,
the stones in which the bodies were enclosed
of men who never will be without fame
unless the universe is first dissolved,
and everything plunged in a general ruin—
all hope that you will mend each single flaw.
O you great Scipios, O faithful Brutus,
how glad you'll be, if in the world below
there's word of such an excellent appointment!
How joyful I believe
it makes Fabritius to hear the news!
He says, "My Rome's recovering her beauty."

And, if heaven spares a thought for things below,
the souls who are now citizens above
and left behind their bodies here on earth,
beg you to end this lasting civil hatred
that leaves the mass of people insecure,
and closes off the routes to the saints' shrines,
which once were so revered and now, through war,
have been made almost into dens of thieves.
The doors are closed only against the good,
and amid altars and denuded statues
there's every form of cruelty on show.
O what unnaturalness!
And fighting's started to the peals of bells
which were hung high above to thank our God.

Women, tears in their eyes, and helpless throngs
of tender children, and the tired old men

37: The Scipios are Scipio Africanus Major, who defeated Hannibal and who is the hero of Petrarch's Latin epic, the *Africa,* and Scipio Africanus Minor, who brought about the final destruction of Carthage in 146 BCE. Lucius Junius Brutus was so faithful to the cause of Republican Rome that he put his own sons to death when they conspired to restore the tyrannical Tarquins.

39: All the Romans mentioned lived during the Republican period, that is, before the coming of Christ. They are therefore condemned to "the world below," rather than being allowed into heaven.

41–42: Gaius Fabritius Luscinus was a Roman statesman celebrated for his incorruptibility.

55: Church bells are being used by factional bands as signals for battle.

who loathe themselves and their too lengthy lives,
and black friars, grey friars, and the white friars too,
and line on line of the distressed and weak,
are crying out, "Help us, our lord, oh help."
And there are the poor people in a daze
who bare to you their numberless afflictions
that would make even Hannibal feel pity.
But if you want to help this house of God
that's now ablaze, you'll put out just a few
firebrands and then those passions
that look now so enflamed will fade away.
And then your actions will be praised in heaven.

Bears, wolves, lions, eagles, and snakes are bent
on damaging a mighty marble column
as often as they can but harm themselves.
For them are tears shed by that noble lady,
who summoned you to uproot from her garden
the evil weeds that have not learned to bloom.
By now more than the thousandth year has passed
since she was left without those inspired souls
who raised her to the place that was her due.
Ah, upstarts of unlimited presumption,
with no respect for such a wondrous mother!
You be husband, be father;
your hand must be the one to give her aid,
since the great father's otherwise engaged.

It rarely happens that high enterprise
is not obstructed by malicious fortune,
who ill accords with actions of great spirit.
Since she has cleared an entry for you now,

60: Various orders of friars: the black are probably the Dominicans, the white the Augustinians, and the grey the Franciscans.

66–70: The house of God here is Rome. It will be sufficient to execute the ringleaders for the conflicts to die down.

71–73: Symbolic representation of the opposition to Petrarch's patrons, the Colonna family, on the part of other noble Roman families. Petrarch draws on their names and their blazons. The bears are "orsi," the Orsini; the wolves and eagles are two branches of the family of the Counts of Tusculum; the lions are the Savelli; and the snakes are the Caetani.

84: A sardonic reference to the pope (probably Benedict XII), who prefers to remain in Avignon rather than bring the papacy back to Rome.

I can forgive her many another crime,
since this time she's not been her usual self.
For never in the memory of the world
has such a road toward eternal fame
opened for any mortal man but you;
you can restore, unless I see things falsely,
the noblest government to its proper state.
What glory then to say,
"Others helped her when she was young and strong,
but in her old age I saved her from death."

My song, you'll see on the Tarpeian Rock
a knight who's honored by all Italy,
who thinks of others rather than himself.
Tell him, "One who's not seen you face to face,
but feels only the love that fame inspires,
says that Rome constantly,
with tears of suffering in her eyes,
begs you for pity from all seven hills."

99: The Tarpeian Rock is cited as the heart of ancient Rome. It is on the Capitol, one of the two summits of the Capitoline Hill, which is one of the seven hills mentioned in line 106.

54

Perch'al viso d'Amor portava insegna

Since she had Love emblazoned in her eyes,
a pilgrim caused my vacuous heart to beat
and made me think all others of less merit.

And following her up through the green grass,
I heard a voice calling from far away,
"Ah, what a waste this walking in the wood!"

At which I shrank into a beech tree's shade,
full of concern. And looking all around
I saw how perilous my progress was,

and turned back almost halfway through my day.

Only the main lines of this attractively enigmatic *madrigale* can be decoded with any confidence. Petrarch falls in love with Laura (cast as a pilgrim), but then realizes that he is wasting his life on earthly distractions (the grass). The wood is a Dantesque wood of sin and ignorance. The beech may symbolize solitude and meditation. The day is the normal span of life, i.e., seventy years. Notionally, therefore, the poem was written in 1339 or just before, when Petrarch was almost thirty-five.

61

Benedetto sia 'l mese e 'l giorno e l'anno

A blessing on the month and day and year,
and on the season, on the time, hour, moment,
on all that region and the place where I
was captured by two eyes that hold me fast.

A blessing on the first sweet perturbation
I suffered as my being fused with Love,
and on the bow, the arrows piercing me,
and on the wounds that reach right to my heart.

A blessing on the many words that I
have broadcast calling out my lady's name,
and on my sighs, my tears, and my desire.

And blessings fall on every single page
where I win fame for her, and on my thoughts;
all are of her, and leave room for no other.

1–4: According to Petrarch, the day was April 6, 1327, and the place the Church of St. Clare in Avignon (see Introduction, section 1).

62

Padre del ciel, dopo i perduti giorni

Father of heaven, after the wasted days,
after the nights spent vainly floundering,
with that wild passion that flared in my heart
when I saw beauties that could only harm me,

be pleased to shine your light and help me turn
back to another life and finer projects,
that, having laid his nets out to no purpose,
my hardened adversary may be humbled.

The eleventh year, my lord, is now beginning,
since I was put beneath the ruthless yoke
that is most savage to those most submissive.

Have pity on my shameful tribulations;
bring errant thoughts back to a better place;
remind them you were crucified today.

Like other "anniversary" poems, this sonnet dates itself (perhaps fictionally) in relation to Petrarch's first sight of Laura on Good Friday in 1327. Line 9 indicates that this particular Good Friday is that of 1337.

8: "adversary"—the devil.

10: "the ruthless yoke"—love.

72

Gentil mia donna, i' veggio

My noble lady, I can see
a sweet light in the movement of your eyes,
which shows to me the road that leads to heaven.
As has long been the way,
within them where I dwell alone with Love,
your heart casts light that's almost visible.
This is the vision that draws me to virtue,
and gives me guidance to the final glory,
only this parts me from the common herd.
No human tongue could ever
express in language what those two divine
lights always make me feel,
both when the winter sprinkles all with frost,
and then when youth comes to the year again,
as at the time of my first qualms of love.

I think, "If there, so high above,
where dwells the eternal mover of the stars
who deigned to show this work of his on earth,
the other works are as fine,
then let the prison open where I'm held
that bars me from the way to heavenly life."
Then I resume my normal inner turmoil,
but thanking Nature and my day of birth
that have assigned me such a privilege,
and thanking her who raised
my heart to such high hopes. Till then I weighed
irksomely on myself.
From that day on I found myself a pleasure,

This is the second of a sequence of three *canzoni* on Laura's eyes, which are often called the three sisters after the image in the last lines of this poem.

16–21: The thrust of the argument is that if God's creations in heaven are as beautiful as what he has created with Laura, then Petrarch would be happy to be released from the prison of the body in order to see them.

with a delighting, lofty thought to fill
the heart whose key those lovely eyes possess.

Never was any state of joy
granted by Love or rapid-changing Fortune
to those whom they most favored in the world,
which I would not exchange
for one glance from the eyes from which comes all
my peace, just as a tree comes from its roots.
Quick sparks of angel light, touching with bliss
this life of mine, lighting a flame of pleasure
by which I'm sweetly melted and consumed!
Just as where your light shines
all other lights must fade from sight or flee,
so from this heart of mine,
when so much sweetness penetrates its depths,
all other things, all other thoughts depart,
and Love is left there by himself with you.

If all the sweetness were combined
that hearts of lucky lovers ever felt,
it would be nought compared to what I feel
at those moments when softly,
from where your blackness and your whiteness meet,
you shine the beams in which Love loves to play.
I do believe heaven's providence prepared,
when I was in my swaddling clothes and cradle,
this remedy for my flaws and adverse fortune.
But the veil does me wrong,
as does the hand I see so often pass
between my highest joy
and my own eyes, from which both day and night
desire pours floods of tears to ease a heart
ruled by her slightest changes of expression.

Since I can see, though I regret it,
that any natural gift cannot avail me,
or make me worthy of one precious look,
I struggle to become
someone who's fit for this exalted hope,
and for the noble love with which I burn.

50: Laura is imagined as dark-eyed. Perhaps here Petrarch is referring to the blackness of the retina in the white of the eye.

If I can make myself, through careful effort,
quick to serve virtue, slow to the opposite,
one who despises what the world desires,
perhaps my reputation
could help me win from her a kinder verdict.
Of course an end to weeping,
which this heart begs in pain from no one else,
will come when those eyes at last sweetly tremble,
the supreme hope of lovers who love true.

My song, one sister came out earlier.
I feel the third is in that selfsame lodging
getting ready. And so I pen more paper.

76–78: Petrarch takes leave of the poem, mentioning the other two in the sequence. The first "sister" is the preceding *canzone;* the one to follow is imagined already preparing herself in the "lodging" of his mind.

78

Quando giunse a Simon l'alto concetto

When the sublime idea came to Simone
that put his pencil in his hand for me,
if he had granted to his noble work
the powers of speech and thought as well as form,

he would have rid my heart of many a sigh
that makes me scorn what most men hold most dear.
For in her eyes she shows humility,
and her expression promises me peace.

And then when I come to converse with her,
she seems to listen sympathetically,
only she can't reply to what I say.

Pygmalion, what delight you must have felt
your image give you, if a thousand times
you had what I wish could just once be mine!

The artist Simone Martini, whom Petrarch knew in Avignon, apparently drew Laura's portrait for him, perhaps in 1339–1340. The portrait was presumably a drawing rather than a painting, given the drawing pencil of line 2. It is the subject also of Poem 77 (not in this volume) and is mentioned again in the *Secretum* (see note 25 there).

12–14: Aphrodite (Venus) made the sculptor Pygmalion fall in love with a statue he had made, then she kindly brought it to life and they married.

81

Io son sí stanco sotto 'l fascio antico

I am so tired beneath the same old bundle
of my misdeeds and my pernicious habits
that I'm afraid I'll falter on the journey
and that I'll fall into my enemy's hands.

A great friend did come to deliver me
out of supreme, ineffable concern.
And then he soared away beyond my sight,
so that in vain I struggle to behold him.

But here below his voice is still resounding,
"O you who labor, look, here is the way.
Come you to me, unless your path is barred."

What grace, what love, or else what destiny
will give me wings to make me like a dove,
that I may rest and rise up from the earth?

4–5: The enemy is the devil, the "great friend" Christ.

10–11: Echoing Matt. 11:28, "Come to me, all who labor and are heavy-laden, and I will give you rest."

13–14: Echoing Ps. 55:6, "And I say, 'Oh that I had wings like a dove! I would fly away, and be at rest.'"

88

Poi che mia speme è lunga a venir troppo

Since what I hope for is so long in coming,
and life is over in so short a space,
I wish I'd had my wits at the right moment,
and fled back faster than a horse can gallop.

I'm fleeing now, though so weakened and lame
on one side, where desire has twisted me.
I feel secure, but still show in my face
scars where I suffered in the fight with passion.

So I advise you who are on the road,
"Retrace your steps," and you aflame with love,
"Don't wait until the heat becomes extreme.

Though I live, not one in a thousand makes it.
My enemy had a real power to resist,
and I saw her, too, wounded in the heart."

5–6: He is wounded on the left side, the side of the heart.

90

Erano i capei d'oro a l'aura sparsi

Her golden hair blew freely in the wind
that wrapped it in a thousand gentle tangles,
and the seductive light burned beyond measure
in those fair eyes from which it's almost vanished.

Her face, I thought, took on a tinge of pity,
though I don't know if that were true or false.
I had the tinder in my breast for love.
What wonder if I blazed up straightaway?

She did not walk as does a mortal being
but like an angelic form; and her words
had not the sound of a mere human voice.

It was a heavenly spirit, a living sun
which I saw then: should that not now be so,
a wound is not healed when the bow goes slack.

This sonnet was apparently written at a time when Laura was suffering from an eye infection.

9–11: Echoing Virgil, especially the words of Aeneas when he sees his mother Venus appear, "For you have not a mortal face, nor does your voice have a human sound" (*Aeneid* 1.327–28).

91

La bella donna che cotanto amavi

The lovely lady whom you loved so much
has taken unexpected leave of us,
and, I may dare to hope, has risen to heaven,
so sweet, so gentle was she in all things.

It's time now to recover both the keys
to your own heart, which she possessed in life,
and follow her along the straight, clear way:
let no more earthly burdens weigh on you.

Since you're delivered of the heaviest load,
you can put all the others down with ease,
and rise up like an unencumbered pilgrim.

Now you well see how each created thing
hurries to death; as for the soul, it has
to travel light toward that perilous crossing.

This poem is thought to have been written for Petrarch's brother Gherardo on the death of the woman he loved, after which Gherardo entered the Carthusian monastery at Montrieux, probably in April 1343.

5: She held the key to his happiness and the key to his unhappiness.

9: "the heaviest load"—the weight of earthly love.

125

Se 'l pensier che mi strugge

If the thought wasting me
could clothe itself in words
as piercing and as hard as that thought is,
she who burns me and flees
perhaps would feel the heat
and Love would waken there where now he sleeps.
The steps would be less lonely
of my exhausted feet
over the fields and hills,
my eyes not so wet always,
if she burned who is like a block of ice
but leaves no drop of me
that is not fire and flame.

Since Love takes all my powers
and strips me of my skill,
the verse I speak is harsh and bare of sweetness:
but branch does not in bark,
nor in its leaf or blossom,
always reveal its natural potency.
Let Love and those fair eyes
in whose shadow he sits
see what my heart encloses.
If the pain seeking outlet
does overflow in tears or in complaints,
the first hurt me, the second
her, since they show no art.

O sweet and stylish poems
that I used at the first
assault of Love, when I lacked other arms,
who will come forth to shatter
the hardness round my heart

24–26: "complaints"—the inadequate poems that Laura finds displeasing.

so that at least I find relief again?
For there within I seem
to have one who depicts her
always and speaks of her.
But I have not the power
to paint her and the effort leaves me weak.
Alas, thus my sweet aid
has slipped away from me.

Like a baby who almost
articulates his babble,
who cannot speak but cannot bear to hush,
so my desire drives me
to speak, wanting my sweet
enemy to hear me out before I die.
But if her every joy
is looking at herself
shunning all other faces,
then hear me, you green bank,
and send my sighs winging so wide and far
people will always say
how you were once my friend.

You know so fair a foot
has never touched the earth
as that by which you were imprinted once:
and hence my weary heart
drags back my tortured body
to share with you the thoughts that they conceal.
If only you retained
some lovely traces scattered
amongst the flowers and grass
so that my bitter life
could find a spot where it could rest and weep!
But my scared, changeful soul
finds what relief it can.

In every place I look
I find a gentle calm,
when I think, "Here that dancing light has glanced."
Any grass or flower I pluck

38: "aid"—the sweeter poetry he once wrote.
49: "green bank"—presumably of the river Sorgue in Vaucluse.

has roots, I can believe,
in ground where once it was her way to walk
between the hills and river
and sometimes make herself
a cool, green, flowery seat.
Thus nought is really lost,
and a more certain knowledge would be worse.
What are you, blessèd spirit,
if you have such effects?

O my poor song, how unrefined you are!
I think yourself you know it:
hide away in these woods.

75–76: The sense is that at least he finds consolation in his imagination, whether what he imagines has a basis in truth or not.

126

Chiare, fresche et dolci acque

Clear waters, cool and sweet,
where she who is for me
the one real mistress placed her lovely limbs;
noble branch, where she chose
(the memory comes with sighs)
to lean her lovely profile like a column;
grass and flowers that were hidden
by her delicate clothing
and her angelic breast;
sacred, unclouded air,
where Love opened my heart with lovely eyes;
together now attend
to these afflicted final words of mine.

If really it's my fate,
and such is heaven's intent,
that Love will close these eyes by dint of tears,
may some grace hide away
the vile corpse among you
and let the soul go naked to its home.
Death will be made less brutal
if I go with this hope
to that fearsome transition.
For my exhausted spirit
could never find a more reposeful port
or a more tranquil hollow
in which to quit the travailed flesh and bones.

The time might yet return
when to her former haunt
the wild thing comes back beautiful and gentle,

1–12: Petrarch is probably remembering Laura actually bathing in the waters of the river (the Rhône or the Sorgue) rather than simply standing and sitting on the bank.

and there where she perceived me
on that now blessèd day,
may turn a look of pleasure and desire,
seeking me. And (the pity!)
when she sees now mere earth
among the stones, Love might
inspire her then to sigh
so sweetly that she wins mercy for me
and forces heaven to yield
when with her lovely veil she dries her eyes.

From the branches came down
(sweet in the memory)
a rain of blossom over all her lap.
And she stayed seated there
humble amid such glory,
till covered by the love-rich downpour.
Some flowers fell on her hem,
others on her blond tresses,
that were rubbed gold and pearls
to look upon that day.
Some settled on the ground, some on the stream,
and some drifted around,
and circling seemed to say, "Here is Love's kingdom."

How many times did I
say full of terror then,
"Surely she is one born in paradise."
So heavy was the trance
that the divine demeanor
and face and words and sweet smile had imposed,
so severed was I from
all image of the truth,
that I kept saying, sighing,
"How did I come? Or when?"
thinking I was in heaven, not where I was.
Since then this grass gives me
such pleasure that I find no peace elsewhere.

39: "lovely veil"—This may be literal, but the phrase also suggests the veil of chastity that Laura always interposes between herself and passion.

If you had all the finery you want,
you could walk boldly from
the woods, and go about among the public.

66–68: The *congedo*, or leave-taking, which, as is normal in Petrarch, is addressed to the poem it concludes, echoes the *congedo* of the preceding poem (Poem 125), with which this one is closely linked thematically and formally.

128

Italia mia, benché 'l parlar sia indarno

My Italy, though speaking will address
in vain the mortal wounds
I see so densely covering your body,
I want my sighing words to voice hopes of
the Tiber and the Arno,
and of the Po, where I sit slumped and grieving.
Ruler of heaven, I ask
that with the pity that brought you to earth
you turn now to your special, much loved land.
Look, generous Lord, and see
what cruel warfare springs from trivial causes!
Hearts that proud, savage Mars
has hardened and keeps locked—
open them, Father, soften and unknot them.
And let them hear your truth
voiced by my tongue, however weak I am.

And you into whose hands Fortune has given
rule over our fine regions,

This is the last and most famous of the three political *canzoni* that Petrarch included in the *Canzoniere*. It was almost certainly occasioned by a messy war in 1344–1345 for control of Parma between Azzo da Correggio and Filippino Gonzaga, which drew in most of the other northern princes on one side or the other, though the troops on both sides were mostly German mercenaries—as is much regretted in this poem. Petrarch was trapped for a time in the city, but he made what appears to have been a dramatic night escape that eventually brought him to Bologna. He tells the story in *Familiares* (*Letters on Familiar Matters*) 5.10. His subsequent patrons include figures on both sides.

4–6: He hopes that his poem will be heard appreciatively in various regions of Italy, symbolized by the names of rivers: Rome and the center (Tiber), Florence and Tuscany (Arno), and Lombardy (Po).

7–14: Petrarch addresses God in three different ways: Ruler of heaven (7), generous Lord (10), Father (14).

17: "you"—the northern Italian princes.

for which you seem to feel no twinge of pity,
what are so many foreign swords doing here?
Is it so this green land
should now be stained red with barbarian blood?
A vain delusion fools you.
You see little and think you see a lot,
looking for love and faith in venal hearts.
The one who has most troops
is most surrounded by his enemies.
O deluge that amassed
from unknown alien wastes
to inundate the sweet fields that are ours!
If our own hands bring this
upon us, who will then be there to save us?

Nature provided well for our estate,
making the Alps a shield
she placed between us and the rabid Germans.
But blind desire, set against its own good,
has so contrived things that
the healthy body suffers with the scab.
Now in a single coop
wild beasts and peaceful flocks are housed together,
and always it's the righteous who must groan.
All this, to make it worse,
comes from descendants of the lawless people
in whom, as we can read,
Marius made such a wound
that memories are vivid still of how,
weary and thirsty, he
drank from the river as much blood as water.

I say nought of Caesar, who everywhere
turned the green grass to crimson
with their veins' blood, when he sent in our swords.
It now seems, through some force of baleful stars,

20–27: Petrarch upbraids the princes for inviting and relying on mercenary soldiers from Germany.

39: "coop"—Italy.

42–48: Petrarch had read in Florus (first to second century CE) how Marius defeated the Teutons at Aquae Sextiae (Aix-en-Provence) in 102 BCE, killing more than 100,000 of them.

49–51: A generic mention of Julius Caesar's various campaigns against the Gauls.

that heaven feels hatred for us,
with help from you, who hold so much in trust.
Your discordant ambitions
ruin the most lovely part of the whole world.
What fault, what judgment or what destiny
warrants you to harass
poor neighbors, to persecute weak, afflicted
unfortunates, to look
abroad for troops and like it
if they shed blood and sell their souls for money?
I speak to tell the truth,
not out of hatred, nor yet to disparage.

Aren't you alert yet, given so many proofs,
to the Bavarians' deceit?
They raise their fingers and just play at fighting.
The shame, in my view, is worse than the damage.
But it's your blood that flows
more freely, for a real rage whips you on.
Think in the early hours
about yourselves and you'll soon see how dear
he holds mankind who rates himself so cheap.
You are high Latin blood—
empty it of these damaging obsessions,
don't idolize a glory
that's empty of all substance.
For wild men from the North, the backwoodsmen,
to show more wits than us,
must be our fault and not a natural thing.

Is this ground not the ground that I first touched?
And this not my first home,
where I was nurtured with such tenderness?
This too the fatherland in which I trust,
kind, pious motherland,
which covers now my father and my mother?
By God, let this somehow
affect your thinking. Look with pity at

67: Raising the finger is a sign of surrender. The Germans are not taking the fighting seriously.

71: "early hours"—The literal sense is from dawn to the third hour. The princes need to reflect only for the hours of the day when the mind is at its clearest for them to see the error of their ways.

the tears of all the suffering populace,
which hopes for respite solely
from you after God. And if you only show
some sign of your concern,
valor will take up arms
against brute rage and the fight will be brief.
For the old strength of spirit
is not yet dead in these Italian hearts.

My lords, regard how time is flying by,
how life is on the run,
and death is following closely at our backs.
You're here today. Think about the departure.
For the soul must arrive
alone and naked on that fearsome road.
Passing along life's vale,
be glad to set aside the hate and pride
that just bring turmoil where there could be calm,
and let time that's now spent
on cruelty to others be directed
to more worthwhile pursuits,
whether of mind or body,
to action promising
renown, to some honorable endeavor.
So here below there is
enjoyment, and the road to heaven is opened.

Song, my advice to you
is to be courteous when you put your case,
for you must travel amongst haughty men,
who are fully committed
only to vicious, ingrained habit,
always opposed to truth.
You'll try your luck among
the few great-hearted souls who love the good.
Ask them, "Who will protect me?
I come calling a cry of 'Peace, peace, peace.'"

129

Di pensier in pensier, di monte in monte

Love guides me on from one thought to another,
from one peak to another, for I find
each marked path counter to the tranquil life.
If on some lonely slope there is a stream
or spring, or a valley between two hills,
there my bewildered soul is pacified;
depending on Love's promptings,
it laughs or weeps, takes fright or finds new hope.
And my expression, following its lead,
clouds over and then clears,
staying but briefly in a single state.
So, seeing me, one practiced in such things,
would say, "This one's on fire, and quite unstable."

Among high peaks and in wild woods I find
some sort of rest. Each populated place
my eyes view as a mortal enemy.
And every step produces a fresh thought
about my lady, which often converts
the torment I endure for her to pleasure.
No sooner do I wish
to change this sweet and bitter life of mine
than I say, "Love may still be saving you
for some much better time.
Someone may hold you dear, though you do not."
And with that I continue onward, sighing,
"Could it be true then? If so, how? And when?"

Where a tall pine or hill offers its shade,
I sometimes halt and on the nearest stone
I mentally depict her lovely face.
When I'm back in myself again, I find
my breast is wet with tears, and say, "Alas,
what have you come to! And from what been taken!"
But whilst I still can keep
my wandering mind fixed on that prior image,

and gaze on her, and quite forget myself,
I feel Love so close by,
my soul is happy in its own delusion.
I see her beauty in so many places,
I only ask the error should continue.

I've often (but will anyone believe me?)
seen her, a living being, in clear water,
or on green grass, or in a beech tree's bole
or in a white cloud, and so lovely that Leda
would have agreed her daughter is eclipsed,
like some star that the sun hides with its rays.
And the more wild the place
I find I'm in, the more remote the hill,
that much more lovely does my fancy paint her.
Then when the truth dispels
the sweet illusion, I sit my cold self down
there on the spot, dead stone on living stone,
looking like one who broods and weeps and writes.

Where no shade from another mountain reaches,
up to the highest ridge and clearest view
I keep being drawn by an intense desire.
From there my eyes start measuring the extent
of all I've lost, while with my tears I vent
the compressed fog of pain around my heart,
as I look out and think
of how much air divides me from the face
that always is so close, and yet so far.
Then to myself I murmur,
"Alas, what can you know? For there perhaps
someone is sighing that you're far away."
And at that thought my soul can breathe again.

My song, beyond that mountain
there where the sky is joyful and serene,

43: Leda was the mother of Helen of Troy, the supreme example of beauty in antiquity.

51: "living stone"—a phrase that recurs in Latin poetry, presumably meaning here "natural stone" as opposed to the mortally inert stone he has become. The Italian word for stone, *pietra,* may also allude to his name, Petrarca.

66–70: The poem is set in Italy. Petrarch represents himself looking toward the Alps, beyond which are Provence and the river Sorgue. He had planted a laurel tree by his house in Vaucluse, but there is of course also an allusion to Laura.

you'll once more see me by a flowing stream,
where a scent in the air
blows from a fresh, sweet-smelling laurel grove.
There my heart is, and she who steals it from me.
Here you can see my image, nothing more.

132

S'amor non è, che dunque è quel ch'io sento?

If it's not love, then what is this I feel?
But if it's love, by God, then what thing is it?
If it's good, why the deadly, dire effect?
If bad, how come each torment is so nice?

If I burn gladly, why the tears and groans?
If I don't want it, what's the use complaining?
O death alive, O pleasurable evil,
how come you rule me if I don't consent?

And if I do consent, I'm wrong to grumble.
Amongst these clashing winds I find myself
far out to sea in a frail, helmless boat,

so light in wisdom, so weighed down with error,
that I myself just don't know what I want,
and shiver in midsummer, burn all winter.

This sonnet was adapted by Chaucer as the lament of Troilus in his *Troilus and Criseyde* (400–21). It is the first poem of Petrarch to appear in English.

133

Amor m'à posto come segno a strale

Love's made me like the target for an arrow,
like snow in sunlight, like wax on the fire,
and like mist in the wind. And I'm now hoarse
beseeching you, lady, and you don't care.

The fatal shot came from those eyes of yours
against which there's no time or place can help me.
Only from you proceed—you think it trifling—
sunlight and fire and wind with such effects.

My thoughts are arrows, and your face a sun,
and desire fire. With this array of arms
Love shoots me, dazzles me, and melts me down.

And the angelic singing, and the words,
and the sweet breath I've no defense against,
are air that blows my fleeing life away.

6: It is no help to wait for time to pass or to go away.
14: "air"—the Italian *l'aura* puns on the name Laura.

134

Pace non trovo, et non ho da far guerra

I find no peace and have no means for war.
I fear, and hope, and burn, and am all ice,
and fly the heavens and lie flat on the earth,
and grasp on nothing, and embrace the world.

This jailer neither opens up nor locks,
neither retains me nor unties the knot.
Love neither kills me, nor untwists his sword,
neither wants me alive, nor pulls me clear.

Eyeless I see, and have no tongue and shout,
and long to perish and call out for help,
and loathe myself and just adore another.

I feed on pain, and, through my tears, I laugh.
I'm equally appalled by death and life.
And I'm like this because of you, my lady.

7: "untwists his sword"—i.e., pulls it from the wound he has made.

136

Fiamma del ciel su le tue treccie piova

May flames of heaven rain upon your tresses,
you crook, who've quit acorns and river water
and now are rich and great through starving others,
since evildoing gives you so much pleasure.

You nest of treachery, in which there breeds
all evil spreading through the world today,
you slave of wine, of soft beds, of good foods,
who try the limits of debauchery.

Young girls and old men wildly romp around
your chambers, and then through their middle flits
Beelzebub with bellows, fire, and mirrors.

You weren't brought up in feather-cushioned shade,
but bare to the wind, shoeless among thorns.
Live on like this for God to catch the stench.

This is the first of a group of three sonnets denouncing the corruption of the Catholic Church in Avignon, possibly written in 1351–1353, in the period just before Petrarch made his definitive move from Provence to Italy.

11: The devil adds mirrors to his wiles to heat up even more the fires of lust in the aging prelates.

14: The implied hope is that God eventually will be offended enough to take appropriate action.

139

Quanto più disïose l'ali spando

The stronger the desire to spread my wings
and fly to you, sweet company of friends,
the stickier the lime that Fortune lays
to stop my flight, and drive me off my course.

My heart, which I can send out all the same,
is always with you in that sunny valley,
where land most stretches to enfold our sea.
I left it tearfully two days ago.

I took the left road, it kept to the right one,
force dragging me, while it was led by Love;
it went to Jerusalem, I to Egypt.

But resignation helps to deal with pain:
our well-established rule only permits us
to be together rarely, and not long.

The sonnet is probably addressed to the monks of Montrieux. Petrarch had visited his brother there in 1347.

3–4: The metaphor is the traditional one of a bird being caught in lime smeared on branches by a hunter.

6–7: Perhaps Hyères, where the land at the end of the valley of the river Gapeau (in which Montrieux is situated) creates a kind of lagoon.

11: Jerusalem (to which the exiled Jews eventually return in the Bible) is the positive image for the abode of his heart and his friends, whereas Egypt (the biblical place of exile) represents the corruption of the papal court at Avignon, which Petrarch had denounced in the three preceding sonnets.

140

Amor che nel penser mio vive e regna

Love, who's the living ruler of my thoughts
and in my heart has his main seat of power,
sometimes steps fully armed into my face.
There he arrays himself, there plants his banner.

She who instructs us how to love and suffer
and wants immense desire and burning hope
to be reined in by reason, shame, and reverence,
is inwardly affronted by our daring.

At which Love runs in terror to my heart,
dropping all his designs, and cries and trembles.
He hides there and won't show himself again.

What can I do, if my lord is afraid,
except stay with him till the final hour?
He makes a good end who dies loving true.

145

Ponmi ove 'l sole occide i fiori e l'erbe

Put me there where the sun kills flowers and grass,
or where he's overcome by snow and ice.
Put me where he drives light and temperate,
where he's returned to us or where he's hidden.

Put me low down in life or on the heights,
in clear sweet air, or air that's dark and dismal.
Put me in night, in long days or in short ones,
in my maturity or unripe years.

Put me in heaven, on earth, or in the depths,
high on a hill, low in a marshy valley,
a spirit set free or tied to its body.

Put me with fame or with obscurity.
I'll be what I have been, live as I've lived,
continuing my fifteen sighing years.

The whole sonnet reworks Horace, *Odes* 1.22, the conclusion of which will then be echoed strongly in Poem 159. The last line of this sonnet dates it to 1342 (since Laura was first seen in 1327), but Petrarch was almost certainly working on both poems well after her death in 1348.

1–3: Respectively the hot zone (line 1), the cold zone (2), and the temperate zone (3).

4: The east, from where dawn returns the sun to us, and the west, which hides it away.

9: "the depths"—may be those of hell.

14: The sighing may be literal, but it is also a metaphor for writing poetry.

148

Non Tesin, Po, Varo, Arno, Adige e Tebro

Not Ticino, Var, Po, Arno, Adige, Tiber,
Euphrates, Tigris, Nile, Hermus, Indus, Ganges,
Tana, Ister, Alpheus, Garonne and its breakers,
Rhône, Ebro, Rhine, Seine, Albia, Loire, Eurus,

no ivy, fir, pine, beech, or juniper,
could soothe the fire of anguish in my heart,
as can a stream whose waters weep with me,
and the small tree I praise and preen in rhyme.

I find no other succor in the assaults
of Love, which force me to live under arms
this life that hurries by in such great bounds.

So may the laurel grow on the cool bank,
and he who planted it, pen in its shade
exalted fancies to the waters' sound.

1–4: The list of rivers, all given their ancient Greek or Roman names, begins in line 1 with what for Petrarch was northern and central Italy, though the Ticino is now in Switzerland and the Var in southeast France. The rivers in line 2 are all in Asia, the Hermus being now the Gediz in Turkey. Lines 3 and 4 put together rivers of various European countries: the Tana is the Don, the Ister the Danube, the Alpheus the main river of the Peloponnese in Greece, the Albia the Elb, and the Eurus, which is in northern Greece, has become the Maritsa. The "breakers" at the end of line 3 (literally, "the sea that it breaks" in the original, a phrase perhaps dictated in part by the difficult rhymes he has chosen) may refer to the estuary of the Garonne, that is, the Gironde. In the original the lines are metrically correct, although the sound effects are deliberately outlandish.

7–8: "a stream"—the Sorgue, which rises at the Fontaine de Vaucluse where Petrarch had his house and where he planted a laurel ("the small tree").

154

Le stelle, il cielo, et gli elementi a prova

The stars, the heavens, the elements competed
to put their total skills and utmost efforts
into the living light that's Nature's mirror,
and the sun's too, who nowhere sees the like.

The work is so sublime, refined, and novel
a mortal gaze looks at it nervously,
such an excess of grace and sweetness Love
seems to pour in the beauty of her eyes.

The air around, struck by their gentle rays,
is fired with purity and turns to something
that quite defeats our language and conceptions.

No one feels low desires arising there,
only honor, and virtue. When before
was ever cheap lust quelled by supreme beauty?

156

I' vidi in terra angelici costumi

I saw on earth ways only angels have
and heavenly beauties unique in the world.
But I recall them with both pain and pleasure,
since all I see now seems just dreams, smoke, shadows.

For I saw those two eyes begin to weep
that have so often made the sun feel envy,
and I heard through the sighs words being said
that could make mountains move and rivers halt.

Love, Wisdom, Merit, Pity, Suffering,
sang in the tears a sweeter sounding concert
than any other that the world has heard.

The skies were so bent to the harmony
that no leaf seemed to stir on any branch,
so steeped in sweetness were the air and wind.

159

In qual parte del ciel, in quale ydea

What part of heaven was it, what idea
contained the model from which Nature took
that lovely face, in which she was resolved
to show on earth what she could make above?

What bathing nymph, what goddess in the woods
loosed to the wind hair of such perfect gold?
When did one heart combine so many virtues,
although the highest's guilty of my death?

A man looks for divine beauty in vain,
if he has never seen those eyes of hers,
and felt the pleasure of the looks she casts.

He does not know how Love can cure and kill,
if he is ignorant of how sweet she sighs,
and how sweet, too, she speaks and sweet she laughs.

1: The "idea" is a Platonic one, a pure form located in heaven of which things in this world are mere imitations.

8: Laura's highest virtue is her sexual purity.

13–14: The lines echo the conclusion of Horace, *Odes* 1.22 (the poem that formed the basis of Poem 145), "I shall love my sweet-laughing, sweet-speaking Lalage."

160

Amor et io sí pien' di meraviglia

Love and myself are full of wonderment,
as if we'd seen something incredible,
gazing upon her when she speaks or laughs,
since she's unlike all others but herself.

In that clear sky her tranquil lashes frame
there's such a sparkle in my trusty stars,
there is no other light to fire and guide
one who's intent on highest forms of love.

What miracle it is when like a flower
she sits amid the grass, or when she presses
against a green bush with her pure white breast!

What sweet delight it is in early spring
to see her walk alone wrapped in her thoughts,
plaiting a circlet for the bright, curled gold!

6: "stars"—her eyes.
14: "gold"—her hair.

162

Lieti fiori et felici, et ben nate herbe

Fortunate, happy flowers and lucky grass,
often pressed by my lady lost in thought;
meadow who can hear sweet words that she says,
and bear some imprint of her passing feet;

trim saplings and green foliage just in leaf,
pale violets who are little signs of love;
woods rich in shade, on which my sun's light beats,
making you tall and stately with her rays.

O mellow part of earth, and O pure river,
who bathe her lovely face and clear, bright eyes,
and take on something of her living light.

How much I envy you that dear, chaste presence!
And not a rock of yours will not have learned to feel
the burning of the flame that burns in me!

14: "the flame"—the fire of love.

164

Or che 'l ciel et la terra e 'l vento tace

Now that the sky and earth and wind are silent,
and birds and beasts are held in check by sleep,
and Night is circling in her starry cart,
and in his bed the waveless sea lies still,

I watch, brood, burn, weep. And my destroyer
stands always there before me for sweet torture.
I'm in a state of war, of rage and anguish,
and only thoughts of her give me some peace.

Thus from the one spring of clear living water
flow bitterness and sweetness, which I feed on.
One single hand heals me again, then wounds me.

And to prevent my sufferings ever ending,
I die and live a thousand times a day,
so far away am I from my salvation.

166

S'i' fussi stato fermo a la spelunca

If I had been more steadfast at the cave
in which Apollo learned to prophesy,
Florence perhaps would have her poet today,
not just Verona, Mantua, and Arunca.

But since my ground no longer grows the reeds
fed by that mountain's water, I must follow
a different star, and harvest from my plot
teazles and prickles with a bent bill-hook.

The olive tree is withered and the waters
springing from Mount Parnassus have changed course,
though once those waters made the olive bloom.

So my misfortune or my faults deprive me
of any good fruit, if eternal Jove
does not rain on me some part of his grace.

The poem plays with learned allusion and metaphor. It was originally a sonnet replying to another by a poet whose name we do not know. The obscurity stems partly from the fact that in the original Petrarch keeps to the difficult rhymes of the first poem, as was the convention in exchanges of this sort.

1: The cave of Delphi where Apollo, the god of poetry, learned his art.

3–4: The parallels, via their home cities, are with various famous Latin poets. Florence (where Petrarch was not born but which was his family's city) would have its poet in the same way that Verona has Catullus, Mantua Virgil, and Sessa Aurunca the satirical poet Lucilius. At the time "poet" (*poeta*) suggested the idea of a serious poet in Latin.

5–6: The water is that of the Castalian spring, the source of poetic inspiration flowing down Parnassus (line 10) from the cave of line 1.

7–9: The poor "harvest" is probably love poems in vernacular Italian, contrasted with poetry in Latin, which is symbolized by the "olive tree" of wisdom in line 9.

13: Jove is used here for the Christian God.

168

Amor mi manda quel dolce pensero

Love sends to me that captivating thought
that's our longstanding secret go-between,
and comforts me, and says he never was
so keen to grant me what I hope and long for.

I, who have sometimes found the words he says
turn out a lie, and sometimes turn out true,
don't know if I believe him, and am torn,
and yes and no both ring false in my heart.

Meanwhile time is passing, and in the mirror
I see myself heading toward the time
that's hostile to his promise and my hopes.

What will be will be. I don't age alone,
and my desires don't change as I grow older.
But I am scared so little life is left us.

10: "time"—old age.

12: "alone"—Laura is aging too.

14: He is apparently frightened that there will not be time enough for this imagined shared love to come to fruition.

170

Più volte già dal bel sembiante humano

Seeing her face concerned, I've several times
felt bold enough to stir my trusty troops
and launch a careful, noble speech toward
my enemy, who seems so meek and gentle.

And then her eyes render my project vain,
since all that chance or fate can deal me,
my good, my ill, my life, my death, have been
placed in her hands by the one power who can.

Hence I could never shape a single word
that any but myself could understand,
so tremulous and whispery has Love made me.

And now I see how highest love, once blazing,
throttles the tongue and steals away the wits.
The fire that can be spoken barely burns.

2: "troops"—his thoughts, which he thinks at such moments he can translate into words.

8: "the one power"—Love.

180

Po, ben puo' tu portartene la scorza

You, River Po, can certainly bear off
my hide on your fast-flowing, powerful waves,
but I've a spirit hidden deep within
that spurns your force, and that of anyone.

Not needing to change tack from port to starboard,
blown straight by breezes favoring its will,
it wings its way toward the gilded branch
and overcomes wind, water, sail, and oars.

King over others, proud, superior river,
who meet the sun when he brings us the day
and westward leave a light of greater beauty,

you bear off on your horn my mortal part.
The other in the feathered garb of love
flies back to rest in its sweet dwelling-place.

A poem of absence from Laura and Provence, written during a journey eastward down the Po.

7: "the gilded branch"—Laura with her golden hair, figured, as in many other poems, in the guise of a laurel tree.

9: The Po was called the king of rivers by Virgil.

11: "a light"—Laura.

12: "horn"—i.e., the current of the river. Classical poets often used bull imagery for powerful rivers.

183

Se 'l dolce sguardo di costei m'ancide

If a sweet look from her can kill me dead,
or just a few soft, subtly chosen words,
and if Love gives her such power over me,
merely then when she speaks, or when she smiles,

oh, what will happen if she should avert,
through a mistake of mine, or unkind fate,
her eyes from any mercy, and then threaten
death to me, though she offers comfort now?

So, if I quake, and feel chill in my heart,
those times I see a change in her expression,
the terror's born of past experience.

Woman by nature is a fickle thing,
and I know very well that loving feelings
don't last long even in the best one's heart.

189

Passa la nave mia colma d'oblio

My ship sails on, packed with forgetfulness,
over wild seas in a dark winter night
by Scylla and Charybdis, and my lord,
or rather enemy, sits at the helm.

At each oar there's a loose and nasty thought
that seems to sneer at storms and final ends.
The sail's ripped by an endless rainy wind
of sighing and hoping and sheer desire.

A downpour of tears, and a fog of frustration
soak and slacken the by now wearied ropes
made up of error twined with ignorance.

The two sweet stars that guided me are hidden.
Reason and skill have died amid the waves.
I'm starting to despair of reaching harbor.

Though the details are ambiguous, the main lines of the boat allegory are clear. Laura, here cast as a siren, has made Petrarch forget his duties (1). He is now at the mercy of Love (the lord of line 3), and left with reckless fantasies (5), his passions (7–9), and his illusions (10–11). He no longer has the guidance of Laura's eyes (12), no longer has any rational human resources (13), and he is losing hope of salvation (14). This poem is best known in English in Sir Thomas Wyatt's version, "My galley chargèd with forgetfulness."

3: "by Scylla and Charybdis"—archetype of the dangerous sea passage, represented by Scylla, the cliffs on the Calabrian coast near Messina, and Charybdis, the whirlpool on the Sicilian side of the strait.

190

Una candida cerva sopra l'erba

A doe of shining white appeared to me
on the green grass, with two horns all of gold,
between two streams, within a laurel's shade,
at sunrise in the early time of year.

She was so sweet and so sublime to see
I left all other tasks to follow her,
like some miser who in his search for treasure
feels a delight that soothes away the effort.

"Let no one touch me," round her lovely neck
she wore inscribed in diamonds and in sapphires,
"My Caesar's pleasure was to make me free."

The sun had reached its midway point by then,
and gazing tired my still unsated eyes,
when I fell in the water, and she vanished.

The main symbols may be interpreted as follows: The doe is Laura, a golden-haired figure of shining purity (1–2), who is first seen by Petrarch in Avignon, with its two rivers, the Rhône and the Durance (3), in his youth (4). She distracts him from serious study and composition (6), though she is destined to remain pure (9), free from carnal desire as God (Caesar) wished her to be (11). Halfway through his life (12), that is, at the age of thirty-five, he was brought face to face with reality (14)—though the precise significance of falling in the water is disputed—and the illusory figure he had been a prey to vanished. Sir Thomas Wyatt adapted this poem in his "Whoso list to hunt, I know where is an hind."

192

Stiamo, Amor, a veder la gloria nostra

Let's linger, Love, to look upon our glory,
at things more high and strange than Nature makes.
Look well what sweetness has streamed into her,
look at a light that heaven reveals on earth.

Look how much art begilds, impearls, and blushes
this chosen and unprecedented being,
who walks with sweet looks and sweet steps around
this shady valley in its cloistering hills.

The green grass and the many-colored flowers
scattered beneath that ancient dark-leaved oak
keep begging that her foot should press or touch them,

and all around move lucent sparkling stars
through the high heavens, which visibly show joy
to feel such lovely eyes make them serene.

5: Divine art has made her hair gold, her teeth pearls, and given color to her cheeks. The word I have translated as "blushed" literally means "empurple" or "encrimson," and may reflect an ideal of female beauty that is different from ours.

8: The valley of the Fontaine de Vaucluse.

12–14: The miracle that is Laura seems to cause the sky to become so clear that the planets can be seen on their courses even during the daytime.

211

Voglia mi sprona, Amor mi guida et scorge

Lust spurs me on, Love guides me and directs me,
and Pleasure pulls and Habit hurries me,
and Hope's there, wheedling and encouraging,
stretching his hand out to my weary heart,

which the fool takes and doesn't realize
our escort is both blind and treacherous.
The senses are in charge and reason's dead,
and from one restless urge another's born.

Virtue, Honor, Beauty, a noble way,
sweet words—these brought me to the branches,
which trap the heart in pleasurable lime.

It was in 1327, precisely
at the first hour on the sixth day of April,
that I entered the maze. I see no exit.

5: "the fool"—his heart.

6: "our escort"—Love.

10: "branches"—of the laurel. A sticky lime was spread on branches to trap birds.

12–14: For the date of Petrarch's first encounter with Laura, see Introduction, section 1.

219

Il cantar novo e 'l pianger delli augelli

The fresh songs and the moaning of the birds
ring round the valleys as the daylight comes,
and there's a murmuring from crystal waters
that tumble down their cool, quick, shining streams.

And she whose face is snow and hair is gold,
in whose love there were never tricks nor flaws,
wakes me to music of a dance of love,
combing the white locks of her agèd spouse.

So I bestir myself and greet the dawn,
and then the sun, and more the second sun
that dazzled me when young and does so still.

On certain days I've seen the two of them
together rise, and, in a single moment,
one dim the stars, the other quite dim him.

5–8: The goddess of the dawn, Aurora, fell in love with the mortal Tithonus, who was granted immortality by the gods but at the cost of endless aging.

10: The second sun is Laura.

226

Passer mai solitario in alcun tetto

No sparrow on the roof, nor woodland beast
has ever felt as lonely as I am,
since I can't see her face, the only sun
I know, and the one focus for my eyes.

Unceasing tears are my supreme delight,
laughter is pain, my food wormwood and gall,
night is exhaustion and clear sky a murk,
and bed the hard ground of a battlefield.

Sleep, as the saying has it, really is
a relative of death, and steals the heart
from that sweet brooding keeping it live.

You calming, happy place, sole in the world,
green banks in full flower, hillsides rich in shade,
you hold the joy that I can only cry for.

1–2: Echoes Ps. 102:8, "I lie awake, I am like a lonely bird ['sparrow' in other translations] on the housetop."

9: Petrarch probably has in mind Virgil, *Aeneid* 6.278, "Sleep, blood-relative of Death."

234

O cameretta che già fosti un porto

My little room, who had become a harbor
to flee to from my savage daytime storms,
you're now a spring which flows each night with tears
that I keep hidden out of shame all day.

My little bed, who were repose and solace
in many a trouble, now what urns of pain
Love empties on you with those ivory hands
that torture only me, and so unfairly.

I run now from my hideaway and haven,
but also from myself and from the thoughts
pursuing which at times I winged the heights.

And common people, whom I loathe and scorn,
are where (incredibly) I look for refuge,
so scared am I to be alone again.

6: "urns of pain"—tears.

7: "hands"—of Laura.

11: "heights"—of spiritual love or poetry.

245

Due rose fresche et colte in paradiso

Two new-bloomed roses, picked in paradise
two days ago, as Mayday was first dawning,
became the fine gift of a wise old lover,
divided equally between two juniors

with such sweet words and with such a smile
as might have brought a bumpkin to feel love.
It sparkled with a light of radiant passion,
and suddenly each face was drained of color.

"The sun won't see another two such lovers,"
he said, and laughed and at the same time sighed.
And clasping both, he looked at each in turn.

Thus he distributed his words and roses;
my heart is still delighted and still fearful.
O happy eloquence, O day of joy.

The identity of the older lover who presents the roses is unknown. The incident has an aura of mystery and has no parallels in the *Canzoniere*.

4: "juniors"—presumably Laura and Petrarch.

13: "fearful"—perhaps because the relationship risked becoming more public than convention allowed.

248

Chi vuol veder quantunque pò Natura

Let anyone who wants to see what Nature
and Heaven can do here, come to gaze at her,
for she alone's a sun, not just for me,
but for the blind world in its moral void.

Let them come fast, for Death's a thief who steals
the best ones first and lets the bad ones be.
She's wanted in the kingdom of the gods,
a passing mortal beauty that can't last.

They'll see, if they arrive in time, all virtues,
all beauties, and all royal qualities
amazingly configured in one body.

And then they'll say these poems of mine are mute,
my wits bedazzled by excess of light.
But if they wait, they'll have to weep for ever.

14: Anyone who misses seeing her alive will only be able to weep over the loss caused by her death.

250

Solea lontana in sonno consolarme

From far away she'd come to soothe my sleep,
my lady in that sweet angelic form
she has. But now she scares and saddens me,
and I've no help against the pain and fear.

For often in her face I seem to see
real pity mingled with severe distress,
and seem to hear things that convince my heart
it must divest itself of hope and joy.

"Don't you recall that very final evening,"
she says, "when I left your eyes wet with tears,
and had to go because it was so late?

I could not tell you then, and did not want to;
I say it now as something tried and true;
don't hope to see me ever here on earth."

260

In tale stella duo belli occhi vidi

The stars were such when I first saw two eyes,
brimming with sweet attraction and true honor,
that, since Love nestles there, my wearied heart
feels a contempt for any other beauty.

None may equal her, not those most admired
in other times or in exotic lands,
not she who was so beautiful she brought
trouble to Greece and cries of death to Troy,

no, not that lovely Roman who tore open
her chaste, disdainful bosom with the sword,
not Argia, Polyxena, Hypsiphile.

This excellence gives, I would claim, to Nature
great glory, and to me supreme delight.
Only it comes late, and at once is gone.

1: "The stars were such"—i.e., under such an astrological conjunction.

7: "she who was so beautiful"—Helen, whose capture by Paris led the Greeks into war and hence to the eventual destruction of Troy.

9–10: Lucretia, who killed herself after her rape by Sextus Tarquinius.

11: Argia was the wife of Polynices, son of Oedipus; Polyxena was the daughter of Priam, loved by Achilles; and Hypsiphile, the daughter of the king of Lemnos, was loved by Jason en route to find the Golden Fleece.

14: There may be an allusion to Laura being born in the last age of the world, immediately prior to the Last Judgment.

263

Arbor vïctoriosa trïumphale

Victorious, triumphal laurel tree,
honor of emperors and of great poets,
how many days you've filled with pain and joy
out of this brief and mortal life of mine.

True lady, you who only care for honor,
and harvest it more richly than all others,
you fear no trap of love, no noose or nets,
and trickery is feeble to outwit you.

Nobility of birth and other things
valued among us—pearls, and gold, and rubies—
you spurn them all as vile impediments.

The lofty beauty, unique in the world,
would trouble you, if it seemed not to drape
and deck the lovely trove of chastity.

This sonnet concludes the first part of the *Canzoniere*. It is addressed to the laurel, which, in Petrarch's version of the myth, furnishes the crowns for triumphant emperors and laureate poets (see Introduction, section 2). In the poems immediately preceding (such as Poem 260) the emphasis has been on the human Laura reaching the end of her life. Here the tree and the human figure are fused.

Poems from the *Canzoniere*

Part II

264

I'vo pensando, et nel penser m'assale

I keep on thinking and in thought I'm struck
by such a powerful pity for myself
that I'm brought frequently
to shed tears quite unlike those I once wept.
Seeing the end come closer every day,
a thousand times I've asked God for the wings
on which the human mind
can soar up from this mortal jail to heaven.
But up to now I've had no benefit
from any of these prayers or sighs or tears.
And it is right that this should be the case;
one who could stand but falls along the way,
deserves to lie there though he may not want to.
I see those pitying arms
in which I put my trust are open still.
But I'm in anguish thinking
of others' ends, and tremble at my state,
for someone spurs me, and perhaps I'm done for.

One of my thoughts speaks to my mind and says,
"What, longing still? Waiting for help? From whom?
Pathetic! Don't you know
what a disgrace it is to let time pass?
Be sharp, make a decision, make one now,
and tear out of your heart every last root
of those pleasures that never

This great *canzone*, introducing the second part of Petrarch's collection, has the appearance of having been written during Laura's lifetime, that is, before April 6, 1348, when she died, though it may actually have been written later. It is closely connected with the debate in the *Secretum*, Book 3.

4: "tears"—The new tears will not be tears of frustrated love.

14: "arms"—of God or Christ.

17: "others"—people who have not escaped the penalties of sin.

18: "someone spurs me"—Love or the devil.

can make it happy and won't let it breathe!
If you've been troubled for a long time now,
and tired too, by that false, fleeting sweetness
this traitor of a world can give to people,
why any longer put your hopes in something
that lacks all peace and all stability?
Whilst life is in the body,
you have the reins there in your thoughts' control.
Pull on them while you can,
delay is dangerous, as you well know,
and starting now will barely be in time.

You know already what a sweet sensation
your eyes felt when she first came into view,
the one I'd wish were yet
still to be born that we might have more peace.
You well recall, and well indeed you must,
the image of her when she first came bursting
into a heart where flames
that others lit perhaps could not have entered.
She fired it. And if the deluding passion
burned on for years while waiting for a day
that, for our greater good, has never come,
now raise yourself to a more blissful hope,
gazing upon the heavens that circle round you,
deathless and beautiful.
Human desire is happy with its ills
on earth and is appeased
by one glance, or a few words, or a song.
How great's that joy, if this one's so intense?"

Then there's another bittersweet concern,
bringing a wearying, delightful burden.
Settling within my soul,
it bows my heart with longing, feeds it hope,
and, set on highest glory,
is not aware whether I freeze or burn,
lose color or lose weight,
and if I kill it, it's reborn still stronger.
It has grown with me every day I've lived,
since I was sleeping in my swaddling clothes,

40: "we"—the thought and the mind.

46–47: If Laura had yielded herself to Petrarch, he would have put his soul at risk.

54: Joy in heaven must be so much greater than the most intense joy here on earth.

and one grave will, I fear, enclose us both.
For once my soul has been stripped of my limbs,
this craving can accompany it no more.
But then if Greek and Latin
speak of me after death, it's only wind.
Hence, since I fear to keep
assembling what a moment will disperse,
I'd like to embrace truth, let shadows be.

But it's the will to love that fills my being
and stunts all resolutions with its shade,
though meanwhile time flies by,
while I write of another and neglect myself,
and that light in those lovely eyes that melts me
so gently in its warm untroubled calm,
restrains me with a bridle
against which neither wits nor force can help.
So what good is it if I grease the keel
of my small boat, since it is still held back
amongst the rocks by two such knots as these?
You who have utterly released me from
the rest that bind the world in various ways,
my Lord, why do you not
remove now from my face this mark of shame?
Like someone in a dream,
I seem to have death there before my eyes:
I want to fight him off and have no weapons.

I see what I am doing, nor am tricked
by misconception, no, I'm driven by Love
who never lets the path
of honor be pursued by his believers.
But often I sense entering my heart
a finer self-disdain, harsh and severe,
which drags each secret thought
into my face for anyone to see;
for loving mortal things with that devotion
that we should duly only give to God
least suits one with the highest aspirations.

68–69: It is futile to acquire immortal fame as a writer and to be celebrated in Latin and Greek, the two great literary languages known by Petrarch.

83: "two such knots"—desire for glory and desire for Laura.

85: "the rest"—presumably, the other deadly sins apart from lust.

And this disdain then loudly summons back
my reason, which has strayed after the senses.
But though it hears and thinks
it should return, bad habit drives it on
and pictures to my eyes
the one born only to provoke my death,
because she pleased me (and herself) too much.

I don't know either how much time heaven gave me
when I came as a fresh young soul to earth
to bear the brutal war
I've somehow engineered against myself,
nor through this veil of mortal flesh can I
foresee the day that will close off my life.
Yet I see my hair changing,
and feel all my desires are changing too.
Believing now the moment of departure
is close at hand, or not so far away,
like one whom loss has made more shrewd and wise,
I think back over where I left the course
on the right hand that leads to the safe harbor.
On one side I feel stabs
of shame and pain that push me back to it;
I'm not free on the other
from a pleasure that's so entrenched in me
it dares to try to strike a deal with death.

My poem, that's where I am. Dread makes my heart
colder than frozen snow,
feeling for sure that I am perishing.
I've spooled away in vain deliberation
most of the little thread given me to weave.
There is no heavier weight
than what I'm bearing in the state I'm in;
for with death at my side
I'm looking for some new plan for my life,
seeing what's better, clinging to what's worse.

126: "strike a deal"—i.e., for love to continue and death to stay away.

131: "the little thread"—his life.

136: A recasting of a famous antithesis of Ovid, "I see the better and approve, and I follow the worse" (*Met.* 7.20–21).

267

Oimè il bel viso, oimè il soave sguardo

Oh for her lovely face, oh for her look,
oh for the graceful grandeur of her walk,
oh for that voice that humbled ignorant,
violent minds and gave the feeble courage.

And oh that smile from which the arrow flew,
that now I only hope will bring me death.
You royal soul, right for imperial rule,
if only you had not come down so late!

All of you I must burn for, find rest in,
for I was always yours, and if I've lost you,
there's no disaster that can hurt me more.

You filled me both with hope and with desire
when I last left that living supreme beauty.
But the wind carried what we said away.

This sonnet is cast as the first poem written after Laura's death on April 6, 1348. It is the third poem in Part II of the *Canzoniere,* not, as we might expect, the first. For the structure of the collection, see Introduction, section 2.

7–8: Laura's soul was worthy to have ruled over the Roman Empire, but she was born too late.

9: "All of you"—all the qualities and parts of Laura he has just addressed.

13: "living supreme beauty"—Laura, who was then alive.

268

Che debb'io far? che mi consigli, Amore?

What must I do? What do you counsel, Love?
It's really time to die,
and I've delayed more than I'd ever wish.
My lady's dead and carried off my heart.
Wanting to follow it,
I must cut short these vitiated years,
since there's no hope I'll ever
see her in this life, and the waiting's torture.
Now that my every joy
has turned to tears because of her departure,
all sweetness has been taken from my life.

Love, you too feel (that's why I'm grieving with you)
how harsh and hard the loss is.
I know you're bowed and bruised by my misfortune,
or rather ours, since on one single rock
we've had our ship break up,
and in one instant seen our sun grow dark.
What genius has the words
that could be equal to my sorry state?
Ah, blind, ungrateful world,
you have great cause to shed your tears with me,
for any beauty in you died with her.

Your glory's fallen, and you cannot see it,
nor were you worthy, while
she lived on earth, to have acquaintance with her,
or to be touched by sacred feet like hers,
for such a lovely being
should have adorned the heavens with her presence.
But I, alas, who do
not love myself or mortal life without her,

6: The only solution is suicide.

8: "waiting"—to enter the life beyond and perhaps be reunited with her.

call her back in my tears.
That's all that's left to me from so much hope,
and only that still keeps me here alive.

Oh, now her lovely face is turned to earth,
though once for us it was
a warranty of heaven and bliss above.
Her unseen form is now in paradise,
delivered from that veil
that cast its shade here in her life's high bloom.
But she will put it on
a second time, never to take it off;
and we shall see her then
that much more caring and more beautiful
as sempiternal outdoes mortal beauty.

More lovely and more fine than ever, she
returns to me, as if
I am the one the vision pleases most.
This is one column that supports my life:
her bright name is the other,
ringing with such sweet music in my heart.
But when the thought returns
that all the hope is dead which was alive
during her flowering time,
Love knows the effect on me, which she, I hope,
sees too, since now she has God's truth so close.

Ladies, you who gazed here upon her beauty
and her angelic being
that brought divine comportment to the earth,
grieve for me, and let pity overcome you,
not though for her who's risen
into such peace, and left me all at war.
If for long years some power
will block the road for me to follow her,
then what Love whispers to me

36–44: Her soul ("form") is now freed from her body ("veil"), which she will recover at the Last Judgment, made still more beautiful than it was on earth, in so far as it will then be immortal.

54–55: Laura in heaven is close to the divine truth of God and therefore can see into Petrarch's heart.

62: "power"—God or Nature.

is all that stops me severing the knot.
But he discourses in this way within me,

"Rein in the grief that's carrying you away,
for from excess of passion
you'll lose the heaven to which your heart aspires,
and where she who seems dead is now alive;
she smiles to think of all
that beauty lost, and only sighs for you,
and begs you not to let
the fame which still has life thanks to your words,
die silently away,
no, you must give her name yet further luster,
if once her eyes were dear or sweet to you."

Avoid things bright or green,
keep far from where there may be song or laughter,
my nonpoem, my lament.
You have no place with animated people,
widowed, disconsolate, in your black clothing.

65: "severing the knot"—killing himself.

269

Rotta è l'alta colonna e 'l verde lauro

Shattered are the high column and green laurel,
that granted shade to my exhausted thoughts.
I've lost what I can't hope to rediscover,
not North or South, in India or Morocco.

You've taken from me, Death, the double treasure
that made me live life happy and walk proud,
and it can't be replaced by land or empire,
by eastern gems or by the power of gold.

But if there's destiny's assent to this,
what can I do but let my soul be sad,
my eyes be always wet, my gaze cast down?

O life of ours that looks so fine to see,
how easily it loses in one morning
what it takes years of effort to acquire!

Petrarch's friend and patron Cardinal Giovanni Colonna died on July 3, 1348, a few months after Laura. He is the "column" of line 1, she the "laurel."

4: India and Morocco symbolize East and West.

272

La vita fugge et non s'arresta un'ora

Life's running by and doesn't stop a moment,
and death comes on behind in mighty marches,
and I keep battling over present things
and things now past and others still to come.

Recalling and awaiting wrench my heart
this way and that, so that, to tell the truth,
if it were not for pity for my soul,
I should be free from these concerns by now.

There comes before my eyes what little pleasure
my wretched heart has felt, and then again
I see winds buffeting around my course,

I see storms in the harbor, and my helmsman
now worn out, and mainmast and guy-ropes broken,
and lovely beacons I once watched snuffed out.

7–8: He would have found escape by killing himself if he were not aware that suicide is a sin that leads to damnation.

11–14: He picks up again the metaphor of life as a voyage. He sees no hope of a calm ending (the "storms in the harbor"), with his reason (the "helmsman") exhausted, and no strength of will or other positive qualities (the broken mast and ropes) remaining, while the guiding lights of Laura's eyes have been put out by her death.

273

Che fai? che pensi? che pur dietro guardi?

What's this? What's on your mind? Why still look back
to times which cannot ever now return?
Disconsolate soul, why still keep on
adding wood to the fire on which you burn?

The gentle words and sweet looks that were hers,
which you've described and pictured one by one,
have risen from earth. It's late, it's the wrong time
to seek them here again, as you well know.

Don't give new verve to what is killing us,
don't chase a vague, deceitful fantasy,
but something sure that leads to a good end.

Let's seek for heaven, if we like nothing here;
for it was bad for us to see that beauty,
if she must steal our peace alive and dead.

9–14: The "we" in these lines consists of Petrarch and his soul.
12: "here"—on earth.

278

Ne l'età sua più bella et più fiorita

At her most beautiful, her most blossoming,
at that age when Love's at his strongest in us,
leaving on earth her earthly covering,
my vital inspiration went from me,

and living, lovely, naked, rose to heaven.
From there she rules me, drives me on from there.
Why is my mortal part not stripped away
by my last day, which is the next life's first?

For, as the thoughts I have go after her,
so may the soul too follow—light, untrammeled,
joyful—and I be free of all these troubles.

All this delay is just to do me down,
to make me weigh the heavier on myself.
A third year's starting since I should have died!

3–4: Laura, "my vital inspiration" (*l'aura* in the Italian, with the usual pun on her name), has left her "earthly covering," that is, her body.

14: It is April 6, 1350, the second anniversary of Laura's death.

279

Se lamentar augelli, o verdi fronde

If I hear sad birds singing, or green branches
tenderly stirring in the summer breeze,
or husky murmuring of limpid waters
flowing in some cool, flower-bordered stream,

there where I sit brooding on love or writing,
I see one that heaven showed us and earth hides,
I see her, hear her, know that, still alive,
she's answering my sighs from far away.

"Oh, why destroy yourself before your time?"
she pityingly says, "Why keep on pouring
a painful river from your wretched eyes?

Don't cry for me, for dying made my days
eternal, and within the inner light
I opened eyes I seemed here to have closed."

13: "inner light"—the purely spiritual light of God.

280

Mai non fui in parte ove sí chiar vedessi

I've never been where I could see so clearly
what I've so wished to see since last I saw it,
nor where I found myself so unconstrained
or filled the skies with such cries of desire;

I've never seen a valley with so many
secure and secret hideaways to sigh in;
I can't think Cyprus or some other isle
offered to Love such a seductive haunt.

The waters speak of love, and airs and boughs
and singing birds and fish and flowers and grass,
all beg me to continue always loving.

But you, my noble one who call from heaven,
remind me how you died before your time
and beg me scorn the world and its sweet snares.

1–4: The general sense is that he feels more free to give himself over completely to erotic imaginings of Laura than he has previously done since her death.

7: "Cyprus"—the island sacred to Venus.

281

Quante fiate, al mio dolce ricetto

How many times I've run to my retreat,
away from people, and perhaps myself,
tears streaming down my breast onto the grass,
and sighs disturbing all the air around!

How many times alone I've nervously
set off through overshadowed, gloomy places,
pursuing in my thoughts the high delight
that I keep calling back but death has stolen.

I've seen her in the form of nymph or goddess
rise from the clearest reaches of the Sorgue
and seat herself upon the riverbank.

I've also seen her walking through cool grass,
treading down flowers as does a living woman,
and showing in her face she's sad for me.

1: "retreat"—his house in Vaucluse near the river Sorgue, in line 10.
7: "the high delight"—Laura.

284

Sí breve è 'l tempo e 'l pensier sí veloce

The time's so short, the thought so quickly gone,
which bring my lady, who's so dead, before me,
that it's too weak a medicine for the pain.
Yet while I see her, I can feel no hurt.

Love who has bound and pinned me to his rack,
trembles to see her stand at my soul's door,
where she can kill me, still so able to,
so sweet to see and so soothing to hear.

She comes proud as a mistress to her home,
dispelling with untroubled calm the bleak
imaginings of my dark, heavy heart.

My soul, which cannot bear so great a light,
sighs and says, "Blessèd be every hour that day
you opened up this entry with your eyes!"

13–14: The day is either the day when Petrarch first saw Laura in life or when her image first returned to him after death. Whichever it was, it was then that she opened the way for her image to enter his heart.

289

L'alma mia fiamma oltre le belle bella

My tonic flame, of lovelies loveliest,
whose friend and patron here on earth was heaven,
too soon for me has made her journey back
to her true home and to her rightful star.

I'm starting to awaken now and see
that she fought for the best with my desires,
and tamed those burning lusts that young men feel
with looks that were at once sweet and severe.

I thank her for it, and the high resolve
that with her lovely eyes and soothing anger
made me think of salvation, though on fire.

What handsome artistry, what right results,
for one to work with words, and one with glances,
I shaping her renown, and she my virtue!

4: Her home is heaven and her star Venus, the destination of souls particularly suited to love.

13–14: He has won glory for her through his poems; she has made him virtuous through not giving in to him.

291

Quand'io veggio dal ciel scender l'Aurora

When I see Dawn descend the height of heaven,
her brow of roses and her hair of gold,
Love sets upon me, blanching me of color,
and I say sighing, "There is Laura now."

Happy Tithonus, you well know the time
when your dear treasure is to be recovered,
but I, what shall I make of the sweet laurel?
To see it once again, I have to die.

The partings of you two are not so hard.
At least at night she regularly returns
and does not find your now-white hair distasteful.

But my nights are made bleak, my days made dark,
by one who has departed with my mind,
and left me of her self only her name.

1–5: Tithonus is the immortal but ever-aging husband of the immortal and ever-young Aurora, the dawn.

292

Gli occhi di ch'io parlai sí caldamente

The eyes of which I spoke so passionately,
and then the arms and hands and feet and face
which from myself had so divided me,
and made me singularly distinct from others,

the hair in ringlets of pure shining gold
and the brief flash of an angelic smile,
that used to make a paradise on earth,
are now a little dust that has no feeling.

And I still live, at which I grieve and rage,
left unlit by the star which I so loved,
in a wild storm and on an unrigged boat.

Here let my song of love come to its end:
the vein of inspiration has run dry,
and now my lyre is only turned to mourning.

14: The line takes up Job 30:31, "My lyre is turned to mourning."

298

Quand'io mi volgo indietro a mirar gli anni

When I turn round to look back down the years
that in their flight have scattered all my thoughts,
and dashed the fire in which I blazed and froze,
and ended a repose replete with troubles,

with faith in the deceits of loving shattered,
my life's one good thing split into two parts,
one being in heaven, the other in the earth,
and any profit from my losses lost,

I shake myself and find I am so bare
I'm envious of the worst unfortunate,
such fear and pity seize me for myself.

O star of mine, O fortune, fate, and death,
O for me always sweet and savage day,
how you have brought me low as low can be!

7: Laura's soul is in heaven, her bodied buried in the earth.
13–14: The day is April 6, when he first saw Laura and also the day she died.

301

Valle che de' lamenti miei se' piena

Valley, who are so filled with my laments,
river, who swell so often with my tears,
beasts of the woods, birds that fly free, and fish
constrained by the green banks on either side,

clear air that feels the heat of all my sighs,
sweet path that in the end turns out so bitter,
hill I delighted in where now I suffer,
but out of habit Love keeps leading me,

I recognize in you your usual forms,
but not, alas, in me, who have become
after such joy the home of endless pain.

From here I'd see her, and now track back
to see again where she rose bare to heaven,
leaving on earth the trappings of her beauty.

1–2: Presumably the valley containing the Fontaine de Vaucluse and the river Sorgue.

12–14: The path leads him to a point from which he once could watch the living Laura. Now he can see from these same tracks the place where she died, that is, presumably Avignon, though the lines are also metaphorical.

302

Levommi il mio penser in parte ov'era

My thinking raised me to a place where was
the one I look for and can't find on earth.
There, among souls enclosed in the third circle,
I saw her looking lovelier and less aloof.

She took my hand and said, "You'll yet be with me
here in this sphere, if what I want is right.
I'm she who caused you so much inner war,
and ended her own day before its evening.

My bliss exceeds the human intellect.
I'm waiting just for you and for the veil
you loved so much that's stayed down there below."

Why did she say no more and free her hand?
For hearing such compassionate and chaste words
I needed almost nought to stay in heaven.

3: "the third circle"—the third heaven, that of Venus.

8: "my own day"—her life.

10: "the veil"—her body, which will be restored to her at the resurrection of the dead at the Last Judgment.

303

Amor che meco al buon tempo ti stavi

Love who came with me in the better days
along these banks—so friendly to our musings—
and, trying to make our old accounts add up,
went talking through them with me and the river,

flowers, fronds, green grass, shades, caves, waves,
soothing winds,
closed valleys, hills above, and sunny slopes,
the harbor from my laborings in love,
from all the many heavy storms I sailed through,

oh quick inhabitants of the green woods,
oh nymphs, and you whom the cool, weedy depths
beneath the liquid crystal lodge and feed,

my days were once so bright, are now as dark
as death, whose fault it is. Thus each man gets
what chance assigns him from the day he's born.

6: "closed valleys"— alludes to the literal meaning of Vaucluse.

9: "quick inhabitants"—normally taken to be birds.

10: "you whom the cool, weedy depths"—normally taken to be fish.

306

Quel sol che mi mostrava il camin destro

That sun that showed to me the rightful way,
by which to mount to heaven with steps of glory,
returned to the great Sun, and shut my light
and her own earthly jail in a few stones.

Hence I've become a woodland animal,
and walk with lonely, wandering, weary steps,
my heart weighed down, tears in my downcast eyes,
here through a world I think a mountain waste.

I search again like this in every place
I saw her, and just you, Love, who afflict me,
come with me, and point out where I must go.

I don't find her, but find her holy traces,
all leading to the road that rises high,
far from the pools of Styx and Lake Avernus.

1: "That sun"—Laura.

3: "the great Sun"—God.

4: "earthly jail"—her body.

13: "the road"—to heaven.

14: Classically, the Styx is the principal infernal river, and Lake Avernus is near a point of entry to the underworld.

308

Quella per cui con Sorga ò cangiato Arno

The one for whom I chose Sorgue over Arno,
free poverty instead of servile riches,
changed to a bitter diet the hallowed sweetness
on which I once lived but now waste and fade.

I've tried and tried so many times in vain
to paint her sublime beauties in my songs
so future times might love and value them,
but her face won't be captured by my pen.

She possessed glories that were quite unique,
and shone in her like stars across the heavens;
at times I dare to sketch out one or two,

but when I reach that part which is divine,
that was a bright and brief sun to this world,
at that point daring, wits, and art all fail.

1–2: Because of Laura he preferred to be free and poor in Vaucluse, rather than wealthy and a servant in Florence. The reason is perhaps specious, but in 1351 Petrarch did turn down an invitation from the Comune of Florence to move there, accepting instead papal patronage in Avignon.

12: "part which is divine"—her soul.

309

L'alto et novo miracol ch' a' dí nostri

She was a new, high miracle that appeared
in our time in the world but would not stay,
for heaven gave us a glimpse, then took her back
to add adornment to its starry cloisters.

Love wants me to depict and show her plain
to those who missed her, first loosing my tongue,
and then in vain a thousand times directing
wits, time, pens, ink, and paper to the task

Our verse has still to reach to such a height.
I know it in myself and so must all
who to this day speak or write about love.

Let any thinking person silently
guess at a truth beyond words, and sigh, "Then
eyes that saw her alive were truly blessed."

4: "starry cloisters"—suggesting a heaven that is a monastery where God is constantly worshiped.

310

Zephiro torna, e 'l bel tempo rimena

Zephyr is back, bringing once more fine weather,
with flowers and greenery, his sweet attendants,
and Procne's chatter, Philomel's laments,
and all the dazzling white and red of spring.

The meadows smile, the sky turns bright and clear,
Jove gazes at his daughter happily,
and earth and air and water fill with love;
love's rediscovered by each living thing.

But back to me there come the heaviest
of sighs, which she who took its keys to heaven
draws from the very bottom of my heart.

And singing birds and hillsides flowering
and charms of lovely, honorable ladies
are all just wilderness and savage beasts.

1: "Zephyr"—the mild west wind associated with spring in classical Latin poetry.

3: The sisters Procne and Philomel were changed into birds, the first into the swallow, the second into the nightingale, according to the version of the story in Ovid (*Met.* 6.428–668).

6: In spring, the planets Jupiter ("Jove") and Venus ("his daughter") are favorably positioned with respect to each other.

311

Quel rosignuol, che sí soave piagne

That nightingale, so tunefully lamenting
perhaps its offspring or beloved partner,
fills all the sky and fields around with sweetness,
making such exquisite and moving music.

It seems to keep me company all night
reminding me how hard my lot's become.
And I have no one but myself to blame,
thinking Death didn't govern goddesses.

How easily the confident are tricked!
Those two fair lights, much brighter than the sun,
who thought to see them turn to obscure earth?

I know now that my brutal destiny
wants me to learn from living on and weeping
how here below nothing delights and lasts.

1–2: Behind these lines is another allusion to the story of Philomel. (See notes to Poem 310.)

8: "goddesses"—such as Laura.

10: "lights"—Laura's eyes.

312

Né per sereno ciel ir vaghe stelle

Not planets moving through unclouded heavens,
not smoothed keels speeding on a tranquil sea,
not knights in armor riding through the land,
not lithe and happy beasts in pleasant woods,

not long-awaited good news just arrived,
not love poems in some high elaborate style,
not sweet song from fine honorable ladies
in spots where springs are clear and meadows green,

not these nor anything can reach my heart,
that she so well entombed when she was buried,
she who was once my eyes' one light and mirror.

Life is so bleak and lasting a vexation,
I call for it to end, out of desire
to see once more one better never seen.

315

Tutta la mia fiorita et verde etate

My green and flowery days were almost past,
and I could feel the fires burning my heart
were less intense, having come to the point
when life tips down toward its final fall.

Little by little my dear enemy
was starting to feel that she safely could
discount her fears, and her sweet rectitude
was making my sour pains a kind of fun.

The time was close when love and chastity
can meet, and lovers find they can just sit
together, and talk over what's going on.

Death took a grudge against my happy state,
or hopes of one; when they were half-born, he
charged at them like an enemy fully armed.

3–4: "the point"—i.e., somewhat past the midpoint of life, probably in his mid-forties.

9: "The time"—later life, when sensual desire becomes less of a threat.

318

Al cader d'una pianta che si svelse

When an uprooted tree collapsed,
as does one torn away by gale or axe,
spreading its glorious foliage on the ground,
leaving its squalid roots bare to the sun,

I saw another that Love made my object,
and Calliope and Euterpe my subject.
It wound around my heart, made it its home,
as ivy creeps around a trunk or wall.

That living laurel, where superior thoughts
would nest, as did my burning sighs
that never stirred one leaf upon its boughs,

translated into heaven, has left its roots
here in its faithful home. So there is still
one sadly calling, though no one replies.

1–8: The sight of an uprooted tree reminds him of the dead Laura whom he loved and whom the muses made the subject of his poetry (Calliope is the muse of epic, Euterpe of lyric).

5: "another"—the laurel, i.e., Laura.

11: The never stirring leaves suggest an image of Laura remaining chastely unmoved by the force of his passion.

13: "faithful home"—his heart.

319

I dí miei più leggier' che nesun cervo

My days were fleeter footed than a deer
and fled like shadows, seeing happiness
pass in a blink, with just brief hours of calm
which I conserve as bittersweet mementos.

Dismal, impermanent, cocksure world,
one who sets hope by you is simply blind.
In you I lost my heart, and she who holds it
is earth now, with no bone and sinew joined.

But the best part of her that lives on still
and will forever, there in the high heaven,
has beauties that entrance me more and more.

And so my hair turns white, as I stay brooding
on what she is today, on where she is,
on what her lovely veil is now to see.

8: Petrarch draws on Job 10:11, "Thou didst clothe me with skin and flesh, and knit me together with bones and sinews."

14: The "veil" is the body, which in her lifetime was the beautiful covering of her soul.

320

Sento l'aura mia anticha, e i dolci colli

I sense the air that once was mine and see
the sweet hills rising where the light was born
that filled my eyes, while heaven so wished, with joy
and with desire, as now with gloom and tears.

O hopes condemned to fail, O crazed delusions.
The grass is widowed and the waters soiled,
and cold and void's the nest in which she lay,
in which I live and wanted to lie dead,

hoping at last from gentle-stepping feet
and from those eyes that burned my heart away,
some measure of repose from all my troubles.

I've served a master who is hard and mean;
I burned then, when I had my fire before me,
now I just cry over its scattered ashes.

1: "air"—the Italian *l'aura* is (as elsewhere) also Laura.

6–11: The images in these lines offer a negative version of the desire to die and be buried in the countryside frequented by Laura that appears in the second and third stanzas of Poem 126. The "nest in which she lay" (7) is usually taken to mean the place where she lived.

12: "master"—Love.

13: "fire"—Laura.

323

Standomi un giorno solo a la fenestra

Standing alone one day beside the window,
I saw so many and such novel things
I was already tired simply with gazing,
when from the right I saw appear a beast
whose human face might have set Jove ablaze,
chased by two hounds, one black, the other white,
which bit the noble beast
so fiercely on one side and then the other
that soon they brought her to the final pass,
where a too early death
conquered great beauty, sealed it under stone,
and made me sigh over its cruel fate.

And then I saw a ship on the high sea
with shrouds of silk and with a sail of gold,
fretted with ivory and ebony,
and the sea was calm, and the breeze was kind,
the sky as when there is no wisp of cloud,
and she sailed laden with a rich chaste cargo.
Then from the east a storm
suddenly so churned up the air and waves
the ship came crashing down upon a rock.
O what a weight of grief!
A moment overcame, a small space hides,
high riches that were second to no others.

This *canzone* consists of a sequence of allegorical visions, each of which is concerned with the destruction of a different manifestation of earthly beauty. Not all relate directly to Laura, although her death is the recurrent and underlying theme.

1: "the window"—normally taken to be a metaphorical visionary window.

4–6: "the right"—the side of moral virtue. The two hounds pursuing the beautiful beast (Laura) are generally thought to symbolize time, the black one representing night and the white one day.

18: "rich chaste cargo"—her virtue.

19–20: The storm symbolizes the Black Death of 1348, which came to Europe from the east.

In a wood of new trees the sacred branches
blossomed upon a young, straight-growing laurel,
that seemed one of the trees of paradise,
and from its shade there came so sweet a singing
of different birds, and so many delights,
that I was taken quite out of the world.
And as I gazed and gazed,
the sky changed all around, and, turning dark,
flashed thunderbolts that struck that happy tree
and straightaway tore out
its roots and all. And so I live in grief,
for such a shade can never be recovered.

There was a clear spring in that selfsame wood
that rose up from beneath a stone and poured
out cool, fresh waters, gently murmuring.
And to that secret, shady, dark-tinged spot,
shepherds and country bumpkins did not come,
but nymphs and muses singing to its music.
There I sat down, and when
I was enjoying most the harmony
and the display, I saw a cavern yawn
and sweep into itself
both spring and setting. I've not yet recovered,
and merely at the memory quake with fear.

A rare exotic phoenix, its two wings
coated in purple and its head in gold,
I saw proud and alone stalking the forest:
I thought I saw a deathless heavenly being
at first, until it reached the torn-out laurel
and the spring waters that the earth holds hidden.
All things fly to their end,
for seeing there the branches scattered round
the trunk split wide, those living waters dry,
as if enraged, it turned
its beak upon itself and vanished in a trice.
At which my heart was fired with love and pity.

37–48: The spring may be literally the Fontaine de Vaucluse. It is also the fount of poetry and poetic inspiration.

49–60: The phoenix (symbolizing the idea of poetic immortality) here seems to destroy itself once and for all in the face of Laura's death rather than dying only to be reborn, as in the normal version of the myth.

Lastly I saw pass through the flowers and grass,
absorbed in thought, a light and lovely lady
for whom I think I'll always burn and tremble,
modest herself, but arrogant to love,
wearing a pure white dress with broidery
that made it seem a blend of gold and snow,
although her highest parts
were all enveloped in a darkening mist.
A little snake then bit her in the heel.
Like a plucked flower that fades,
she took leave gladly, and with confidence.
O nought, except for tears, lasts in this world!

My song you may well say,
"These six visions that I contain have made
my master feel a sweet desire to die."

61–70: Laura now reappears cast as Orpheus' wife Eurydice who, like the Laura here, died from a snakebite. The "white dress" (65) suggests purity, the "darkening mist" (68) around "her highest parts" (67) probably signify that her soul was already absorbed in thoughts of death, suggesting the impending tragedy. But unlike Eurydice, this Laura accepts death, glad to leave this world and confident about her heavenly destination.

328

L'ultimo, lasso, de' miei giorni allegri

The last, alas, of the few happy days
that I have seen in this brief span of life,
had come, and turned my heart to melting snow,
guessing, perhaps the bleak black times to come.

Like one with joints and blood and mind enfeebled
about to be attacked by chronic fever,
was I, not knowing then how easily
my still imperfect happiness would end.

The lovely eyes, bright now in heaven and raptured
by light from which life and salvation pour,
leaving my own deprived and dismal here,

told them with a strange and virtuous sparkle,
"Stay on alone in peace, dear friends;
here never more, but we shall meet elsewhere."

1: The day is that of the poet's last meeting with Laura.

12: "them"—his eyes.

14: "elsewhere"—in Paradise.

336

Tornami a mente, anzi v'è dentro, quella

Back to my mind comes she who's always there,
she who cannot be banned from it by Lethe,
just as I saw her in her flower of life
alight with rays descending from her star.

She looks as lovely and as chaste as first
I saw her, so self-enclosed, so apart,
that I cry out, "It's her, she's still alive!"
and ask her for the gift of her sweet voice.

Sometimes she answers, sometimes does not speak.
And I like one who errs and then thinks straight,
address my mind and say, "You are deceived.

You know well that in 1348
on April 6th, at the first hour of day,
that blessèd soul departed from her body."

2: "Lethe"—the river of forgetfulness from which souls drink after death.

4: "her star"—Venus.

337

Quel, che d'odore e di color vincea

The one whose perfume and whose tints outdid
the perfume-bearing, shining-colored East,
outdid its fruit, flowers, herbs, leaves (so the West
took the first prize for all rare excellence),

that sweet laurel of mine, once the home
of every beauty, of all passionate goodness,
would see my master seated in its shade
together with my goddess honorably.

And I too made a nest for my best thoughts
within that fostering tree. And I was happy
through fire and ice, whether I burned or shivered.

The whole world was full of its perfect honors,
when God reclaimed it to enhance his heaven.
And it deserved to be so used by him.

2: The East is the source both of precious perfumes and of the dawn.

7: "master"—Love.

8: "goddess"—Laura, who is both distinguished from the laurel tree (5) and identified with it.

11: "fire and ice"—the fire of passion, the ice of rejection.

342

Del cibo onde 'l signor mio sempre abonda

The food my lord has always in abundance,
is tears and pain, with which I feed my heart,
often atremble, often turning pale,
to think how raw and deep a wound it has.

But she who in her day had no compare,
none who came close, comes to my sickbed now
in such a form I barely dare to look,
and sympathetically sits on the edge.

And with that hand that I desired so much,
she dries my eyes, and with her words she brings
a sweetness mortal man has never felt.

"What use is learning to a self-tormentor?"
she says, "Don't cry. Have you not cried enough?
I wish you'd live, just as I am not dead."

14: He should come to his senses, just as she has come to eternal life.

346

Li angeli electi et le anime beate

The highest angels and the blessèd souls,
the citizens of heaven, on the first day
my lady passed among them, crowded round her
full of amazement and concerned respect.

"What light is this, what beauty never seen?"
they asked each other. "No such lovely soul
has ever come up from the errant world
to this high dwelling in the whole last age."

And she, contented at her change of home,
finds she is placed with those who are most perfect.
Meanwhile she looks back now and then to check

that I am following, and seems to wait.
Hence I raise all thoughts and desires to heaven,
since I can hear her only beg me hurry.

8: "the whole last age"—the final age in the history of the world immediately before the Last Judgment.

10: Laura is in the highest part of heaven.

353

Vago augelletto che cantando vai

Little bird singing somewhere hereabouts,
or maybe crying for your times gone by,
seeing that you've the night and winter near,
and daylight and the brighter months behind,

if you knew my condition—it's like yours—
as well as you know your own heavy troubles,
you'd fly into the lap of one so wretched
to share with him your woebegone laments.

I don't know if the shares would turn out equal,
for she you cry for may be still alive,
while to me death and heaven are much more grudging.

And yet this least appealing hour and season,
and memories of the sweet and bitter years,
invite me to speak pityingly with you.

1: "little bird"—nightingale.

355

O tempo, o ciel volubile, che fuggendo

O time, O whirling heavens hurrying on,
tricking blind, wretched, mortal beings,
O days which have more speed than wind or arrows,
I know your wiles now through experience.

But I excuse you and reproach myself,
for Nature spread the wings you have for flight,
and gave me eyes, which I then just kept fixed
upon what harmed me, hence this shame and pain.

It should be time, or it's well past by now,
to turn my gaze to something more secure,
and put an end to these unending moans.

The soul, Love, does not leave your yoke behind,
only its evils, and you know the cost.
Virtue doesn't just happen. One must learn it.

358

Non pò far Morte il dolce viso amaro

Death cannot make the sweet face unappealing,
but that sweet face can make Death something sweet.
What need of other guides to dying rightly?
She guides from whom I learn all that is good.

And He who was ungrudging of His blood,
and with His foot broke down the gates of hell,
seems to encourage me by having died.
So come then, death. I hold your coming dear.

But don't delay, for it's high time by now.
Or if not now, the time came at that point
when she, my lady, passed out of this life.

Since then I have not lived a single day.
I traveled with her, with her reached the end;
when her feet stopped, I stopped my journey too.

5: "He"—Christ.

359

Quando il soave mio fido conforto

When my soothing, trusted comforter comes
to give some respite to my weary life,
and sits herself upon the bed's left side,
and speaks that sweet perceptive speech of hers,
from awe and anguish I turn deathly pale,
and ask, "Where have you come from, happy soul?"
She takes out from her breast
a small palm branch and then a laurel one,
and says, "I've made myself
leave the serene Empyrean heaven and those
holy parts. I come only to console you."

I humbly show my gratitude in words
and gestures, and then ask, "Well now, how did you
learn of my state?" And she, "The bitter waves
of tears, of which you never have enough,
are blown on by your sighs through all of space
till they reach heaven, where they disturb my peace.
You are too deeply vexed
that I have left behind this misery
and reached a better life.
You should be pleased, if you loved me as much
as in your face and words you seemed to show."

I answer, "I weep only for myself,
since I am left in darkness and in torment,
though just as certain you have risen to heaven
as if I saw it right before my eyes.
How could it be that God and Nature gave
such qualities to one so young in years,
if eternal salvation

3: "left side"—the side of the heart, but also symbolically the more suspect side.
10: "Empyrean"—the highest heaven, the seat of God and the blessed.

had not been destined to reward your goodness?
You're one of the rare souls,
and lived your life sublimely here among us,
and afterward soared up at once to heaven.

But I, what must I do but keep on crying,
wretched, alone, since without you I'm nothing?
I wish I'd died an infant in my cradle
and not had to experience love's workings."
And she, "Why all this crying and self-wounding?
And how much better to fly high from earth,
to take the proper measure
of mortal things and this sweet verbal trash
with which you trick yourself,
and follow me, if it is true you love me,
by gathering now one or two of these branches."

"I meant to ask," I say then in response,
"What do those two fronds mean to signify?"
And she, "You should know the reply yourself,
since your pen honors one of them so much.
The palm is victory, and I, still young,
vanquished both world and self. The laurel stands
for triumph, which I deserve,
thanks to that Lord who granted strength to me.
If other forces press you,
turn now to Him, ask Him to give you aid,
so that we join Him at your journey's end."

"Is this the blond hair, this the golden knot,"
I say, "that binds me still, and those the eyes
that were my sun?" "Don't make mistakes fools make,
she says, "or speak or think the way they do.
I am bare spirit and have joy in heaven.
What you look for has been mere earth for years.
I'm given that form to help
release you, and I'll be the same again,
only more lovely still,
more dear to you for saving both our souls
through being hard on you, and true to God."

41: "trash"—primarily his poems, but perhaps his other writings too.

60: "bare spirit"—her bodiless soul.

63: She will recover her body in its perfected form at the Last Judgment.

I weep, and with her hands
she wipes tears from my face, and sweetly sighs,
and loses patience with me,
with outbursts that would cause a stone to break.
And after that she leaves, and so does sleep.

360

Quel' antiquo mio dolce empio signore

Calling that vicious, sweet, old lord of mine,
to show and plead his case before the queen
who governs the divine
part of our nature from her seat on high,
there, wanting to be gold that fire refines,
I represent myself, weighed down by pain,
by fearfulness and horror,
like one afraid of death who asks for justice.
So I begin, "Lady, when I was young
I stepped left-footed into this one's realm.
Nothing I got from it
but scorn and anger, suffering so many
different torments there,
that in the end that endless fortitude
of mine gave way, and I felt life was loathsome.

So right up to today my time's passed by
in flames of anguish. And what profitable
paths of honor, and what
fun, I turned down to serve this cruel fraudster!
What fertile mind could come up with the words
to express here my miserable state,
and all the grave and righteous
complaints I want to make against this ingrate?
What little honey, how much gall and aloe!
What bitterness he's got my life attuned to

This *canzone* forms a contrasting pair with the preceding one. In its debate form and its thematics, it also complements Poem 264, which introduces Part II of the *Canzoniere*. There are strong links, too, with the *Secretum*, Book 3.

1: "lord"—Love.

2: "the queen"—reason.

10: "left-footed"—contrasted with the more favorable right, and perhaps suggestive of succumbing to sensuality.

24: "aloe"—The aloe's berries produced a particularly bitter purgative.

with the deceitful sweetness
that drew me first into the ranks of lovers.
Unless I trick myself,
I was one fit to rise high from the earth.
He took my peace and landed me in war.

He it is who has made me love God less
than I should and take less thought for myself.
For a lady I've let
every other concern slip out of mind.
He's been the only one to urge that course,
ever honing the desires of my youth
upon a vicious whetstone, from which once
I hoped for respite from his brutal yoke.
Wretch, what use are the bright superior mind
and all the other gifts that heaven gave me?
My hair may turn to grey,
but my ingrained desire I cannot change.
So I am stripped completely
of freedom by this sadist I accuse,
who's made a bitter life a sweet addiction.

He's driven me to probe deserted regions,
to confront beasts and bandits, spiky scrub,
hard people and their ways,
and all the wrong roads that embroil a pilgrim,
mountains, valleys, marshes, and seas and rivers,
with traps in thousands lurking everywhere,
and winters in strange months,
with dangers and exhaustion ever-present,
and neither he nor the she-enemy
I ran from, would leave me for one moment.
If I've not yet succumbed,
before time, to a cruel, painful death,
heavenly pity cares
for my well-being, not this tyrant here
who feeds himself upon my pain and loss.

36–38: Love constantly sharpens his desire through the very fact that Laura (here, the whetstone) is so resistant. Petrarch thus takes up a metaphor of Horace, "And savage Cupid, ever sharpening his burning arrows on a blood-stained whetsone" (*Odes* 2.8.14–16).

46–55: The travels are partly inner ones, but the images also suggest northern Europe, with its cold summers (52) and scrub-covered plains. In 1333 Petrarch traveled through the then-dangerous hills of the Ardennes to reach Ghent and Liège.

Since being his, I've not had one calm hour,
nor hope to have one, and my nights have seen
sleep banished and cannot
recover it by dint of herbs or spells.
He's made himself the master of my spirits
by tricks and force, and no bell rings the time,
whatever town I'm in,
and I not hear. He knows I speak the truth,
for worm has never gnawed away old wood
as he has gnawed my heart, in which he nests,
threatening it with death.
This is the source of all the tears and woes,
and all the words and sighs,
with which I wear myself (and maybe others) out.
You judge, for you know me and you know him."

My adversary opens with some bitter
remonstrance. "Lady, hear the other party,
who will utter unblemished
the truth from which this ingrate here departs.
In youth he was sent off to learn the art
of selling words, or lying.
It seems he's not ashamed,
though I had my delights replace those tortures,
to moan about me, when I kept him pure
and spotless from self-damaging desires,
while living a sweet life,
which he complains of and calls misery.
And he won no mean fame
only through me, who raised his intellect
to where alone it never would have risen.

He knows that great Atrides, proud Achilles,
and Hannibal, your country's bitter foe,
and then that shining hero

80–81: As a young man Petrarch unwillingly studied law at Montpellier and Bologna and never completed his degree.

85: "self-damaging desires"—in this context, most likely for money and material goods.

91–93: Atrides is Agamemnon (the son of Atreus); he and Achilles competed for the slave-girl Briseis. Hannibal was supposed to have fallen in love with an Apulian girl, and Scipio Africanus ("that shining hero") with one of his slaves.

92: "your country"—Italy, presumably seen here as the home of reason.

whose prowess and success outshone all others',
as was ordained for each one by his stars—
these I degraded with cheap loves for servants,
while for this fool I chose,
out of all the elect, outstanding women,
one whose like won't be seen beneath the moon,
not if Lucretia should return to Rome.
And then I gave her such
sweet speech, and such a rapturous singing voice,
that no base or grim thought
could ever last a moment in her presence.
This was the trickery I turned on him.

This was the gall, the disdain and rebuffs,
far sweeter than full pleasure with another.
Bad fruit I harvest from
good seed, that's how ingrates reward their servants.
Beneath my wings I'd led him to the point
of writing verse that knights and ladies loved.
I raised him up so high
his name's now one the fervent cognoscenti
find exciting, and there are places where
they gladly make collections of his poems.
He might have been a wheezy
legal mutterer, just one of the tribe.
I exalt him, make him known,
by dint of what he learned both in my school
and from her who was peerless in this world.

And finally to cite my major service,
I've saved him from a host of shameful lapses,
for squalid pleasures never
have been in any way attractive to him.
He turned into a modest, pure young man
in thought and deed, once he swore fealty
to her who stamped his heart
with her high imprint, and made him her like.
Anything rare and noble that is in him,
he has from her and from me, whom he blames.

99: "beneath the moon"—on earth.

100: Lucretia is cited here as the supreme example of beauty and chastity, in view of her suicide after being raped by Sextus Tarquinius.

No nighttime fantasy
could be so errant as his view of us.
Since he first came to know us,
he's been in the good grace of God and man.
That's what this rebel moans and groans about.

And then, and this is what beats everything,
I gave him wings to soar up to the heavens,
via those mortal things
which, for the thinking mind, are stairs to God.
Fixing his gaze upon the number and the kind
of qualities his hoped-for love possessed,
he could have raised himself,
image by image, to the high first cause.
He's said as much in verse, and not just once;
now he wants to forget me and that lady
I gave him as a prop
for his frail life." At this I raise a tearful
scream and shout, "Oh yes,
he gave her to me, but soon took her back."
And he, "Not I—God wished her for himself."

Finally turning to the justice seat,
each one concludes, I in a trembling voice,
he sounding loud and harsh,
with, "Noble lady, I await your verdict."
At this she smiles and says,
"I am pleased to have heard the pleas you've made,
but such a weighty case requires more time."

137–43: In the Platonic tradition, virtue and beauty seen in this world may be the means by which the well-disposed observer, or lover, may progress through higher and higher forms of love and eventually contemplate their true divine form.

361

Dicemi spesso il mio fidato speglio

My trusted mirror often says to me,
as do my tired mind, my changed exterior,
and my decreasing nimbleness and strength,
"No hiding any more. You're getting old.

Obedience to Nature's best in everything,
and time is sapping us, though we resist."
Then suddenly, as water puts out fire,
I wake up from a long and heavy sleep,

and see quite clearly that our lifetime flies,
and more than once a person cannot be,
and in my heart I hear resound a word

from one released now from her lovely bonds,
who in her days on earth was so unique
no other woman seems worth speaking of.

11: "a word"—it is left unsaid what the word is.

12: "her lovely bonds"—her body.

362

Volo con l'ali de' pensieri al cielo

I fly upon the wings of thought to heaven
so often that it almost seems to me
I'm one of those who have their treasure there,
leaving the tattered veil behind on earth.

Sometimes my heart trembles with a sweet chill,
hearing the one who drains all color from me
tell me, "Now, friend, I love and honor you;
you've changed your habits, as your hair has greyed."

She leads me to her Lord, and I then kneel,
praying in humbleness to be allowed
to stay looking at her face and at His.

And the reply: "Your destiny is sure.
Waiting another twenty years or thirty
you'll think too long, and yet it won't be much."

3: "treasure"—the soul.

4: "veil"—the body, the veil around the soul, which is torn apart at the moment of death.

13–14: Twenty or thirty years is nothing in comparison with eternity.

363

Morte à spento quel sol ch'abagliar suolmi

Death has put out the sun that dazzled me;
the clear, unsullied eyes are now in darkness,
she's earth from whom I took my heat and cold;
with laurels shriveled, I've just oaks and elms.

I see the good in this and still I grieve.
There's no one here to make me think rash thoughts
or frightened ones, no one to freeze or fire them,
or fill them full of hope, or else with pain.

Out of the hands of one who stabs and soothes,
who tore my self in pieces for so long,
I find myself in sweet and bitter freedom,

and to the Lord I gratefully adore,
whose merest nod rules and supports the heavens,
I turn back tired of living, sated too.

4: The unique laurel has been replaced by commoner trees.

5: "in this"—in Laura's death, which sets him free.

9: "one"—Love.

12: "Lord"—God.

364

Tennemi Amor anni ventuno ardendo

Love kept me twenty-one years in his fire,
happy to burn, and, if hurt, full of hope,
and, when my lady and my heart together
rose up to heaven, he kept me ten more weeping.

I'm weary of it now and blame myself
for errors that have almost killed all seeds
of good in me, and, God above, I duly
render this last part of my life to you,

saddened and contrite for the wasted years,
which ought to have been spent to greater profit,
seeking for peace and keeping clear of passion.

Lord, who have shut me in this earthly prison,
release me safe from everlasting torment;
I know my fault, and I make no excuses.

1–4: The sonnet (perhaps fictitiously) dates itself to 1358, since Petrarch first saw Laura in 1327 and she died in 1348.

365

I'vo piangendo i miei passati tempi

I keep on crying for my bygone years
which I spent on the love of something mortal,
not rising up in flight, though I had wings,
to show the world perhaps what I could do.

You who can see my abject sinfulness,
invisible, immortal King of heaven,
succor a feeble, misdirected soul,
and fill with your grace its deficiency,

so that, if I lived life in war and storms,
I die in peace and port, and, if the stay
was vain, at least the parting may be decent.

To that short space of life that I have left,
and to my dying, grant your helping hand.
You know that I have hope in no one else.

366

Vergine bella, che di sol vestita

Virgin of beauty, who, enrobed in sunlight
and crowned with stars, so pleased the highest sun
that it was you in whom he hid his light,
love presses me to speak in verse of you,
but I cannot begin without your aid
and that of Him who came in love to you.
I call on her who's always answered kindly
those who've called with true faith.
Virgin, if you have ever
been moved to mercy by an extreme case
of human misery, bend to my prayer,
succor my wartorn state,
though I am earth and you the Queen of Heaven.

Virgin of wisdom, and one of the number
of blessed prudent virgins,
you are the first, and with the brightest lamp;
you are a solid shield to those afflicted,
one which withstands the blows of Death and Fortune,
and under which there's triumph, not just refuge;
you bring a cooling to blind passion blazing

This *canzone* concludes the collection, though it probably was not the last poem to have been written. It is full of reminiscences of the Bible and of traditional motifs of poems and prayers to the Virgin Mary, to whom are applied praise motifs used earlier of Laura.

1–2: The light imagery applied to the Virgin stems ultimately from Rev. 12:1, "A woman clothed with the sun, with the moon under her feet, and on her head a crown of twelve stars."

2: "the highest sun"—God.

6: "Him"—the Holy Spirit.

14–15: Petrarch here applies to the Virgin Mary Christ's parable of the wise and foolish virgins (Matt. 25:1–13). The former had their lamps prepared for the coming of their lord and were admitted to his marriage celebrations; the latter were unprepared and excluded.

here in us foolish mortals.
Virgin, whose lovely eyes
looked sadly on the wounds stamped ruthlessly
upon the sweet limbs of your darling son,
look at me all awry,
coming to you to solve what I cannot.

Pure virgin, who are whole in every way,
daughter and mother to your noble child,
who light this life and are the other's jewel,
through you your son and son of the High Father,
(you window to the shining heaven above)
came down to save us in the world's last age.
Of earthly women to receive him here,
none but yourself was chosen,
Virgin of blessedness,
to make the tears of Eve turn into joy.
Make me deserving of his grace—you can,
who are blessed endlessly,
and crowned already in the realm on high.

Virgin most holy, full of every grace,
who through your true and high humility
rose up to heaven from where you hear my prayers,
you bore the fountain from which pity springs,
the sun of justice that illuminates
humanity beset by dense, dark errors,
you gather in yourself three dear, sweet names,
mother, daughter, and bride;
Virgin arrayed in glory,
the mistress of the King who loosed our bonds
and made the world a free and happy place,
you who can truly bless,
I beg you help my heart rest in His wounds.

32: "last age"—It was commonly believed that Christ's birth ushered in the sixth and last age of the world.

36: Eve's eating of the forbidden fruit led to the fall of man which Christ's coming redeemed.

40: "full of every grace"—The line echoes the Vulgate version of Luke 1:28, "Hail Mary, full of grace."

47: The Virgin is the mother of Jesus, the daughter of God and the bride of the Holy Spirit.

51: There is an implicit contrast with Laura.

Virgin, unique on earth, made on no model
whose beauties caused high heaven to fall in love,
who had no like before and none that followed,
your holy thoughts, and pure compassionate ways
created in fertile virginity
a living temple for the one true God.
Through you my life might yet find happiness,
if at your prayers, Maria,
sweet and devoted Virgin,
abounding grace is given where sin abounded.
Lowering my mind until it's on its knees,
I pray you be my guide,
and right my crooked path to a good end.

Bright Virgin, fixed for all eternity,
star shining out over this stormy sea,
and trusted guide for steersmen who believe,
consider in how terrible a storm
I find myself, alone, without a tiller,
with little time before my final cries.
But still my soul maintains its trust in you,
though sinful, I confess;
Virgin, I beg you stop
my enemy from mocking my discomfort.
Remember that our sinfulness made God
take on, to rescue us,
our human flesh within your virgin cloister.

Virgin, how many tears I've shed in vain,
how much I've praised and flattered, how much begged,
only to hurt myself, do myself harm.
Since I was first born on the Arno's bank,
I've sought peace in one place and then another,
and life has been for me nothing but trouble.
Mortal beauty, and mortal words and deeds
have weighted down my soul.
Virgin, our holy helper,
do not delay, this may be my last year.
My days have rushed by faster than an arrow
and disappeared in sin
and misery, and only death awaits me.

75: "my enemy"—the devil.

Virgin, she who is earth and keeps my heart
plunged in its grief, kept it in tears in life
and did not know one-thousandth of my ills,
and if she had known, still what did occur
would have occurred; her wanting otherwise
meant death for me and disrepute for her.
Now you, heaven's mistress, you who are our goddess
(if the term's right and proper),
Virgin of high perceptions,
you can see everything, and what no other
could ever do, is nothing to your power,
that is, to end my pain,
which will both honor you and save my soul.

Virgin, in whom I place my each and every hope
that you can help me in my need, and want to,
don't leave me as I near the final pass.
Don't think of me but of who deigned to make me,
let not my worth, but that likeness to Him
in me, move you to aid so low a man.
Medusa and my faults made me a stone,
dripping with futile moisture.
Virgin, fill my tired heart
with tears of reverence and piety,
so that at least these last ones fall devoutly,
free from terrestrial mire,
not like those tears of madness I once wept.

Virgin of human kindness, foe of pride,
let love of our shared origin impel you:
have pity on a contrite humble heart.
If I have loved with marvelous faithfulness
a little piece of transient mortal earth,
how should I love you, noble as you are?

96–97: The argument is that if Laura had felt the same lustful passion, and they had both given in to it, he would have risked damnation and she would have lost her good name.

99–100: He is concerned that the pagan term "goddess" may not be appropriate in the Christian context.

107: "pass"—the transition from one life to the next.

109: According to Gen. 1:27, God created man in His own image.

111–12: Laura here becomes the Gorgon Medusa. Petrarch intimates that her gaze has paralyzed him, leaving him with only a capacity for futile weeping.

If your hands help me rise again from this
despicably vile state,
Virgin, I'll consecrate
and cleanse in your name, thought and mind and style,
my tongue and heart, my weeping and my sighs.
Guide me to a good crossing,
and look with pleasure on my changed desires.

The day is coming and cannot be far,
so fast time runs and flies,
Virgin one and unique,
and death and conscience pierce my heart by turns.
Speak kindly of me to your Son, who is
both true man and true God,
that he may take my last breath to His peace.

129: "crossing"—again, like "pass" in line 107, the transition to the next world.

The Triumph of Eternity

The Triumph of Eternity

Since I saw nothing under heaven that was
secure and stable, I turned then to myself
in deep dismay and asked, "What do you trust in?"

I answered, "In the Lord, who never breaks
a promise made to those who trust in Him.
But I see plainly that the world has mocked me,

and realize what I am and what I was,
and see time going by, or rather flying,
and would complain, but don't know who to blame.

The fault is mine alone. I should have opened
my eyes sooner, not lingered till the end,
for truly I've let too much time go by.

But never has divine grace come too late.
I hope that such grace will still work in me
exalted and exceptional effects."

That's what I said. But now, if there's no rest
for these things changing as the heavens direct,
what end will follow after all the changes?

I thought and thought, and, as my mind reached deeper
into itself, I saw a world appear,
new in immobile and eternal time;

the sun and all the heaven and stars around
dissolved, and so too did the land and sea,
and were remade more pleasing and more lovely.

What wonder did I feel when I saw stay
in one sole moment what has never stopped,
but courses on in total transformation!

17: "these things"—all things in this world subject to the influences of the stars and planets, or alternatively, the stars and planets themselves.

26: "what has never stopped"—time.

I saw its three parts concentrate together
in one alone and that one motionless,
no longer hurrying by as it did once,

and saw, as if on ground stripped bare of grass,
no "will be," "was," "ever," "before," or "after,"
that make our lives unstable and infirm.

My thoughts pass onward like the sun through glass,
or faster still, since nothing hinders them.
O what grace it will be, if I should win it,

to see the divine goodness fully present,
and none of those ills time alone supplies,
that take their leave with time and with time come!

Taurus and Pisces will not host the sun,
whose movements are the reason why our labors
begin and end, diminish and increase.

Blessed are those spirits who will stand, or stand
already, in the highest choir, so ranked
to make their names eternally remembered!

O happy is that man who finds the ford
by which to cross this rushing mountain torrent
that is called life and is so much adored!

And wretched are the sightless vulgar herd
who set their hopes here on the things that time
with such abruptness takes away from them!

O you are truly deaf and bare and frail,
impoverished in reason and resolve,
utterly sick and wretched mortal men!

There's one who governs heaven with his glance,
who raises up and calms the elements,
whose wisdom is beyond not just my grasp,

31: "grass"—suggesting seasonal change.

37: "divine goodness"—God.

40: Taurus and Pisces seem here simply to stand for the signs of the Zodiac as a whole. The probable sense is that the sun's changing position in the sky dictates the cycle of daily and seasonal work—beginning in the morning, ending in the evening, decreasing in winter, and increasing in spring.

but that of angels, who rejoice and revel
to see one in a thousand of its parts,
absorbed in gazing and desiring more.

O febrile mind, still famished at the end,
why all that worrying? An hour disperses
what years of labor barely scrapes together.

What presses on our souls and burdens them,
"then," "now," "yesterday," "tomorrow," "morn," "night,"
will all pass in one moment like a shadow.

There'll be no "was," "will be," or "used to be,"
but only "is," "present," "now," and "today,"
and just eternity, entire and whole;

as if the hills before us and behind,
blocking our sight, were leveled, there'll be nothing
for hopes and memories to rest upon.

Their seesawing leads us into delusions,
when life seems a charade, and we just ponder,
"What shall become of me? What was I once?"

Time will not be divided into portions
but be one whole, with no summer or winter;
time will be dead, and place will be transformed.

Years won't hold in their power the governance
of human fame; no, he who once wins glory
will have that glory for eternity.

O happy are those souls who are, or will be,
traveling the way that leads them to the end
of which I speak, whenever that may be!

Among those lovely, special travelers
most blessed of all is she whom Death cut down
so long before she reached her natural limit!

And then there will appear the angel features,
the virtuous language, and the unsullied thoughts
that Nature planted in her youthful heart.

86: "she"—Laura.

So many faces death and time have wasted
will come back in the flower of their lives,
and they will see, Love, her you bound me to.

So they will point their fingers at me, saying,
"Here's one who always wept, but in his tears
was blessed beyond the laughter of all others!"

And she for whom I still sing and still weep
will feel enormous wonder at herself,
to see how she is praised above the rest.

When this will be, I do not know. But since
the trustiest disciples were not told,
who can begin to plumb so deep a secret?

I think the day draws near, when the accounts
of true and false gains will be duly settled,
for both will be no more than spiders' webs.

It will be clear how vain are our obsessions,
how futile are our labor and our sweat,
and how much individuals are deceived.

No one may hide then or repress a secret,
and every conscience, whether clean or stained,
will stand bare and exposed to all the world.

And One will judge the balance and know all.
Then we shall see the sinners take their way,
like hunted beasts running into the woods.

And we shall see how paltry noble crests
that puff you up with pride, and gold, and land,
have done you down and not brought betterment,

while to one side stand those who willingly
accepted modest limits and enjoyed
inner contentment with no outward pomp.

100–1: Christ did not inform His Apostles when precisely the Last Judgment would take place.

105: The image of the spider's web may be intended to suggest fragility or transparency.

Five of these Triumphs we have seen below
on earth, and finally, if God so wills,
we'll see the sixth of them in heaven above.

And time which is so quick to shatter things
and death which is so greedy for its dues,
will both be brought to suffer death together.

And those who shone with fame that they deserved
but Time destroyed, and those lovely faces
time and the bitterness of death had ravaged,

will then return more beautiful than ever
and leave oblivion and bleak ugliness
to the brute force of death and thieving days.

In the full bloom and greenest years of life
they'll have eternal fame and deathless beauty.
But first amongst those to be made anew

is she for whom the world cries out in tears,
using my tongue and my exhausted pen,
while heaven's one longing is to see her whole.

Beside a river rising in Gebenna,
Love threw me into chaos for so long
I can't erase the memory from my heart.

Happy the gravestone covering that face!
And when she wears again the body's veil,
if it was bliss to see her here on earth,

what will next seeing her in heaven be?

121: The reference is to the subjects of the five preceding poems in the sequence, that is, Love, Chastity, Death, Fame, and Time, each of which triumphs over the one that precedes. All are now triumphed over by Eternity.

131–32: The destructive effects of time and death will be left to the two negative powers and vanish with them.

138: Laura will be whole when her body and soul are united at the Last Judgment.

139: The Durance, which flows into the Rhône at Avignon (where Petrarch first saw Laura), has its source in Mount Geneva ("Gebenna").

Secretum

Book 3

Secretum, Book 3

AUGUSTINE: If anything I have said so far has been of any benefit to you, now I beg and beseech you to make yourself receptive to the remainder and to put aside your propensity to argue and sulk.

FRANCISCUS: Consider it done. I feel that your admonitions so far have freed me from a great part of my worries. So I am all the readier to go on and hear the rest.

AUGUSTINE: I have not yet probed some chronic injuries to the very depths of your being that are highly resistant to treatment, and I am fearful of doing so. I remember how contentious and complaining my touching on less serious matters made you. However, I have hopes, on the other hand, that if you gather your strength, you will now be able to bear this harsher examination with greater fortitude and equanimity.

FRANCISCUS: Have no fear. I have become accustomed both to hearing my diseases called by their names and to tolerating the helping hand of the doctor.

AUGUSTINE: Your own hands are still weighed down by two chains of glittering steel, which do not let you give due attention to either life or death. I was always afraid that they would drag you to total destruction. My mind is still not at rest on this score, and will not be until I see you moving in total freedom, with the chains shattered and thrown aside. I do not think that is impossible, though it is certainly a hard task. Still, if it were impossible, I would be wasting my words now. They say that using a goat's blood helps to break up diamonds.[1] In the same way we can soften up inflexible obsessions of this sort with a remarkably effective treatment that breaks down and penetrates the rebarbative heart as soon as it touches it. But I have my doubts, since the matter requires your active assent, and that is something that you cannot give, or rather, to tell the truth, which you do not wish to give. My main fear is that the dazzling, beguiling radiance of the chains themselves is an obstacle. I suspect that you will turn out to be like a miser kept in prison in chains of gold, wanting to be freed but unwilling to lose what binds him. The law regulating your imprisonment says that you cannot go free unless you throw off the chains altogether.

[1] Pliny, *Natural Histories* 37.4.59.

Franciscus: Good heavens! I am in a more miserable state than I thought! Can there be two chains that I do not realize are pinning me down?

Augustine: No, you know what they are very well, but their beauty gives you such pleasure that you judge them riches, not chains. To take up the simile I have just used, you are in the position of one bound by golden manacles and fetters who happily contemplates the gold and does not see the bonds. Now you do see plainly what binds you. But, being a blind fool, you are delighted by the ties that are dragging you to death, and the most dismal thing of all is that you glory in them.

Franciscus: But what are these chains that you talk about?

Augustine: Love and glory.

Franciscus: Ye gods above! What is this I hear? Do you call these chains? And, if I let you, is it these you will cast off?

Augustine: That is what I am working for. But I am doubtful about the outcome. The other chains that bound you were weaker and less seductive. So you were quite willing for me to snap them. But these give pleasure even as they cause harm. They trick with their outer show. So more effort is obviously needed. You will dig your heels in, as if I wanted to strip you of your most valuable possessions. However, I shall do my best.

Franciscus: What have I ever done to you to make you want to rob me of the loveliest things I have ever devoted myself to, and to condemn the most serene part of me to perpetual darkness?

Augustine: You poor fool! Have you lost sight of the philosophical maxim which says that the peak of unhappiness is when false arguments lead to the fatal conviction that things are as they should be?

Franciscus: I have not forgotten it at all. But that maxim is not to our purpose in the slightest. Why should I not judge that things should be as they are? I have never thought more rightly, and never will do, than when I judge the two attachments that you throw in my face to be the noblest there are.

Augustine: Let us keep the two things separate for a little while. I do not wish when looking for the remedies to be pulled this way and that, and so come down on either of them singly with less force. Tell me then—since love was the first to be mentioned—don't you think it the most extreme madness there is?

Franciscus: To keep strictly to the truth, I consider that, given the diversity of objects toward which it can be directed, love may be called either the most baleful of passions or the most noble action of the psyche.

Augustine: The matter needs to be put more concretely. Be specific.

FRANCISCUS: If I am fired with passion for some disgusting, disreputable woman, my passion is decidedly unhealthy. But if I am attracted by some rare model of virtue and give myself over to loving and worshipping her, what do you think? Won't you make a distinction between things that are so different? Has respect for female modesty evaporated? To speak for myself, I judge the first case a grave and dangerous weight to labor under, but I can think of no happier event than the second. If you perchance should think the opposite, let each of us keep to his own ideas. As you know, there exists an immense range of points of view and an equally large freedom to make individual judgments.

AUGUSTINE: Opinions may differ over matters in dispute. But the truth remains always one and the same.

FRANCISCUS: I admit that it is indeed so. And what leads us astray is that we obstinately stick to our old ideas and resist being torn away from them.

AUGUSTINE: If only your notions on the whole question of love were as right-minded as you are on this point!

FRANCISCUS: What more needs to be said? I seem to myself to view the issue correctly, and I have no doubt that those who think differently are out of their minds.

AUGUSTINE: But it is the height of madness to take an inveterate falsehood to be true and to reckon a newly discovered truth to be false, as if time were the one source of authority.

FRANCISCUS: You are wasting your efforts. I will have none of it. I draw comfort from Cicero: "If I err in this, I err willingly, and I do not wish to be disabused of this error as long as I live."[2]

AUGUSTINE: When Cicero used words something like those, he was discussing the immortality of the soul. He was voicing the finest view of all on the matter. He wished to show that he had no doubts at all that the soul was immortal, and would refuse to hear anything to the contrary. You are abusing what he said in support of a disgraceful and baseless prejudice. For surely, even if the soul were mortal, it would still be better to believe it immortal, since an error that will instill love of righteous behavior may well be felt to be salutary. When there is no prospect of reward, virtue is still to be sought for its own sake, but the desire to be good would fade with the prospect in view of the death of the soul, whereas the promise of a future life, even if mendacious, would appear a not ineffective stimulus to the human spirit. Surely you can see the consequences of this error of yours. You will fall prey to all sorts of insanity: you will lose any sense of shame and fear

[2] Cicero, *On Old Age* 23.85.

and be completely bereft of reason and awareness of the truth, which commonly act as brakes on the driving force of desire.

FRANCISCUS: I said earlier that you would be wasting your efforts. I do not recall ever having felt love for anything base. I am aware only of having loved something of supreme beauty.

AUGUSTINE: It is without doubt possible for beautiful things to be loved basely.

FRANCISCUS: But I have not sinned either in the object or in the manner of my love. Do not persecute me any further.

AUGUSTINE: So now what? Do you wish to breathe your last, joking and laughing, like some people who are out of their wits? You are still mentally and morally sick. Don't you prefer to be offered a cure?

FRANCISCUS: Of course I will not turn down the cure, if you can show me that I need one. But it is often dangerous to press treatment on the healthy.

AUGUSTINE: When you begin to get better, you will be like many other people and admit that you have been seriously ill.

FRANCISCUS: In the end, I cannot be dismissive of someone whose advice I have often found to be sound, particularly in these last few days. Go on then.

AUGUSTINE: Well, first of all I should like you to be forbearing, if I should be obliged by the matter in hand to utter harsh words concerning your heart's delight. I can already foresee the painful impact truth will have on your ears.

FRANCISCUS: Listen for a moment before you begin. Do you know who we are going to speak of?

AUGUSTINE: I have given due and careful thought to everything. Our coming conversation will regard a mortal woman, on the adoration and celebration of whom you have, I am sad to say, spent a great deal of your life. I am astounded that an intelligence like yours has submitted to so great and so long-lived a madness.

FRANCISCUS: Please spare the jibes. Thais and Livia were both mortal women too.[3] Do you realize that you have alluded to the one woman who is unaware of earthly concerns, whose ardor is entirely heavenly, whose beauty, if there is any truth anywhere, exemplifies divine beauty, whose life is the model of perfect chastity, whose voice and irresistible eyes have no trace of the mortal in them, and whose step has a more than human quality?[4] Please

[3] Thais is a licentious concubine in Terence's *Eunuch*. Livia was the upright wife of the emperor Augustus and the mother of the emperor Tiberius.

[4] Petrarch praises Laura in very similar terms in Poem 90 of the *Canzoniere*.

think it over a few times. Then I think you will come to see what sort of language is appropriate when speaking of her.

AUGUSTINE: You are out of your mind. Isn't this how you have used pretty words to fan the flames for over fifteen years?[5] Italy's famous foe[6] posed a long-term threat to the country centuries ago, and the country itself underwent invasions and was frequently set ablaze. In recent years you have been even more subject to the flames and fury of passion. In the end someone was found to drive Hannibal out. But who is going take the yoke of your Hannibal from your neck, if you forbid him to leave and spontaneously offer him servile invitations to stay? You are in the unhappy state of delighting in your misery. But when those eyes whose beauty will be your downfall have closed for the last time, when you gaze on her face changed by death and see her wan lifeless body, you will be ashamed to have tied the immortal part of yourself to transient flesh and will remember red-faced the fantasies that you now so obstinately construct.

FRANCISCUS: God let it not happen! I shall not see it.

AUGUSTINE: But these things will inevitably happen.

FRANCISCUS: I know, but the stars are not so set against me as to overturn the order of nature by her death. I entered on life before her; I shall leave it first too.

AUGUSTINE: I think you can remember a time when you feared the contrary. Your grief inspired you to compose a lament for her as if she were on the very point of dying.

FRANCISCUS: Of course I remember. The pain was intense. I still tremble at the memory. I was outraged to think that what I see as the noblest part of my soul should be mutilated and that I should survive the being who made life sweet with her mere presence. That was the subject of a verse lament that poured from me amid a rain of tears. I remember its matter, though the words are harder to recall.[7]

AUGUSTINE: We are not enquiring just how many tears or how much pain the fear of her dying may have caused you. I have raised the issue to make you understand that the fear that inflicted such a blow to you once may well return, the more so since every day that passes is another step for her toward

[5] This suggests, since Petrarch claims to have first seen Laura on April 6, 1327, that the *Secretum* was composed in 1342. But neither date is to be trusted.

[6] Hannibal, who led the Carthaginians into Italy in 218 BCE and was only forced out by the Romans in 203 BCE.

[7] Probably a Latin elegy in rhyming couplets, which can be found in E. H. Wilkins, *The Making of the Canzoniere* (Rome: Edizioni di storia e letteratura, 1951), 302–3.

death, and that exceptionally beautiful body of hers, worn out by sickness and frequent childbirths, is not as irresistible as it once was.

FRANCISCUS: I too feel more burdened by care and am more advanced in years. She may be coming closer to her death, but I am preceding her.

AUGUSTINE: What lunacy, to deduce the order in which we die from the order in which we are born! What makes old age more bereft for parents than the sudden deaths of their sons in early manhood? What makes aged nurses grieve more than the snuffing out of their infant charges,

> whom, reft of sweet life and torn from the breast,
> black day bore off and plunged in early death.[8]

But a few years' precedence has given you the totally vacuous hope that you will die before the woman who fired your mad passion. And this you imagine is the unchanging order of nature.

FRANCISCUS: Not so unchanging that I do not recognize that the opposite may happen. But I pray constantly that it does not. Whenever I think of her death I am helped by this verse of Ovid:

> Let that day come late, and when my life's done.[9]

AUGUSTINE: I have not the strength to hear more of these inanities. Since you realize that she may die first, what will you say if that does happen?

FRANCISCUS: Only that the catastrophe has plunged me into abject misery, but that I shall find some consolation in remembering times past. But may our words be carried away on the winds, may storms come and disperse the evil omen!

AUGUSTINE: You blind fool! Do you not yet understand how insane it is to make the soul subject to mortal things, which inflame it with desire but cannot bring rest, which do not last through to the end, which promise to soothe but really torture with their constant turmoil?

FRANCISCUS: If you have a more effective argument, out with it. You will never scare me with this sort of talk. Anyway I have never given myself over to a mortal thing in the way you think. Let me tell you that I have never loved her body so much as her soul. I have been entranced by a character that transcends human limitations, that gives me an idea of what it is to live among the beings of heaven. And so, if—and the mere sound of the words is torture—if she were to die first and abandon me, what would I do, you ask? I should find consolation for my unhappiness after the example of Laelius,

[8] Virgil, *Aeneid* 6.428–29.

[9] *Metamorphoses* 15.868.

the wisest Roman of them all, who said, "It was his moral virtue which I loved, and that has not died."[10] That is what I would say, and then the rest of what I understand he said after the death of the friend whom he had loved with quite remarkable intensity.

AUGUSTINE: You are entrenching yourself in an almost impregnable citadel of errors, from which it will require no little effort to evict you. I can see that your disturbed state means that you will listen much more patiently to whatever is said about yourself than to what is said openly about her. Well, you can pile as much praise as you like on your insignificant female. I shall make no objection. She may be a queen, a saint, she may be

a goddess surely,
or Apollo's sister or from the race of nymphs.[11]

But her immense virtues will not provide the slightest excuse for your own errors.

FRANCISCUS: I'm trying to work out what new disagreement you're engineering between us.

AUGUSTINE: There can be no doubt that beautiful things are often loved in a disgusting fashion.

FRANCISCUS: You have already had the reply to this earlier. If the love ruling me had a face that could be seen, it would be very like her face, the face of one I have praised lavishly but still inadequately. This lady,[12] in whose presence we are speaking, is a witness that in my love there has never been anything disgusting, nothing obnoxious, nothing blameworthy, apart from its immensity. Set a limit to it and nothing finer can be imagined.

AUGUSTINE: I could reply with that phrase of Cicero that "you're looking to set a limit to vice."[13]

FRANCISCUS: Not to vice, but to love.

AUGUSTINE: But when he said that, he was talking about love. Do you remember where?

FRANCISCUS: Of course. I read it in the *Tusculan Disputations*. But he was offering his view of common human love. In mine, however, there are some special features.

[10] Cicero, *On Friendship* 27.102 (slightly misquoted by Petrarch). Laelius is speaking of Scipio Africanus.

[11] Virgil, *Aeneid* 1.328–29.

[12] The silent figure of Truth.

[13] Cicero, *Tusculan Disputations* 4.8.41 (slightly misquoted by Petrarch).

Augustine: Maybe others think the same about themselves. It's plain that everyone is an indulgent interpreter of his own position in relation to love, even more than happens with the other passions. Even if it was written by a writer of doggerel, it's not foolish to give credit to the couplet

> Each one's got his bride and I've got mine;
> each one's got his love and I've got mine.[14]

Franciscus: Do you want me, if there is time, to spell out a few of the many things that would compel you to feel admiration and wonder?

Augustine: Do you think that I am ignorant of the fact that

> lovers themselves shape their own dreams?[15]

That's from a poem that every schoolboy knows. It's painful to hear these insanities from the mouth of someone one could reasonably expect to think and speak with more depth.

Franciscus: There is one thing—whether it is to be ascribed to gratitude or ineptitude, I don't know—which I must say. What little merit you see in me I have thanks to her. I would never have achieved the name or renown, such as it is, that I have, if she had not inspired noble feelings in me, which nourished the feeble seeds of virtue that nature planted in my breast. She made me recoil from anything squalid, hooked me back, as they say,[16] and forced me to turn my gaze to higher things. How could I not be transformed by taking on the habits of my beloved? The backbiter is yet to be found who can sully her good name, or to dare to say that he has seen something to reproach in a gesture or word of hers, let alone in her behavior. Those who leave nothing unbesmirched have ceased to try with her, lost in wonder and veneration. So it is not at all surprising if her remarkable reputation produced in me, too, the desire to become gloriously famous, and took the sting out of the unstinting efforts that were needed for me to achieve my goal. As a young man all I wanted was to be found pleasing by her and her alone, who alone gave pleasure to me. For that to happen, I scorned a thousand enjoyments I might have had. You yourself know how many tasks and obligations I took on at a too early age. And yet you are bidding me to forget the person who separated me from the vulgar herd, or at any rate to love her less, when she is my guide in everything, the one who spurred my dull wits into action and put some life into my sluggish spirit.

[14] A pair of lines quoted by Cicero (*Letters to Atticus* 14.20.3), who ascribes them to Atilius, a writer of comedies he considers to be stylistically harsh.

[15] Virgil, *Eclogues* 8.108.

[16] The image of love using hooks to pull the lover in one direction or another appears occasionally in prose and poetry of the time.

AUGUSTINE: You miserable creature! How much better it would have been not to have spoken at all! Although I would have been able to see into your heart anyway, your persistent effrontery is outrageous and quite nauseating.

FRANCISCUS: Why, may I ask?

AUGUSTINE: Because wrong views are a mark of ignorance, but shamelessly to make false assertions is a mark not just of ignorance but of pride.

FRANCISCUS: What evidence is there that I have thought or pronounced things that are so mistaken?

AUGUSTINE: Only everything you say! First of all, when you say that you are what you are because of her. If you mean that she gave you this being that you have, you are definitely telling a lie. But if you mean that she has not allowed you to be any more than that, you are speaking the truth. Oh, what a great man you might have turned out, if she had not held you back with the charms of beauty! So what you are was given by the goodness of nature. What you might have been she has snatched from you, or rather you robbed yourself. She is innocent, but you find her beauty so seductive, so delectable, that all the healthy growth that would have sprung from the natural seeds implanted in you has been wasted by the combination of the heat of arid desire and the floods of tears you have shed. Then you were wrong to boast that she pulled you back from all forms of disgraceful behavior. She may have pulled you back from many, but she pushed you into worse miseries. Someone who warns against taking a path fouled by various kinds of filth but who leads us on over a precipice, or who heals lesser sores but inflicts a lethal wound in the jugular vein, must be called a killer rather than a liberator. She whom you proclaim your guide may have deflected you from a host of defilements, but only to drive you into a magnificent abyss. As for having taught you to raise your sights, or having set you apart from the herd, does that mean anything except that she made you obsessed with her, so bewitched by her attractions, that you were dismissive and wearily indifferent toward everything else? As you should know, there is nothing more damaging to human society. Then you also say that she led you to become involved in countless laborious tasks. There is some truth in that, at least, but think what marvelous benefits you've had. Since there are manifold labors in life that cannot be avoided, how demented it is to go looking for new ones of one's own accord! As for boasting that you became all the more eager for glory because of her, that's an error of yours I can sympathize with. I shall show you, though, that none of the things weighing you down are as deadly as this. But our discussion is not yet at that point.

FRANCISCUS: The quick fencer feints and then strikes. I am troubled as much by the feint as the wound. I am already feeling seriously off balance.

Augustine: How much more you'll wobble when I wound you really seriously! Anyway, she, the one you praise to the skies, to whom you claim to owe everything, she is the one destroying you.

Franciscus: Good God, by what means can I be persuaded of that?

Augustine: She has alienated you from love of heaven and turned your desires away from the Creator toward the creature created by Him. This has always been the fastest way to death.

Franciscus: Please, I beg you, no hasty judgment. Surely loving her helped me to love God.

Augustine: No, it inverted the order of things.

Franciscus: In what way?

Augustine: While the whole of creation is to be loved out of love of the Creator, you went against the rule. You were captivated by the allure of a creature and loved the Creator in an inappropriate fashion. You wondered at her Maker as if He had made nothing more beautiful, when physical beauty is the lowest form beauty can take.

Franciscus: I call on Truth here to be my witness, with my conscience as co-witness, that, as I said earlier, I have never loved her body more than her soul. That will be evident to you from the fact that, the more mature in years she has become—and age inevitably undermines physical beauty—the stronger I have felt my attachment to her. Although her youthful bloom has visibly faded with the passage of time, her inner beauty has increased with the years. It was that which gave my love its start, which made me persevere with it once it had begun. Of course, if I had been running after her body, the time to change direction would have come long ago.

Augustine: Are you making fun of me? Would you have been attracted to her in the same way if the same inner person had dwelled in a grisly, misshapen body?

Franciscus: I don't dare to say exactly that. The inner being is not directly discernible, and a physical exterior of that kind would not have encouraged me to imagine that it was as I have described. But if it were visible, I would certainly love the beauty of the inner person, even if it had an ugly dwelling-place.

Augustine: These are just words to bolster yourself up with. If you can only love what appears to the eyes, then you have loved her body. But I wouldn't deny that her character and behavior added fuel to the flames, just as her very name increased this madness of yours, in fact added to it enormously, as I shall go into shortly. With all the passions, but especially this passion of love, the result is that very often an enormous blaze springs from a few small sparks.

FRANCISCUS: I can see where you are driving me. You want me to admit with Ovid that "I have loved her body and soul."[17]

AUGUSTINE: You must also confess that you have loved neither in moderation, nor in a way that was appropriate.

FRANCISCUS: You will have to have me tortured before I confess that.

AUGUSTINE: And furthermore that you have been reduced to a grossly wretched state on account of this love of yours.

FRANCISCUS: That is something I will not confess, even if you hoist me on the rack.

AUGUSTINE: Oh no, you will soon confess to both of your own accord, unless you choose to pay no attention to my arguments and my questioning. Tell me, then, do you recall your boyhood, or has the memory vanished amid the throng of your current worries?

FRANCISCUS: Let me tell you that my childhood and boyhood are as plainly before my eyes as yesterday.

AUGUSTINE: Do you remember how much in those days you feared God, how much you thought about death, how strong your religious feelings and your love of righteousness were?

FRANCISCUS: I certainly remember. I am sorry that my good qualities have diminished as the number of years has grown.

AUGUSTINE: Indeed. I was always afraid that a chill spring wind would scatter such precocious blooms. If the plant had stayed whole and intact, in due course it would have brought forth some marvelous fruit.

FRANCISCUS: Do not digress. What has this to do with what we began with?

AUGUSTINE: I shall tell you. Silently go over—since you feel the memory is perfect and as fresh as ever—go over the whole span of your life and recall when this enormous variance in your behavior first started.

FRANCISCUS: There, in one nervous blink, I have surveyed the number and sequence of the years of my life.

AUGUSTINE: So what do you find?

FRANCISCUS: That the theory of the so-called Pythagorean letter, which I have heard and read about, is not an empty one.[18] I was following the straight path upward, and I arrived at the fork an unassuming, self-controlled per-

[17] Ovid, *Amores* 1.10.13.

[18] The Pythagorean letter is Y, the fork representing the choice that must be made at a certain point in life between the path of virtue and the path of pleasure. Petrarch had read about it in Isidore's *Etymologies* (1.3.7) and elsewhere.

son. I was told to take the right path, but—shall I call myself rash or simply headstrong?—I turned off to the left. The words I had often read as a boy were of no help. I mean these:

> Here is the place where the way divides in two.
> The right leads to the walls of mighty Pluto.
> This takes us to Elysium. But the left
> leads to the pains of miscreants and vile Tartarus.[19]

I had read these lines before, but I did not understand them until I had direct experience. I have been astray since that moment on a crooked, sordid path. Though I have often looked back through my tears, I have been unable to hold to the right way. The moment that I left it, yes, of course, that was the moment when my moral being was thrown into confusion.

Augustine: But at what point in your life did this occur?

Franciscus: Halfway through the turbulence of early manhood. If you wait just a moment, I shall easily remember which year of my life it was.

Augustine: I am not asking for such precise numbering. I want you rather to give a clear answer to this question: When did you have your first vision of that woman's beauty?

Franciscus: Oh, that is something I never want to forget.

Augustine: Then put the two times together.

Franciscus: To tell the truth, her appearance and my losing direction occurred at the same time.

Augustine: Now I have what I wanted. You were stunned, I think, and the extraordinary radiance dazzled your eyes. They say that being astounded in that way is the beginning of love. The great poet was very aware of natural processes. He wrote:

> Sidonian Dido was stunned at her first sight of him.[20]

Then he has:

> Dido is on fire with love.[21]

The whole story may be fictitious, as you well know, but in his fiction the poet respected the order of nature. But, granted that you were so dumbfounded at that first encounter, why particularly did you take the left turning?

[19] Virgil, *Aeneid* 6.540–43.

[20] Virgil, *Aeneid* 1.613. Virgil is the "great poet" mentioned immediately above.

[21] *Aeneid* 4.101.

FRANCISCUS: I think that it seemed smoother and wider. The right road is steeper and narrower.

AUGUSTINE: So it was the effort that you were afraid of. But that celebrated woman, who you imagine to be your quite unfailing guide to the heavens above, why did she not put you right in the midst of the doubts and fears? Why did she not hold your hand, as we usually do with the blind, and indicate where you should go?

FRANCISCUS: She did all that she could. After all, what else was she doing when she stayed unmoved by my entreaties, and shrugged off my attempts at seduction? She maintained her honor as a woman, and stayed firm and impregnable, in spite of both our ages and the many other different pressures that you would have expected to bend a spirit of adamantine steel. Yes, that strength of character in a woman was a lesson to any man. It ensured that, in my commitment to an ideal of sexual purity, I should not be without either a model or a reason for self-criticism, to use a phrase of Seneca.[22] In the end, when she saw that I had snapped the reins and was hurtling downhill, she chose to let me go rather than follow me.

AUGUSTINE: So from time to time you did want something disgusting, which you denied earlier. But this is the cheap and common passion of those madly in love, who are, to be more accurate, simply maniacs. The only thing they can be said to say is, "I want it, no, I don't, I don't want it, yes, I do." But what they want or don't want, nobody knows.

FRANCISCUS: I thoughtlessly fell into the trap. However, if perhaps my wishes were once somewhat different, I was driven on by youth and passion. But now I know what I want and firmly desire, and I long ago made myself stop hesitating in that way. On the other hand, she remained resolute and unchanged, and that firmness of purpose in a woman is something I admire the more, the better I understand it. Perhaps I once complained about her determination, but now I am glad and give thanks for it.

AUGUSTINE: It is not easy to regain trust in one who has once failed. You may have changed your behavior, habits, way of life, but can you persuade me that you have changed within? You may be milder and less ruffled on the surface, but the fire is certainly not out. You attribute so much merit to your beloved, but do you not realize how much you condemn yourself when you absolve her of responsibility? Let us freely grant that she is sainted, so long as you confess to being out of your mind and immoral, or that she is blissfully happy, so long as we recognize that you are plunged in misery thanks to your love for her. This, if you remember, is how I began.

22 Perhaps Petrarch has in mind *Letters to Lucilius* 11.8–10, but the correspondence is not exact.

FRANCISCUS: Yes, I do remember. I have not the power to deny that the situation is as you say. I can see the point to which you have gradually brought me.

AUGUSTINE: Now concentrate, so that you can see things clearer still. There is nothing like love of temporal things to produce both forgetfulness and contempt of God, especially that Love which is given a proper name or is actually called a god (which is a sacrilege that surpasses all others). No doubt that is so that human madness can have some heaven-granted excuse and great wrongdoing can be justified as divinely impelled. One should not be surprised that this emotion has such power in the human breast, since other attractions, too, depend on the beauty of the image seen, the expectation of enjoyment to come, and the sheer force of the imagination. However, as well as these factors, with love there is also the ignition of reciprocal passion. If the hope of that is taken away, then love itself must diminish. So, if in other instances there is simply your own desire, in this case you are desired in return. The mortal heart is goaded, as it were, from two sides. Hence I do not think that our friend Cicero was beside the point when he wrote that "of all the passions certainly none is more overwhelming than love."[23] He must have been quite sure, since he added that "certainly" when he had spent four books defending the Academy, which was skeptical about everything.

FRANCISCUS: I have marked that passage several times and wondered about the fact that he should have termed this passion the most overwhelming of all.

AUGUSTINE: You would not wonder at all, if you had not been so forgetful. You need a few admonitory words to bring back to your mind the memory of your many troubles. Think now of everything that has happened since that disease took hold of you—how you quickly surrendered yourself totally to moaning and groaning, and reached such an extreme of wretchedness that your one nourishment was weeping and sighing; how you took a deathly pleasure in all that, not sleeping at nights, with just the name of your beloved on your lips all night long; how you disdained everything, hating life and wanting to die; how you conceived a bitter love of solitude and wanted to avoid other human beings, so that the words used by Homer about Bellerophon could just as well be applied to you.

> One who wandered wretched and mournful in foreign fields,
> eating his heart out, and shunning the traces of men.[24]

Then there was the pallor, the wasting, the premature fading of youthful bloom, the heavy-lidded, eternally tearful eyes, the mental confusion, the

[23] Cicero, *Tusculan Disputations* 4.35.75.

[24] Homer, *Iliad* 6.201–2. The lines were known to Petrarch through Cicero's quotation of them in Latin (*Tusculan Disputations* 3.26.63). The now accepted text of Cicero is slightly different from that used by Petrarch.

restless slumbers, the weeping protests when you did sleep, with your voice made feeble and hoarse by your crying, and your speech broken and halting, and all the other even worse forms of turmoil and misery that can be imagined. Do these seem to you to be the signs of well-being? What do you make of the fact that she was the one who made your days happy or sad from beginning to end? At her approach the sun came out, and when she went away night returned. The slightest change in her expression changed the way you were feeling, and you became gloomy or cheerful depending on her mood. To sum it up, you hung on her every whim. You know that I am citing things that are true and that are known to all and sundry.

But, since you were not content with the mere sight of the face that was the source of all your woes, what could be more insane than to have an image of it made by an artist of genius, which you could carry around everywhere with you so that you always had something to cry over?[25] You were afraid that your tears might dry up, and took care to collect anything that would provoke them and were quite indifferent to everything else. And then—and here I come to the high point of all your insanities and carry out the threat I made a little earlier—who could denounce as much as it really deserves the insanity of your estranged mind, which was so taken by the splendor of her name, no less than by that of her person, that, with incredible futility, you adored everything that sounded at all like it? You became enamored of both the imperial and the poetic laurel crowns because she was called by the same name.[26] Since then barely a single poem has issued from you that does not mention the laurel, as if your home were on the banks of the Peneus or you were a priest of Cirra.[27] It was out of the question for you to aspire to the imperial crown, but you lusted after the poetic one, which promised to be the reward of your literary efforts, no less outrageously than you did after your mistress. If you think about it now, you will be shocked at how much effort you put into obtaining it, even though your native talent carried you some of the way. But I am aware of what is going on in your mind. I can see you have a reply ready and are even now thinking of opening your mouth. You are thinking that you had dedicated yourself to study and writing before you felt the heat of passion, and that you had been excited since boyhood by the idea of being awarded that form of poetic honor. I am

[25] Petrarch apparently had a portrait of Laura painted by Simone Martini, perhaps in 1339–1340; if it ever existed, it is now lost. It is the subject of Poems 77 and 78 of the *Canzoniere*.

[26] In Petrarch's Latin the words for "Laura" and "laurel crown" are identical (*laurea*). In ancient Rome victorious generals and emperors were crowned with laurel leaves, as well as the more familiar laureate poets. Compare here Poem 263 of the *Canzoniere*.

[27] Peneus is the river in Thessaly, and the river-god the father of Daphne, who was changed into the laurel. See Introduction, section 2. Cirra is one of the peaks of Parnassus, the Greek mountain sacred to poetry.

not trying to cast doubt on that fact or discount it. But really the custom had fallen into disuse many centuries ago, and this present age is hostile to serious engagement with poetry. Then there were the perils of the long journey, which almost ended in imprisonment and death. What with the risk of other dangerous mishaps, you might well have postponed the attempt or perhaps let it be altogether, if that sweet name had not constantly nagged at your mind, making you shrug off all other concerns, and dragging you over land and sea past many a dangerous rock until you reached Rome and Naples, where you obtained at last what you so ardently ached for.[28]

Anyone who thinks that all these are signs of a merely moderate madness is, I am sure, completely out of his senses. I am deliberately leaving aside the lines that Cicero was not ashamed to borrow from Terence's *Eunuch,* where he said:

> There are all these bad things in love: wrongs,
> suspicions, enmities, periods of truce,
> war, then peace again. [29]

You will recognize your own insanity in these words, especially jealousy, which indisputably has pride of place within the disease of love, just as love has the prime place among the passions. Perhaps you will interrupt and say, "I wouldn't want to cast doubts on that, but reason may be present too, and the bad things are mitigated at its command." Terence anticipated your response. He went on:

> If you ask for reason to make
> these incoherent things cohere, you will only
> be trying to be rationally mad.

Now that that's been said—and without any doubt you feel it to be completely true—unless I'm mistaken, all your avenues of escape have been blocked. These are the sorts of miseries there are in love. A precise count is not needed for anyone who has experienced them, and would not be credible for someone who has not. However, to return to where we began, the worst thing of all is that it makes one forget both God and oneself. How can a heart and mind that are bent double by such weights of woe crawl their way eventually to the one pure spring of the true good? Since that is the

28 Petrarch was crowned poet laureate on the Capitoline Hill in Rome in 1341. He had previously been examined as to his poetic merits by King Robert of Anjou in Naples, which he had reached after what does not in reality seem to have been a particularly arduous or dangerous journey. Letter 5 gives a full account of the coronation and the events leading up to it.

29 The quotations from Terence in this section all come from Act 1 (lines 56–73) of Terence's *Eunuch,* which Petrarch probably knew from Cicero's lengthy quotation of the passage in its entirety in *Tusculan Disputations* (4.35.76).

case, stop now wondering at Cicero for thinking that there was no passion that was more overwhelming.

FRANCISCUS: I am defeated, I confess. I have the impression that you have taken everything you say from the book of my own experience. You have cited Terence's *Eunuch*. I should like to insert some words of regret from the same passage.

> O undignified error! Now I . . .
> feel how wretched I am.
> I suffer and I burn with love, and perish
> thoughtful, aware, alive and with eyes open,
> and I do not know what to do.

I should like to beseech you for advice in the words of the same poet:

> So whilst there is time, think and think again.

AUGUSTINE: I too shall reply with Terence's words, namely,

> It is a thing with neither sense nor measure;
> you can't rule it by being sensible.

FRANCISCUS: What shall I do then? Shall we abandon hope?

AUGUSTINE: We must try every possibility first. Listen while I briefly outline one well-tested strategy I know. You are aware that not only have some of the best philosophers dedicated treatises specifically to this subject, but that famous poets have composed entire books about it. It would be particularly insulting to you who profess yourself fully qualified in such things to inform you where to look or how to interpret their writings. But perhaps it will not be out of place to instruct you on how to turn your reading and understanding to your benefit.

First, then, as Cicero says, there are those who "think that an old love is to be expelled by a new love just as one nail hammers out another."[30] That is a piece of advice that Ovid as a teacher of amorous matters agrees with, advancing the general rule that

> All love is conquered by its new successor.[31]

And without doubt, that is what happens. If your attention is dispersed and spread over many things, then it is directed to each individual one in a less energetic way. It is recounted that the Ganges was split into countless chan-

[30] *Tusculan Disputations* 4.35.75.

[31] Ovid, *Remedies against Love* 462.

nels by a Persian king and thus changed from one fearsome flood into many insignificant streams.[32] In the same way open ranks can be breached by the enemy, or a blaze that has spread far and wide loses its force. Generally, any force gains strength through concentration and loses power through dispersal. But I want you to grasp what I judge to be an objection to this. It must be seriously feared that, supposing you withdraw yourself from one single passion of a nobler kind (if it is right to call it that), you may tumble into a series of others and change from a lover into a fickle womanizer. In my judgment at least, if perishing is unavoidable, it is better to perish from a disease that has something noble about it. You ask for my advice. I do not dismiss the idea of pulling yourself together, and escaping, if you can, and passing from one prison to another. Perhaps there will be some hope of liberty in the transition, or at least of less oppressive subjection. But I do not approve of the idea of tearing yourself free from one single yoke of slavery only to submit to a host of squalid ones.

Franciscus: Will the doctor allow a patient who is aware of his disease to interpolate a few words?

Augustine: Why should I not? Many doctors have found that the words of the sufferer, like certain symptoms, help them to discover an appropriate cure.

Franciscus: Then let me tell you just this one thing: I can have no other object for my love. My inner being is addicted to admiring her, my eyes to gazing at her, and what is not her they find depressing and dismal. Thus if you ask me to love another in order to be free of love, you are setting me an impossible condition. It is all over. I am done for.

Augustine: Your senses are dulled, your will sluggish. So since you have no inner resources, we shall have to apply external remedies. Can you induce yourself to take flight or go into exile, and live without the sight of the places you know so well?

Franciscus: I can, though the hooks that pull me back are very deeply attached.

Augustine: If you can do this you will be saved. Do I need to do more than cite that famous verse of Virgil in a slightly modified form?

> Alas, flee the loved lands, flee the loved shore.[33]

For how can you ever be safe here, where there are so many traces of the wounds inflicted on you, where you are afflicted both by what you can see

[32] The image comes from Seneca, *On Anger* 3.21.

[33] *Aeneid* 3.44. The original says, "Alas, flee from the cruel lands, flee the ungiving shore."

now and by your memories of the past? As Cicero says, "like the chronically ill, you must be treated by a change of place."[34]

FRANCISCUS: Please be careful, I beg you, with what you prescribe. How many times, in my eagerness to be cured and in full awareness of this doctorly advice, have I tried running away! Though I pretended to myself that there were various reasons, the one purpose of all my journeying and rural escapes was to find freedom. In its pursuit I have circled far and wide, gone westward and northward, as far as the edge of the Great Ocean.[35] You can see what good it has done me! A Virgilian simile has often touched my heart.

> Like a doe pierced by an arrow, a rash beast
> struck from afar amid the Cretan woods
> by a shepherd hunting. He unaware
> left the winged dart in her, and she in flight
> traverses the woods and the glades of Crete,
> with the death-dealing shaft fixed in her flank.[36]

I am rather like that doe. I have run away, but I carry what harms me with me everywhere.

AUGUSTINE: What are you expecting me to say? You have answered your own question.

FRANCISCUS: How?

AUGUSTINE: By saying that changing places adds to the toils of one who carries harm with him, instead of bringing well-being. We might apply to you a remark that Socrates addressed to a young man who complained that traveling had been of no benefit to him. "It is because," he said, "you were traveling with yourself for company."[37] So, in your case, you must first of all put on one side this longstanding burden of obsessions and prepare your inner self for the journey. Then you must finally make your escape. For it is an established fact, regarding not just the body but the mind and heart too, that the measures taken are ineffective unless the patient is ready to cooperate. Otherwise you might travel to the furthest reaches of India, but you will still confess that Horace spoke the truth when he wrote,

> Those who run overseas change skies but not themselves.[38]

[34] *Tusculan Disputations* 4.35.74 (slightly misquoted by Petrarch).

[35] Petrarch presumably alludes to his journey to the west of France in 1330, where his patron Giacomo Colonna was Bishop of Lombez, and that to the north in 1333, which took him as far as the coast of Flanders.

[36] *Aeneid* 4.69–73.

[37] Seneca, *Letters to Lucilius* 104.7.

[38] Horace, *Epistles* 1.11.27.

Franciscus: Now I am wonderfully perplexed. You present me with lessons for curing and healing my heart and mind, and tell me that the curing and healing must take place before any eventual escape. Yet we are debating precisely about how this curing is to occur. If it has already happened, what else is required? If it has not, given that changing place does not help, as you yourself assert, you must tell me more explicitly what treatments are to be used.

Augustine: I did not speak of curing and healing but of preparation. Anyway, either your mind and heart will be cured, in which case changing places will make your healthy state continue, or you will not yet be cured, but you will be prepared and can achieve such a state yourself. On the other hand, if neither of these is the case, what will these changes, this rushing from one place to another, achieve beyond an exacerbation of your condition? I shall continue to call Horace as witness. He says,

> Reason and prudence take away our cares,
> not some spot dominating the open sea.[39]

And it is true. You will go off full of hope and longing to be back, dragging all the snares that you are caught in with you. Wherever you are, wherever you turn, you will see before you the face and the words of the one you have left behind. You will enjoy the abominable privilege of lovers of hearing her and seeing her when you are far apart from each other. Do you expect to quash love with tricks like this? Believe me, it becomes stronger in both parties. That is why writers on love give instructions that lovers should arrange short absences from each other from time to time to avoid the risk of a loss of interest through being constantly in each other's company. I advise you, beg you, and command you to learn properly how to lay down your burdens and so be able to go away without hope of returning. Then you will learn what power absence can have to heal mind and heart. If you found yourself in a physically oppressive place that was rife with plague and your life were constantly a prey to disease, wouldn't you take flight never to return? But it may be, as I seriously fear, that people are more concerned with looking after their bodies than their inner selves.

Franciscus: That is a question for the human race as a whole. However, to go back to the previous point, there can be no doubt that if I fell ill because a place was unhealthy, I would deal with the illness by moving to a healthier spot. I might feel similarly, or rather much more strongly, with regard to my mental and emotional condition. But, so far as I can see, it is much more difficult to find a cure.

Augustine: We have it on the unanimous authority of the great philosophers that this is untrue. It is clear that all the ills of the spirit can be treated,

[39] *Epistles* 1.11.25–26.

unless the patient resists, whereas many bodily illnesses are not treatable by any known means. But I do not wish to digress too much. I persist in my judgment that, as I said, you must prepare yourself inwardly, disposing yourself to abandon the things you are attached to, without nostalgia or regret for old habits. For the lover that is finally to embark on a safe journey, and you know that is what you must do if you want your soul to be saved.

FRANCISCUS: Just so you may feel that I have taken in everything you have said, you are saying that traveling does no good to one who is inwardly unprepared, but heals one who is prepared and protects one who is healed. Is this a fair summary of your three main injunctions?

AUGUSTINE: That is just what I am saying. You have put in a nutshell the various things we have been saying.

FRANCISCUS: Fine. But I might have worked out the first two points for myself without someone else pointing them out. But I do not grasp the third, why, that is, distance is needed for one who is already healed and out of danger. But perhaps concern for a relapse induced you to say that.

AUGUSTINE: And does that seem trivial to you? If it can happen with physical illness, how much more is to be feared with those of the spirit. The relapse happens much more easily and is much more dangerous. Almost nothing Seneca said was more naturally healthy than these words in one of his letters: "He who wishes to be rid of love, must avoid anything that calls the beloved's person to mind," adding as the reason that "nothing springs back to life more readily than love."[40] Oh, there is something so true in that, something mined from the depths of personal experience! But you do not need me to produce external witnesses in that regard.

FRANCISCUS: I admit the truth of what he says. But, if you look more closely, you will see that he is not referring to someone who has rid himself of love already, but to someone who is making the effort to do so.

AUGUSTINE: He was speaking of those most at risk. Every knock is to be feared with any wound before the scar tissue has formed, and with any illness before it is fully cured. Yet even when the most dangerous point has passed, the risks cannot safely be underestimated. Since examples from close to home affect us more deeply, think about your own case. You, who are speaking like this now, thought you were cured, and would have been largely cured if you had gone away. But how many times you walked through the familiar streets of this city,[41] which may not have been the cause of your troubles but was certainly where they were forged into shape. Think how the mere sight of certain places brought back all the old inanities. No one

[40] *Letters to Lucilius* 69.3.

[41] Avignon.

appeared, but you went into a daze, and sighed, and stopped, and could barely hold back the tears. Then after a little while you went off hurt, saying to yourself, "I can tell that my old enemy has left traps of some sort hidden hereabouts. There are traces of death housed here." If you were taking in what I am saying, you would not think it a good idea to stay in these parts any longer, even if you were well, which you are very far from being. It is absurd for someone just out of his chains to hang around the prison doors, when the head jailer is going round constantly laying snares, with his mind particularly set on the feet of those who he regrets have escaped. His door is always open.

> The descent to Avernus is easy,
> and the dark gate of Dis gapes night and day.[42]

If the healthy, as I said, should take preventive measures, how much more should those whom the disease has not yet abandoned! Those were the ones whom Seneca had in mind. He was offering advice where the danger was greatest. It would have been superfluous to address those caught in the full fire of passion who do not think in the slightest about saving themselves. He aimed at the next category, those who are still burning but are thinking hard about how to come out of the flames. Many on the way back to health are harmed by a little sip of water, which would have done them good before they became unwell, and a light push often floors a battered opponent, though it would not have shifted him at all when he had all his strength. What trivia sometimes plunge the emerging spirit back into its miseries! The glimpse of senatorial purple on another's back can reawaken ambition, the sight of a little pile of coins revitalize greed, seeing a beautiful body rekindle lust, and a fleeting sidelong glance prod sleepy passion back into life. These plagues enter the soul easily because of human witlessness, and, once they know the way in, they return more easily still. Since that is how things are, you must not only leave the site of infection, but you must make sure you avoid anything that draws you back to your old obsessions. You do not want to be like Orpheus returning from the underworld, who looked back and lost the Eurydice he had recovered.[43] That is the sum of my advice to you.

Franciscus: I accept it gladly and thank you for it. I feel that it is the right remedy for my malady. I shall now think seriously about flight. I am unsure, though, where would be my best destination.

[42] Virgil, *Aeneid* 6.126–27.

[43] Orpheus was allowed to descend to the underworld to bring back his dead wife Eurydice on the condition that he would not look back as he was leading her up into the world. Unfortunately, he was unable to stop himself from turning around, and Eurydice was lost to him.

AUGUSTINE: You have many a road open to you, and havens abound where you could find a berth. I know that you particularly like Italy. You find your native land deeply attractive, and not without reason.

> For the Medes' forests, the richest of lands,
> lovely Ganges, and Hermus thick with gold
> cannot compete with gloried Italy,
> not Bactria, nor India, nor all Pancaia
> fertile with incense-bearing sands.[44]

The eminent poet was speaking the truth as well as writing elegantly, and you yourself have recently developed the theme in a poem to a friend.[45] I advise Italy then. The customs of the country, the sky, the surrounding seas, the Apennine hills running down between the two coasts, and the whole lay of the land make it a most suitable place for you to take up residence in view of your problems. Not that I would have you coop yourself up in one spot. Go happily where you feel like going, and go confidently and quickly, without looking back. Forget the past and concentrate on the future. You have been far too long in exile from your country and from your own self. It is time to return, "for evening falls and night is a friend to robbers," to admonish you in your own words.[46] But there is one thing left that I had almost forgotten. Bear in mind that you must avoid solitude for as long as you feel that any traces of your illness remain. You should not have wondered that your stays in the country were of no help to you. What remedies, tell me, did you expect to find in a lonely rustic retreat?[47] I confess that, often when you were rushing off there by yourself, sighing and looking back to the city, I laughed at you from on high and said to myself, "Look how love has wrapped the poor fool in a fog of oblivion and robbed him of any memory of lines every schoolboy knows! Running from disease he hurries toward death."

FRANCISCUS: I am sure you are right. But what are the lines you are talking about?

AUGUSTINE: They are Ovid's.

> Whoever loves, take note; the lonely places harm,
> beware those lonely places.

[44] Virgil, *Georgics* 2.136–39.

[45] Petrarch, in the voice of Augustine, is referring to a verse letter he addressed to Cardinal Aldobrandini of Padua on returning to Provence after one of his Italian visits (*Verse Letters* 3.25).

[46] Petrarch here quotes from one of his own *Penitential Psalms* (3.10). He finally moved definitively to Italy in 1353.

[47] Petrarch's house near the Fontaine de Vaucluse.

Where are you fleeing to? You can be safer among people.[48]

FRANCISCUS: I remember them well. I have known them almost since I was a little boy.

AUGUSTINE: What is the point of knowledge, if you cannot apply what you know to your own needs? I was all the more amazed by your mistaken pursuit of solitude since you were acquainted with the warnings of the ancients against it and had also found some more recent supplements to what they said. You have complained in many of your writings that solitude did you no good, particularly in that poem that you sang so limpidly about your condition.[49] When you intoned it, I was delighted by its music and was amazed that such a melodious poem could emerge from such demented lips, with all the storms buffeting you within. I asked myself what love it was that stopped the Muses from running from their usual home in horror at the turmoil and distraction of their host. Plato says that "a man in his right mind raps in vain on the doors of poetry," and his successor, Aristotle, holds that "no great genius is without a dose of madness."[50] But the terms are different, and inapplicable to this insanity of yours. We can speak of this question another time.

FRANCISCUS: I acknowledge that what you say is right. But I did not think that I had composed such a musical poem or one that you would find so remarkably pleasing. I am beginning to feel warmly toward it now. But if you have any other sort of remedy, do not withhold it from me in my hour of need.

AUGUSTINE: Spelling out everything you know is more like self-display than giving a helping hand to a friend. And then so many kinds of treatment for diseases of body and mind have been devised that all should not be tried on one single patient. As Seneca says, "Nothing impedes a cure like frequent changes of treatment, and a wound does not scar over when various applications are tried."[51] We should rather have recourse to a fresh treatment when the previous one turns out to have failed. So, although there are many different medicines for this disease of yours, I shall be content to suggest just a few of them, selecting particularly those that I feel will most benefit your case. Not that I shall teach you anything new, but I want you to know what I think are the most effective among those that are most obvious and widely used.

48 Ovid, *Remedies against Love* 579–80.

49 *Verse Letters* 1.14, which is titled "To Himself."

50 Petrarch did not know the original texts of either Aristotle (*Poetics* 17.4) or Plato (*Phaedrus* 245a), but he had read Seneca's version of them in *On the Tranquillity of the Spirit* (17.10).

51 *Letters to Lucilius* 2.3.

As Cicero says, there are three things that put the heart and mind off love—satiety, shame, and reflection.[52] There may be more, there may even be less, but let us not go against such an authority and grant that there are three. It is futile to speak of the first since you will deem it impossible that, with things as they are, you could find yourself at all sated by your love. But if your desires put any trust in reason and considered the future in the light of the past, you would readily admit that with anything, however much we love it, not just satiety can creep over us, but irritation and nausea. However, I have discovered that my efforts in this direction are useless since you might grant that satiety is possible and that when it is present it is the death of love, but you will argue that your own blazing passion is as far as possible from that state. And I shall have to agree with you. But I can say something about the two remaining points. You will not, I think, deny me this—that nature gave you a sincere heart and a sense of decency.

FRANCISCUS: It may be that speaking on my own behalf leads me astray, but I judge what you say to be true. I have often been depressed to think how unsuited I am both to my sex and to my times. As you see, shamelessness reaps all the rewards—honors, prospects, and wealth, before which human virtue and the power of fortune both give way.

AUGUSTINE: Do you not see then what a conflict there is between decency and love? One presses forward, the other restrains, one spurs on, the other pulls the reins in, one has no patience, the other takes a careful look at all the factors involved.

FRANCISCUS: I see it only too well. I am being torn apart by these two conflicting desires. They take turns to come at me, and send my mind spinning first one way and then the other. I am not yet sure which one I can fully commit myself to.

AUGUSTINE: Tell me, please, have you recently looked at yourself in the mirror?

FRANCISCUS: What does this mean, I ask you? Just as much as I usually do.

AUGUSTINE: I hope that is not more often, or more fastidiously, than is reasonable! However, I am asking you whether you have not noticed that your face changes with each day that passes, and that there are white hairs gleaming on your temples.

FRANCISCUS: I thought you meant something out of the ordinary. It is the common experience for everyone who is born to grow up, grow old, and die. I have observed in myself what I have observed in almost all my contemporaries. Somehow men today are aging more quickly than they used to.

[52] *Tusculan Disputations* 4.35.76.

Augustine: The aging of others will not bring back youth to you, and their deaths will not make you immortal. So let us leave them aside and come back to you. Well then, has the visible physical change affected you inwardly at all?

Franciscus: It has shaken me, of course, but altered nothing.

Augustine: What then has been your state of mind or what have you said?

Franciscus: What else do you think but the words of the emperor Domitian? "I bear with fortitude an old man's hair in the years of my youth."[53] An instance of such stature consoles me for my few white hairs. Then I've added a kingly example to the imperial one. Numa Pompilius, who was the second Roman king to be crowned, is believed to have been white-haired from early manhood. Nor have I lacked the example of a poet. Our very own Virgil, who is known to have written the *Eclogues* at the age of twenty-six, speaking of himself in the person of a shepherd, says,

> since his beard fell whitish beneath the razor.[54]

Augustine: What an immense abundance of examples you have to hand! I wish that you had just as many who would lead you to think about death. I do not approve of such examples, which teach you to blot out these white witnesses to the approach of age and harbingers of death. For what else do they persuade you to do but discount the passing of the years and forget the final hour? When I ask you to consider your white hairs, you produce a host of illustrious greybeards. To what end? Only if you had said that they were immortal would you have had some valid precedents for not being afraid at turning white. If I had thrown baldness at you, you would have brought out the example of Julius Caesar.[55]

Franciscus: None other, naturally. What more illustrious example could I have found? I would say that it is a great consolation to feel companions of that caliber at one's side. So I admit that I do not shy away from using such instances as day-to-day supports, as it were. It helps to have something at the ready to console myself with, not just amid the tribulations chance and nature have already inflicted on me, but for those that might be in the offing. The only way for me to get by is through vigorous thought or else by considering the example of someone outstanding. If you had reproached me with being somewhat nervous in the face of thunder, which I could not deny (not the least of my reasons for being so attached to the laurel is its reputation

[53] Suetonius, *The Caesars,* Domitian 18.

[54] *Eclogues* 1.28. Petrarch took the information about Virgil's age from Servius' commentary, which actually makes him twenty-eight.

[55] Petrarch learned about Caesar's baldness from Suetonius, *The Caesars,* Julius Caesar 45.

for being impervious to thunderbolts,)[56] I would have replied that Augustus Caesar was troubled by the same weakness. If you had said blindness and that were the indeed the case, I would have cited Appius Caecus and the prince of poets, Homer; if you had brought up losing an eye, I would have shielded myself behind Hannibal, the Carthaginian leader, or Philip, king of the Macedonians. If it were deafness, I would have cited Marcus Crassus, if intolerance of heat, Alexander of Macedon. It would take a long time to run through them all, but you can imagine the rest from these.

AUGUSTINE: Frankly, I do not disapprove of this abundance of exemplary figures, so long as they do not lead to torpor but dispel fear and gloom. I praise anything that helps you not to fear the advent of old age, or to hate it when it comes. But I thoroughly detest and abhor whatever suggests that age is not the beginning of our leaving of this life, or deters us from meditating on death. I say again that supporting premature greyness with equanimity is a mark of a good state of mind, but it is sheer folly, however common it is, to try to slow down the due process of aging, to pretend to fewer years than one has, to plead that white hairs have come too soon, and to try to hide them or pull them out.

Blind humanity! You do not see with what speed the stars revolve, devouring and annihilating the time of your short lives in their flight, and you wonder that age comes to you, brought on by the rapid passage of every day you live. There are two things that drive you to such idiocy. The first is dividing up this tiny space of life into four stages, or six, or even more, trying through number to extend something minuscule that cannot be quantitatively increased.[57] What use is this chopping? Invent as many parts as you like. They all vanish almost in the blink of an eye.

> Not long born, a lovely child just now,
> already a youth, already a grown man.[58]

Note how this especially clever poet expresses the speed with which life flies by in the onward rush of his words! You all struggle in vain to expand what the law of our common mother nature restricts.

The second reason is that, though growing old, you keep up your games and specious amusements. The Trojans spent their last night in such pleasures and did not realize it

[56] Petrarch often refers to the laurel's supposed invulnerability to thunderbolts, which is mentioned by Pliny (*Natural Histories* 2.56.146) and other ancient authors. Augustus' fear of being struck is mentioned by Suetonius (*The Caesars,* Augustus 90).

[57] Petrarch probably has in mind particularly Seneca's discussion in *Letters to Lucilius* 49.3, though divisions of this type were commonplace.

[58] Ovid, *Metamorphoses* 10.522–23.

when the fateful horse leapt the high walls of Troy,
heavy with armed soldiery carried within.[59]

Similarly you do not notice age passing through the walls of the unguarded body, bringing death, armed and indomitable, in its company, until finally the enemy shins down the rope and

invades a city buried in vinous slumber.[60]

For you are just as buried under the weight of the body and of temporal enjoyment as those Trojans whom Virgil depicted as buried in wine and sleep. Hence Juvenal's neat formulation:

The little flower that is the briefest portion
of our short and wretched life rapidly
slips by. Whilst we drink, whilst we demand garlands,
unguents, girls, age creeps on us unaware.[61]

To return to our subject, are you trying to shut out age, which is creeping up on you and is already taunting you at your door? You plead that it has come up too quickly, without following the due stages of nature. You like anyone you run into who is not elderly and claims to have seen you as a little boy, especially if he claims that it must have been only yesterday or the day before, as people do in conversation. You forget that the same can be said of the most decrepit. Who was not really a boy yesterday, or rather is still not a boy today? Everywhere we see children of ninety squabbling over trivia or still up to childish pursuits. The days fly by, the body wastes away, and inside nothing changes. Everything may crumble, but the inner man never reaches maturity. People say that one person works through many bodies, and it is true. Childhood flies away, but as Seneca says,[62] childishness remains. Believe me, that applies to you too. You are not as young as you think you are. Most men do not reach the age you have now reached. You should be ashamed to be called an elderly lover, to have been an object of common gossip for so long.[63] And then, if the glory of real fame has no attractions for you, and notoriety does not frighten you either, you should change your life out of consideration for the way you make others feel. One should think about one's own reputation, unless I am much mistaken, if only to release friends from the shame of having to tell lies about you. That is a general

[59] Virgil, *Aeneid* 6.515–16.

[60] Virgil, *Aeneid* 2.265.

[61] Juvenal, *Satires* 9.126–29.

[62] *Letters to Lucilius* 4.2.

[63] Petrarch uses very similar words in Poem 1 of the *Canzoniere*.

obligation, but you should be particularly careful, since you have so many people talking about you whom you should relieve of that burden.

> To guard a great fame is a major task.[64]

In your *Africa* you make your hero Scipio hear these words of advice from his ferocious enemy; now let yourself profit from the same advice when it comes from the lips of someone who is full of fatherly concern. Reject childish foolishness, quash the burning passion of youth, stop always thinking about what you were like, and take a look sometimes at what you are like now. Do not think that I raised the subject of mirrors to no purpose. Remember Seneca's *Natural Questions*. "Mirrors were invented," he writes, "so that a man should know himself. Many have derived from them their first knowledge of themselves, and then some good counsel—the good-looking to avoid gaining a bad reputation, the ugly to learn to compensate for their physical defects by their moral qualities, the young to recognize that youth is a time for learning and for acquiring manliness, and the old to abandon things inappropriate to age and to give thought to death."[65]

FRANCISCUS: I have never forgotten those words since I first read them. It is wise advice and worth remembering.

AUGUSTINE: What use has it been to have read and remembered it? It would have been more excusable if you could have claimed the protection of ignorance. Are you not ashamed that, in spite of knowing what you know, white hair has not changed you a jot?

FRANCISCUS: I do feel ashamed, and I feel troubled, and I feel regret, but that is all I am capable of. However, do you know what comforts me somewhat? That she is growing old with me.

AUGUSTINE: I think that remark of Julia, the daughter of Augustus Caesar, has stayed with you. When her father reproached her for being unlike her stepmother Livia, in not having a circle of serious people around her, she sidestepped the paternal admonition with her witty retort, "They too will become old with me."[66] But tell me, surely you do not judge it more honorable to burn with passion for her when she is an old woman and you an old man than to be in love with a slip of a girl? It is more horrible in that the object is less lovable. So be ashamed of yourself; be ashamed that there is no change in your inner self though your body is constantly changing.

[64] *Africa* 7.292. The line is from the speech of Hannibal to Scipio before the decisive battle of Zama between the Romans and Carthaginians.

[65] Seneca, *Natural Questions* 1.17.4 (slightly misquoted by Petrarch).

[66] Petrarch took the story from Macrobius (*Saturnalia* 2.5.6). The wit, such as it is, does not quite pass into English. The Latin translated as "with" here means both "in my company" and "at the same time as me."

But this is all that time allows me to devote to the topic of shame. Besides, it really jars, as Cicero argued, when shame usurps the place of reason.[67] So let us turn for help to the very source of all cures, that is to reason itself. It will be aided by the intense reflection, which was the last of the three deterrents to love that I listed. Now is the moment to hear yourself summoned to the one redoubt in which you can be safe from the incursions of the passions and that lets you truly be called a man.

Think then first of all about the nobility of the mind; I would have to write an entire book on the topic if I wanted to cover it adequately. Think at the same time of the fragility and the squalor of the body, about which there is no less to be said. Think about the brevity of life, on which we have books by great men. Think of the speed with which time passes, which no one could capture in words. Think of the certainty of death and the uncertainty of the hour of our dying, which hangs over us in all places and at all times. Think how men all make the same error of believing that what cannot be postponed is in fact postponable, though no one is so unaware of his nature as to deny that it must happen sometime, should he be asked if he must die. So I urge you not to trick yourself into expecting to live longer, as countless people do, but rather to take to heart, as if it had been pronounced by a divine oracle, that verse which goes:

> Believe each dawning day to be your last.[68]

Yes, each day that dawns on mortal men is either the last or close to being the last. And then think how degrading it is to have people point at you, to be gossiped about by the vulgar herd. Think how different what you profess to be is from your actual behavior. Think what damage that woman has done to your mind and body and career. Think how much you have suffered to no purpose. Think how often you have been tricked, spurned, forgotten. Think how much wheedling and complaining and weeping you have thrown to the winds. Think how she meanwhile remained haughty and unappreciative, or, when she did show a more human side, how little time it lasted, how it was more fleeting than a summer breeze. Think how much you have increased her fame, but how much she has taken away of your life, how you have been concerned for her good name, and how indifferent she has always been to the state you were in. Think how you have distanced yourself from the love of God because of her, and fallen into all the woeful habits I know about but will not speak of, just in case I am overheard, if anyone should poke an ear into our conversation. Think how many commitments you have that you could more profitably and more honorably attend to. Think how many unfinished works you have on your hands that you would do much better to complete as they deserve, instead of dividing up the little you have

[67] *Tusculan Disputations* 2.21.48.

[68] Horace, *Epistles* 1.4.13.

left of your life in such a hodgepodge. Lastly, think what the thing you so ardently desire really is. Truly it is something to think about manfully and vigorously, in order to avoid the risk of escaping and then only finding yourself more tightly bound than before. It happens to many; for the charm of physical beauty finds its way through the slightest chinks, and the illness feeds upon the medicine. Of those who have once sipped the poison of this seductive pleasure, very few can consider the foulness of the female body in a manly enough way, let alone with enough resolution. The mind easily relapses, and, under pressure from nature, falls into the very state in which it was mired for so long. The greatest effort is to be made to ensure that this does not happen. Expel all memory of the past obsessions, dismiss any thought that brings back times gone by, and, as the Bible says,[69] dash your infants on a rock lest, if they grow, they drag you down into the slime. At the same time let heaven resound to your heartfelt cries and God's ears be almost wearied by your devoted prayers. Not a day or night must pass without tearful entreaties, in the hope that the Almighty will take pity and impose an end to all your tribulations. This is what you must do and not do. If you follow my instructions thoroughly, I am hopeful that you will receive divine aid and that the hand of our invincible Liberator will assist you. Given your need, what I have said amounts to little, but, proportionately speaking, given the shortness of the time available, I have spoken at length on this one disease. Now let us go on. There remains one last affliction, which I shall now make an attempt to cure.

FRANCISCUS: Please do. You are the gentlest of fathers, and I do feel a great relief, even if I have not yet been completely freed from my other troubles.

AUGUSTINE: You desire more than you should to win glory among men and for your name to be immortal.

FRANCISCUS: I admit it, but I am incapable of reining in this hunger in myself by any means in my power.

AUGUSTINE: But you should be seriously afraid that excessive longing for this vain immortality will block the path to the real one.

FRANCISCUS: This is one of the things I do indeed particularly fear. I am looking to you to suggest measures that might save me. You have supplied remedies for ills that are much worse.

AUGUSTINE: Let me tell you that none of your diseases is worse, although some are perhaps more repulsive. What do you think this glory is that you are so bent on? Explain.

FRANCISCUS: I am not sure you need a definition. Don't you know what it is better than anyone?

[69] Ps. 136:9.

Augustine: I do. But you know the word "glory," while the thing itself, to judge from your behavior, is unknown to you. If you did know what it was, you would not desire it so ardently. Of course we might say that it is "glittering fame springing from one's achievements which has spread among one's fellow citizens or countrymen or among all races of men," as Cicero puts it in one place, or "fame which is recurrent and involves praise," as he puts it in another.[70] But in both instances you will find that glory is equated with fame. But do you know what fame is?

Franciscus: I do not have it clear in my mind at the moment, and I am afraid of displaying my ignorance. I should prefer not to say what I think comes nearest to the truth.

Augustine: Well, that is one thing you have said in a modest, prudent fashion. In any discussion, especially a serious and difficult one, it is necessary to be as attentive to what not to say as to what is to be said, since praise of what is well said does not balance the reproof for what is said badly. Let me tell you, then, that fame is nothing more than talk about someone that has spread through the populace at large and is on many people's lips.

Franciscus: That is a good definition, or a good description, if you prefer.

Augustine: It is then just a release of breath, a waft of air blowing this way and that, or, to make it more distasteful to you, it is the breath of a host of people. I know who I am addressing. No one could find the way the mass of people behave and the things they do more detestable. Now consider what perversity there is in your judgment; you are delighted by the chitter-chatter of those whose actions you condemn. And if only you just gained pleasure from this and did not set it up as the height of happiness! For what other purpose is there in all that unrelenting toil, all your late nights, and all the passionate energy you put into your studies? You will perhaps reply that you aim also to learn lessons for living. But really you learned all that is needed for life, and for death too, some time ago. You should have been trying to find a way to put those lessons into practice rather than continuing with this wearisome acquisition of knowledge. There are always more hidden corners, more unexplored obscurities, and research has no set limit. Note, too, that you have put special efforts into carrying through projects that might win popular acclaim, in your anxiety to please those whom you particularly disliked. Hence the selections you made from poems, histories, and other writings of all kinds, which you thought would delight the ears of those who heard them.[71]

[70] The first reference is to Cicero's oration *For Marcellus* (8.26), the second probably to his *On Invention* (2.166).

[71] Petrarch (in the voice of Augustine) is referring to collections of passages from other writers rather than from his own work.

FRANCISCUS: Please spare me. I cannot let that pass in silence. I have never, since I ceased to be a child, been happy with anthologies of writers' best sayings. I have registered Cicero's many elegant criticisms of literary robbers,[72] and above all taken note of Seneca's dictum that "It is unworthy of a man to pick other men's flowers, to find props in words that are well known, and to make the ability to remember one's mainstay."[73]

AUGUSTINE: In saying this, I am not charging you with slovenliness or rote learning, only saying that you collected the choicer products of your reading for the pleasure of fellow writers and scholars, and that from that immense pile you selected the more refined parts for use by your close friends, all of which is pandering to vain glory. In the end you were not content with a humdrum activity that demanded a great deal of time but only promised celebrity in the present. You looked into the far distance, and lusted after fame among generations to come. So you set about a great work, and embarked on a series of historical biographies from Romulus to Titus Caesar, an immense project demanding vast amounts of time and effort.[74] When that still had not been brought to its conclusion—so many different incentives to glory were crowding in on you—you took a poetic ferry, so to speak, to Africa. And now, though you cannot leave the others alone, you are working hard at the books of your *Africa!*[75] In this way you give your life over to these two enterprises, not to mention the innumerable others that interfere with them, squandering the most precious and irreplaceable thing of all, and forgetting yourself in writing of others. But do you realize that death may snatch your weary pen from your hand before either work is completed, and that your immoderate pursuit of glory by two paths may mean that you reach your goal by neither?

FRANCISCUS: I have been afraid of that, I admit, at various times. I once fell victim of a serious illness and feared that death was near. But nothing grieved me more when I was in that state than the thought that I was leaving the *Africa* unfinished. I dismissed the idea of allowing others to give it the finishing touches, and decided to consign it to the flames with my own hands, since I could not trust my friends enough to perform the task once my spirit had left my body. I recalled that this was the one request from our beloved Virgil that was turned down by the emperor Augustus.[76] I do not want to delay you, but I too almost set Africa on fire, adding, that is, to the blazing

[72] Perhaps he particularly has in mind *On the Orator* 3.6.

[73] Seneca, *Letters to Lucilius* 33.7.

[74] *On Famous Men,* which Petrarch began in the late 1330s and never finished.

[75] Petrarch's epic poem in Latin on the struggle between Rome and Carthage. Like *On Famous Men,* it was begun in the late 1330s and never finished.

[76] According to Donatus' biography, Virgil did not quite finish the *Aeneid*. Just before he died, he asked for the text to be burned.

heat that it always endures through being closer to the sun and to the Roman flames that three times scorched its length and breadth long ago.[77] But we can speak of this at another time. It is a bitter memory.

AUGUSTINE: You reinforce my assessment with this story. The day of reckoning was briefly postponed, but the argument is still valid. What is more foolish than to pour such efforts into something with an unpredictable outcome? I know, though, that you are persuaded not to abandon what you have undertaken by that very hope of carrying it through. It is a hope that, unless I am mistaken, I shall not easily undermine. But I shall use all the verbal means in my power to show you that even then the result would not correspond at all to your vast expenditure of effort. Imagine that you have time, freedom, and tranquillity in abundance, with mental sluggishness and physical tiredness entirely dispelled, and with a complete absence of the chance hindrances that have often broken the flow of your writing and sent your speeding pen off course. Let everything come to fruition, even beyond what you could ask for in your prayers. What great thing do you think you would have achieved?

FRANCISCUS: At least a work of excellent quality, one that was rare and out of the ordinary.

AUGUSTINE: I would not disagree too much. A work of high quality, let us grant that. But you would be horrified if you realized what greater excellence your lust for fame is hindering you from attaining. I should go so far as to say that more than anything it distracts you from all the better pursuits that you could devote yourself to. Note too that outstanding excellence is neither widely acknowledged nor long-lasting, but constrained by narrow limits of time and space.

FRANCISCUS: I know that worn old fable of the philosophers who say that the whole earth is like a tiny point and that infinite millennia are like one single year and that human fame fills neither the point nor the year, with other things of this sort intended to discourage the love of glory.[78] Please, produce a stronger argument if you have one. I have found this an attractive tale to tell, but not efficacious. I have no thoughts of becoming a god who has eternity before him and could embrace heaven and earth. Human glory is enough for me. That is what I sigh for. Being mortal I want only mortal things.

AUGUSTINE: What a wretched creature you are if you are telling the truth. If you do not want immortal things, if you do not look to what is eternal, you are nothing but earth. It is all over for you. There is no hope left.

[77] Petrarch is referring to the three Punic Wars, from which Rome emerged as the victor over Carthage.

[78] Petrarch's principal source is Cicero's *Dream of Scipio*.

FRANCISCUS: God protect me from such madness! My awareness of my problems is a witness to my having always been fired by love of the eternal. But what I said, or, if I perhaps expressed myself badly, what I meant to say, was that I treat mortal things as mortal things, and I am not looking to do violence to the natural order by indulging some vast, unregulated desire. So I am seeking for glory in the knowledge that both I and it are mortal.

AUGUSTINE: Sensibly put. But it is quite stupid of you to abandon what will last forever for a vacuous puff of air, which is bound to perish, as you yourself say.

FRANCISCUS: I am not abandoning it at all, just perhaps postponing.

AUGUSTINE: But what a perilous postponement, given the speed at which time goes unpredictably by and your own life hurries away from you! I should like you to answer this question: If He who alone has set the limits of life and death were to determine today that you had just one whole year of life left, without it being possible for you to have the shadow of doubt about it, how would you see yourself setting about spending this span of a year?

FRANCISCUS: I should be very sparing and diligent indeed. I would make every possible provision for it to be spent on serious matters. I can barely imagine anyone being so insanely full of themselves to reply differently.

AUGUSTINE: I approve the reply, but human madness in this regard makes me feel an astonishment that it is beyond my own skill to express, as it is beyond the most eloquent writers there have ever been. They could bring to bear all their talents and efforts on this one subject, but words would eventually fail them.

FRANCISCUS: What is the reason for all this amazement?

AUGUSTINE: It is because you are all as mean as you can be with things that are certain, and lavish with uncertain ones, when the opposite should be the case, if you were not completely out of your minds. Of course a year is very brief, but once promised by Him who never misleads or is misled, it could be divided up and spent with a certain freedom, leaving the last moments for taking thought for salvation. But it is the most execrable and abominable madness of all to squander on absurd vanities something that may or may not suffice for the final necessities, as if you had a superabundance of it. Someone who knows that he has one year to live has something certain, modest though it may be. But he who is subject to the ambiguous rule of death, under which all you mortal men spend your days, is not certain about a year, or a day, or a whole hour. With a year to live, even if six months are wasted, there is still the space of another six months. But if you waste today, who will you find to guarantee you a tomorrow? Cicero said that "it is certain we must die; what is uncertain is whether it is today," and that there is no one so young that "it is known whether or not he will make it through to the evening."[79] So I ask you, and I ask the same question of all you mortal men who are agog about your future and careless about the present, who knows

> whether to our today the gods above
> will add tomorrow's hours?[80]

Franciscus: No one, of course, to reply for myself and for all. But let us hope for at least a year. As Cicero views it, no one is old enough not to hope to have that much left.[81]

Augustine: Ah, but he is also of the view that old and young alike are stupidly hopeful and promise themselves things that are uncertain in place of what is certain. But, though it is the most impossible thing of all, let us assume that there has been assigned to you a substantial and at the same time definite space of life. Do you not think that it is an enormous folly to spend your best years, the very prime of your life, on giving pleasure to the eyes of others or in beguiling their ears, and then, as if the freedom of your soul were the last of your concerns, to keep back for God and yourself the last and worst, the ones that are almost good for nothing and which will bring both an end to life and displeasure at existing? Even if the time allotted were assured, does it not seem to you that putting the best second subverts the order of things?

Franciscus: Perhaps, but my project does have some reason to it. I tell myself that, being here on earth, one should try to win the glory that is allowed here. The greater glory is to be enjoyed in heaven, and those who come there will not even wish to think about this earthly version. So I see it as being in the order of things that the first concern of mortals should be with mortal matters, and that what is transient should then be replaced by what is eternal. There is a most orderly progression from the former to the latter, whereas a regression in the other direction has no sense.

Augustine: You brainless little man! So you think that at your nod the pleasures of heaven and earth will flow from both realms toward you with blissful results. Millions have had that delusion and countless souls have sunk to hell as a result. They thought they could keep one foot on earth and the other in heaven, but they were unsteady here, and could not move upward either. So they had a wretched fall. Suddenly the breath of life abandoned them either in their very prime, or else in the midst of planning for the future. Do you think that what has happened to so many cannot happen to you? Good grief, if you were, in the middle of your manifold projects, to suffer such a disaster—which God forbid!—what pain you would feel, what shame, and how late in the day you would be sorry! With your mind on so many things, you would have failed to bring any single one to fruition.

79 Cicero, *On Old Age* 20.74 and 19.67.

80 Horace, *Odes* 4.7, 17–18.

81 Cicero, *On Old Age* 7.24.

FRANCISCUS: May God on high take pity and not let such a thing happen!

AUGUSTINE: Divine pity may grant release from human madness, though it does not excuse it. But I would not have you set too many hopes by that pity. Just as God detests those who despair, so he disappoints those who hope rashly. I am distressed to have heard from your own lips that you think that the old tale, as you put it, which the philosophers tell on the subject, can be discounted. I ask you, is that account then just a tale that uses geometric proof to determine the small size of the landmass of the earth and demonstrates that it is like a rather long but narrow island? Or what about that other one, which states that the earth is divided into five zones (as they are called), and that the largest, the middle one, does not permit human habitation on account of the heat of the sun, as is the case with the two on the left and right, which are afflicted by unbearable cold and permanent ice and frost, leaving only the two between the middle and the extremes to be inhabited? And then there's that other tale, that one of these two inhabitable zones is in the antipodes and inaccessible because of the barrier created by the great ocean. You know how men of great learning have long disagreed whether it is inhabited, and I have expressed my own opinion on the matter in the *City of God,* which I am sure you have read.[82] That leaves one zone entirely habitable by you, though those scholars may be right who think that it is subdivided into two parts, one of which is given over to human use, while the other is shut off by the curved limits of the northern Ocean and hence inaccessible. And what about the story that this habitable zone that you have, tiny though it is, is made smaller by seas and marshes and forests and deserts and empty wastes? If so, doesn't this little patch of earth, on which you strut so proudly, shrink almost to nothing? And perhaps it is a story too, that within the extremely confined space in which you live, different ways of life, opposed religions, mutually incomprehensible languages, and incompatible customs have developed, and that as a result you have been robbed of any chance of being at all widely known? If these are all old tales, all the hopes I had of you are old tales too.

I thought that no one was better informed about these things than you. To leave aside the teachings of Cicero and Virgil and the pronouncements of other philosophers and poets, I knew that you had recently made the point in some excellent verses of your *Africa*. You wrote,

> Hemmed in its narrow bounds, the world
> is like a little island that the Ocean circles
> with its curving flow.[83]

[82] *City of God* 16.9. For Augustine's subsequent remarks about the various zones of the earth, Petrarch draws principally from Cicero's *Dream of Scipio* and Macrobius' commentary.

[83] *Africa* 2.361–63. The Ocean is the vast expanse of water surrounding the inhabited part of the globe.

Then you added some further considerations, which I am amazed you have so constantly asserted if you thought them untrue. What shall I say now about the short span granted to the fame of mortal men and history's stark limitations, since you know that the furthest we can look back extends only a little way into the recent past compared with eternity? I am not referring you to the views voiced by ancient writers about all the fires and floods there have been on earth as developed in Plato's *Timaeus* and the sixth book of Cicero's *On the Republic*. Many scholars find them probable enough, but they are alien to the true religion in which you were raised. Leaving those aside, how many things there are which prevent fame from lasting at all long, let alone for eternity! First of all, there are the deaths of those in whose company we have lived our lives, and there is the loss of memory that is a natural affliction of old age. Then there is always the growing celebrity of fresh arrivals on the scene. Often, as they blossom, they take the bloom from older reputations, as if their rise were dependent on the decline of their elders. Then we can include envy, which unceasingly dogs anyone engaged in enterprises of a glorious kind, we can include hostility to moral greatness and popular dislike of exceptional talent, not to mention the fickleness of popular verdicts. Add also the ruin into which the graves of the dead must fall. All that is needed to split them open is, as Juvenal puts it, "the malign power of a barren fig tree."[84] You rather elegantly call this "a second death" in your *Africa*. To cite the actual words, you have one of your characters say,

> The tomb will crumble soon, and the words
> cut in the marble fail, and thus, my son,
> you will suffer a second death.[85]

That is your shining immortal glory for you, wobbling over at a push from a stone!

And then think about the death of the books in which your reputations are enclosed, whether they are written by yourselves or by others. This death might seem to come much later, since a book has a longer life in human memory than a grave. But the fall into nothing is inevitable; books are subject to the countless forms of destructive action to which chance and nature subject everything else. Even if there were none of these, every book has its own aging, its own mortality to face.

> For all things that mortal labor
> with futile genius has produced must be
> mortal too.[86]

[84] Juvenal, *Satires* 10.145.

[85] *Africa* 2.431–42.

[86] *Africa* 2.455–57.

I am using your own words to try to make you see the puerile error of your ways. Yes, and I shall go on inflicting your own verse on you.

> As the books die, so you too
> will sink away. Thus a third death awaits you.[87]

Well, there you have my verdict on glory. I am sure I have spoken at greater length than either you or I felt was appropriate, but the subject is so important that I have really not said enough about it. But it may be that even so you think that all of this is mere fable.

FRANCISCUS: Not in the slightest. What you have said has affected me in a different way from a fable, injecting in me fresh desire to throw off my old habits. Of course I did know it all and had heard it often enough. As our friend Terence says, "nothing is said that has not been said before."[88] However effectiveness comes from the serious quality of the language, the order in which points are made, and the authority of the speaker. But there is one matter here on which I would like to have a final opinion from you. Would you bid me abandon all my literary activities and live without thought of fame, or would you counsel a middle path?

AUGUSTINE: I shall never advise you to live an inglorious life, but at the same time I shall not advise you to set the pursuit of glory before the pursuit of virtue. You know that glory is, as it were, the shadow of virtue,[89] and so, just as in your world it is impossible for a body not to cast a shadow when struck by the rays of the sun, so it cannot be that virtue does not give birth to glory, wherever the light of God shines. Therefore, anyone who achieves true glory must first have achieved virtue too. Without it human life is bare, and, like that of dumb animals, prone to follow the call of instincts, which is the one desire that beasts have. You must therefore observe this rule: cultivate virtue, and neglect glory. However, as is recounted of Marcus Cato,[90] you will find yourself attaining glory all the more, the less you crave for it. Again, I cannot refrain from citing yourself as witness against you:

> You may refuse, may flee, but it will follow you.[91]

Do you recognize the verse? It is one of yours. Naturally, you would think someone crazy who forces himself to run about in the heat of the midday sun in order to see his own shadow and to show it to others. And the man

[87] *Africa* 2.464–65.

[88] Terence, *Eunuch* 1.41.

[89] From Cicero, *Tusculan Disputations* 1.45.109.

[90] Sallust, *Catiline* 54.6, which Petrarch knew was also cited by Augustine in the *City of God* 5.12.4.

[91] *Africa* 2.486.

is no wiser who struggles laboriously amid life's frenzies to spread his own glory far and wide. What follows? Suppose the runner goes on till he reaches an end; his shadow stays with him all the way. Let the second man make his goal virtue, then glory does not desert him in his pursuit of it. I am speaking here of the glory that is the companion of true virtue. There are forms of glory that can be won through other mental or physical skills (which human ingenuity has created in boundless numbers), but they do not really deserve the name. However, you wear yourself out, even in times like these, with all the efforts involved in writing books, and, I am sorry to say, you have gone far astray. You forget the things that should concern you, and give yourself over entirely to things to do with others. Meanwhile, this brief span of life slips by you all unaware, in thrall to the empty hope of glory.

Franciscus: What shall I do then? Shall I leave my works unfinished? Or is it more advisable to quicken the pace, and round them off, if God is willing? Then I can be free from other involvements and make a clean start on the more important things. But I would find it very hard to abandon in mid-course an enterprise that is so vast and has cost me so much effort.

Augustine: You are lame in one leg, I see. You prefer to abandon yourself rather than your scribblings. But I shall go on with my duty. You will decide how successfully I do it, but I shall have done it faithfully anyway. Jettison the huge burdens imposed by historical works. What the Romans did shines bright enough thanks to the fame of the protagonists and the talents of other writers. Let your *Africa* be. Leave the continent to its inhabitants. You will not enhance either Scipio's glory or your own. He cannot be extolled any higher, and you are scrambling after him up a side path. Putting all this aside, finally restore yourself to yourself, and, to come back to where we started, begin to reflect on death, which you are steadily but benightedly approaching. Tear back the veils, shatter the darkness, and fix your eyes on it. Do not let a day or night go by that does not remind you of your final moment. Consciously relate to this whatever comes before your eyes or into your mind. The sky, the earth, and the sea all change. What hope has that feeble animal man? Time progresses through change and recurrence and never stays in one state. You are wrong if you think that you can stay as you are. Horace put it neatly.

> Swift moons recoup their heavenly losses;
> we, when we fall away, etc. [92]

Whenever you see the summer crops following the spring flowers, or autumn cool the heat of summer, or winter snow the autumn harvest, say to yourself, "These things pass but will come back again and again. I, however, shall go away never to return."Whenever you see the shadows lengthen as

[92] *Odes* 4.7.13–14.

the sun moves toward its setting, say, "Now the shadow of death grows longer as life hurries by. That sun will be here again tomorrow, but this day of mine has flowed away irreparably." Who could number the marvels of a clear night sky? Criminals may have their best chance then, but the virtuous feel it is a time for the greatest reverence. Like the pilot of the Trojan fleet, and trusting in just as trustworthy a vessel, rise in the middle of the night and

> Mark all the stars declining through the heavens.[93]

As you watch them hastening to the west, be aware that you are being driven on with them, and that the only hope of rest you have left must lie in Him who does not move and who knows no setting. Think, too, when you encounter men reaching the pinnacle of their lives whom you knew as boys only a little while ago, that you meanwhile are on the downward path, and that the descent is all the quicker since it is more in accordance with nature's law that heavy weights should fall. If you happen to see some ancient walls, ask yourself first and foremost, "Where are the people who built them?" If you see new ones, ask, "Where will the builders be soon?" Similarly with trees. The person who tended or planted them is often not the one who picks the fruits from their branches. That line from the *Georgics* has often been proved right:

> slowly it grows, to shade remote descendants.[94]

And when you gaze at rivers rushing by, have one of your own lines to hand (to avoid once again directing you to others' words).

> No rivers flow more swiftly than the time
> of life departs.[95]

Do not be tricked by the sheer number of days or complicated divisions of life.[96] However prolonged, human life is like a single day, and not a full one either. Remember as often as you can a certain simile of Aristotle, which I noticed that you particularly like and that you can barely ever read or hear cited without being deeply affected. You can find it strikingly and persuasively expressed in Cicero's version in the *Tusculan Disputations*. The words are these or very similar, given that we do not have a copy of the work at hand. "Aristotle writes," he says, "that by the river Hypanis, which flows into the Pontus on the European side, some tiny creatures are born that live for just one day. One that dies as the sun rises dies young; one that dies

[93] Virgil, *Aeneid* 3.515.

[94] Virgil, *Georgics* 2.58.

[95] Petrarch, *Verse Letters* 1.4.91–92.

[96] See note 57 above.

around midday is already adult; but the one that dies at sunset is old, the more so if it is the solstice. Compare the whole of our human life with eternity, and we turn out to be almost as ephemeral as these creatures."[97] In my judgment, his pronouncement is so true that it has long passed from philosophical discourse into popular usage. Have you noticed how homely, uneducated people have acquired the habit in their day-to-day talk of saying when they see a boy, "It's the morning of his life," or of a full-grown man, "He's reached his high noon," or "His life's at its afternoon peak," or of a decrepit old man, "He's coming to the end of his day and his sun is setting."

My dear boy, think these things over, and any other similar things that come to your mind. I am sure there will be many, since those I have mentioned are just the ones I spontaneously thought of. I do beg of you one further thing. Contemplate very attentively the graves of the old, especially of those whose lives overlapped with yours, in the full certainty that an identical resting-place and permanent chamber will be prepared for you.

> There we all tend. For all it's the last home.[98]

At the moment, you exult in the full flush of life and trample on others. Soon you yourself will be trampled down. Think about it, meditate on it day and night, as befits a serious man who is mindful of his nature, and as befits a philosopher too. That is the sense in which you should interpret the saying that "The whole life of philosophers is spent preparing for death."[99] Reflections of this kind, I tell you, will teach you to disdain mortal things and show you another road you may take. You will ask what road this is and by what paths one comes to it. I shall reply that you do not need lengthy directions. Only listen to your conscience calling and urging you, saying, "This is the way to our homeland." You know what promptings it gives you, what routes and what deviations it indicates, what it declares should be followed or avoided. Obey it if you want to be safe and free. You do not need to weigh it up for long. The nature of the danger demands action. The enemy is both pressing at your rear and taunting you to your face, and the walls of your redoubt are trembling. There is no room for further hesitation. What do you gain from singing sweetly to others, if you do not hear yourself? I shall stop. Avoid the rocks, pull yourself up safely on shore. Follow where your heart carries you. That may be an obnoxious thing to do in other respects, but it is a beautiful thing when the end is good.

Franciscus: If only you had said these things to me at the start, before I turned my thoughts to writing and study!

97 *Tusculan Disputations* 1.39.94. As Petrarch says, the quotation is not exact.

98 Ovid, *Metamorphoses* 10.34.

99 *Tusculan Disputations* 1.30.74.

AUGUSTINE: I did say them often. And in the very first stages, when I saw you had seized hold of your pen, I warned you that life was short and uncertain, that the labor was long and sure, that the task was a major one, and that the fruits would be few. But your ears were blocked by popular acclaim, which I am astounded you listened to and pursued. To finish, since our discussion has been quite a long one, I ask you not to surrender to dull, slovenly decay, if you have found any of my advice acceptable, and not to take it ill, if I have also been hard on you.

FRANCISCUS: I am grateful to you for many reasons, but in particular for these three days of conversation. You have cleared my clouded vision and dispersed the dense fog of ignorance in which I was plunged. And how can I express my gratitude to the lady here,[100] who has heard our long discussion right through to the end with good grace? If she had turned her face away at all, we would have been shrouded in darkness and wandered off track. Your addresses to me would have lacked any foundation, and my understanding of what you said would have been nonexistent. Now, however, since your residence is in heaven, and my own stay on earth is not yet over, though I do not know how long it is to last (and worry anxiously about that, as you see), I beg you not to desert me, however far away I am. Without you, who are the best of fathers to me, my life is misery, and without our patroness here it would be nothing.

AUGUSTINE: Take my presence as granted, so long as you do not desert yourself. Otherwise you will rightly be deserted by everyone.

FRANCISCUS: I shall be as present to myself as much as I can. I shall gather together the scattered fragments of my soul and watch vigilantly over myself. Only now, as we speak, I have many important things waiting to be dealt with, even if they are still mortal ones.

AUGUSTINE: Some things may seem more important to people at large, but there is really no form of reflection that is more beneficial or more fruitful than this. Thinking about other things may turn out to have no point, but the inevitable outcome of life is proof that reflections on oneself are always necessary.

FRANCISCUS: I admit it. I am only eager to deal with other things so that I can come back to this one after resolving them. I am not unaware, as you said I was a short while ago, that it would be much safer to make this my one object and to refuse to be turned aside from the one straight path to salvation. But the desire is too strong for me to control it.

AUGUSTINE: We are falling back into our old disagreement. You call the action of your will impotence. But so be it, since it cannot be otherwise. I pray

[100] The figure of Truth who has remained silent throughout.

to God that he accompany you on your path and guide your steps, errant though they are, to safety.

FRANCISCUS: I only wish that what you pray for happens, and that, with God's guidance, I emerge intact from all the twists and turns of life. Let me follow His call without throwing dust in my own eyes. Let the waves within me subside, the world be quiet, and the clamor of fortune cease.

Letters

1

To Giacomo Colonna (*Familiares* 2.9)

The excitement of your letter has woken me from my sleepy state. I read through all the joking jibes you've packed into it with great enjoyment. But I want to deal at once with the first of the many missiles you've collected to throw at me. You may be like the best of fathers to me, but let me show you how right from the start your words and your intentions part company. You say that you've been amazed for ages how a young man like me manages to trick the world so skillfully, as if this were a skill I was born with rather than the fruit of experience. You might have written a longer eulogy, of course, but you couldn't have thought up one I could glory in more. The world is the deceiver of the human race and commends to us a life that is a tangle of traps baited with a bittersweet coating. Those who go their way through life with their eyes open know this, though we deliberately encourage the deceits and work energetically to go against the advice of Apollo and remain unknown to ourselves.[1] One man might be puffed up with pride behind a high-minded exterior, and another fools himself into malice and fraud, under the cloak of what appears very like prudence. A vicious inhuman beast may simply think himself strong, and a feeble coward might plead humility. Some people are drawn to call their avarice frugality, and some spendthrifts say they are just open-handed. Vices dress in masks and horrid monsters hide in lovely skins. Then there are a host of delightful things that must prove transient, or rather are already passing by and fleeing from us—ambition, which dangles honors, applause, celebrity before us, sexual pleasure with all its enticements, and money that promises an abundance of material goods. There's no hook without bait, no branch without bird-lime, no snare without hope. And then there is human desire—impetuous, mindless, fallacious, and gullible. Let us suppose that, on this uncertain, slippery, and fearful road, we imagine nature or study making a person canny enough to evade the world's deceits and to deceive the world, perhaps by making a display of being like everyone else, while being of a different mind within. What would you make of such a person? And where can we find him? We are looking for exceptional natural gifts, solid, sober maturity of mind, and a capacity for acute observation of others. And yet you put me in this category. It's an immense privilege, of course, so long as you're not making fun of me. But if it's not

[1] "Know yourself" was the precept set above the entrance to the temple of Apollo at Delphi.

the true one for me at present, I pray to God, who has the power even to raise the dead, that it may become true before I die.

But how far do you want to go with your jokes? You say that many people have an enormously high opinion of me thanks to my skillful subterfuges. And I admit that some outstanding individuals have used art of this kind to get their admirers to see their real virtues in the best possible light. Hence Numa Pompilius' conversations with a divine being and the story of the divine origin of Publius Scipio's family.[2] But this is not an art I possess, since I have nothing to put on show. However, I have been pursued since my cradle by the completely vacuous favors of good fortune. I am better known than I would wish, and I am aware that, insignificant though I am, good things and bad things are bandied round about me, by which I'm neither uplifted nor depressed, since I know that popular gossip is all lies. At least that's how it's been so far. But it won't require much effort for the crowd to find me boring.

Your wit doesn't stop there. You say that I don't try simply to take in the dim majority with my pretenses but heaven itself, that I make a display of having lovingly embraced Augustine and his works, but in fact cannot tear myself away from the poets and philosophers. But why should I try to tear myself from them, when I see Augustine himself so attached to them? If that were not so, he would never have based his *City of God*, not to mention his other books, so much on the poets and philosophers, and never have enriched their texture with so many tropes from the historians and orators. And no wonder! For, unlike your Jerome,[3] my Augustine never dreamed of being dragged before the eternal judge and hearing himself denounced as a Ciceronian, whereas when Jerome heard it, he gave his word never to touch books by pagan writers again. You know how punctiliously he kept away from them all, especially Cicero. But Augustine, free from dream prohibitions, felt no qualms about his close familiarity with them, and openly admitted that a great part of our Christian faith is found in Plato's work. He said that it was that book of Cicero titled *Hortensius* that worked a wonderful change in him, ridding him of misguided aspirations, freeing him from the futile disputes between different sects, and converting him to the pursuit of the one and only truth.[4] It was through being fired by that book, he says, that his emotional attitudes were transformed, the pleasures of the flesh

2 Livy says that Numa Pompilius invented the stories of his encounters with the nymph Egeria (*History of Rome* 1.19.5) to bolster his position as king of Rome, and that Scipio Africanus similarly invented a divine origin for his family (26.19.3).

3 Jerome was apparently a favorite author of Giacomo Colonna. In a famous letter (*Epistles* 22.30), Jerome tells how he dreamed that God charged him with being a Ciceronian, not a Christian, and that consequently he stopped reading pagan literature altogether.

4 Augustine, *Confessions* 3.4.7 and 7.9.13. The *Hortensius* is one of Cicero's lost works.

abandoned, and he began to rise above the world. What a wonderful man, one who deserved to have Cicero himself praising him in the forum and publicly thanking him for being one reader ready to show gratitude when so many did not! What magnificent humility, what humble excellence! He was not one to deck himself with other writers' feathers and then insult his masters, no, he was someone driving the imperiled vessel of Christianity past the rocks of heresy, aware in all modesty of his real greatness, and yet ready to acknowledge his real beginnings and early efforts, a great doctor of the Church not blushing at having learned from that man from Arpino with his quite different agenda.[5] But why should he have blushed? No guide is to be spurned who shows the way to salvation. How can Plato or Cicero be an obstacle to the pursuit of truth? It is not just that the school of Plato does not go against the true faith, it teaches it, preaches it, and the writings of Cicero are guides to the way toward it. Similar things might be said of other writers, but I am referring about something very well known and am reluctant to cite superfluous witnesses.

But I would not go so far as to deny that there is much in those authors to be avoided, since even in our Christian writers there are certain perils for the unwary. Augustine himself wrote a vigorous work in which he himself weeds out the patches of error springing up in the fertile fields he had cultivated so successfully in his studies.[6] What deductions are we to make? Simply this, that it is a rare book that is free from risk, unless the reader is illuminated by the light of divine truth, which teaches what to follow and what to reject. If that light is the guide, there is total safety, and what might harm becomes more recognizable than Syrtes, Charybdis,[7] and famous reefs of the deep. So finally to have done with this unfounded calumny, Augustine himself knows whether I have truly taken him to my heart or not, since he is in a place where no one wants to deceive or can be deceived. I think he looks down pityingly from there on my errors and uncertainties, especially if he recalls the inconstancies and aberrations of his own younger years, which the Almighty put back on the right course. Now He has taken him from the sandy shores of Africa, where prolonged indulgence in sinful pleasure was a mortal peril to his soul, and made him an everlasting citizen of the eternally verdant Jerusalem. It is from there that he loves and cares for me. Why should I have any doubts about this, when I hear him saying with unshakeable confidence in his *On the True Religion,* "Whichever of the angels loves God, I am certain also loves me"?[8] Given their contemplation of the God they shared together, he, though still a man, was not afraid to assure himself

[5] Cicero, who was born in Arpino, a small town southeast of Rome.

[6] The *Retractions.*

[7] The shoals of Syrtes (off North Africa) and the rocks of Scylla and Charybdis (in the straits of Messina) are canonical images of danger for classical writers.

[8] Augustine, *On the True Religion* 55.112.

he had the love of the angels, and so I, also a man, shall dare to hope for the human love of that sainted soul who is now enjoying the fruits of Paradise.

And your raillery goes on. You say that since I keep on turning over notions taken from the poets and philosophers, the words of Augustine must seem to me to be just dreamlike. You would have done better to say that, when I reread him, my whole life seems to me nothing but an insubstantial dream and a fleeting fancy. So at times it is as if that reading shakes me awake from a heavy sleep, but under the weight of my mortal nature, my eyelids close once more, and then I reawaken, and then I doze off again and again. My will fluctuates, my desires are at odds with each other and are tearing me apart with their discord. So the outer self battles with the inner,

> redoubling his blows now from the right side,
> now from the left, with neither pause nor respite.[9]

Unless the Eternal father calls a halt to the fight and snatches weary Dares from raging Entellus,[10] the outer self will win. Do I need to add anything further? I am still unsure about the outcome and live in fearful hope, often calling to the Conqueror of Death:

> Unvanquished one, pluck me from these evils . . .
> Give your hand to me in my misery
> and carry me with you over the waves,
> that at least in death I may rest in peace.[11]

But nothing is more flexible or adroit than jibes and jokes. Wherever you turn, they follow. So what about this other remark of yours? You say that the lovely name of Laura is something I invented in order to have someone to speak about and hence, through this female figure, to make hosts of others speak about me. In reality, you say, there is no Laura, only the poetic laurel to which my tireless studies indicate that I have long aspired.[12] As regards this breathing, living Laura, whose beauty I seem to be captured by, you claim that everything is artificial, my poems a fiction, my sighs a pretense. If only this were one thing you were right to joke about! If only it were a pretense and not an insane passion! But, believe me, no one pretends for a

[9] Virgil, *Aeneid* 5.457–58. The lines are taken from the description of the fight referred to in the next note.

[10] The Trojan Dares and the Sicilian Entellus fight a boxing match as part of the games described in *Aeneid* 5. Dares is saved from Entellus' murderous assault only by the direct intervention of Aeneas.

[11] Virgil, *Aeneid* 6.365 and 6.370–71. The soul of the dead Palinurus is here asking Aeneas to take his remains to Italy for proper burial.

[12] Petrarch always makes receiving the laurel crown in Rome in April 1341 (i.e., some four years after this letter was apparently written) one of the major events of his life.

long time without enormous effort, and to make that effort only in order to seem mad is the height of insanity. Then take into account that, when we are healthy, we might imitate the behavior of the sick, but we cannot simulate their pallor. You are very well acquainted with my pallor and my generally troubled state. So I am rather afraid that you are resorting to that Socratic playfulness that they call irony (and in this you are not a whit inferior to Socrates himself) to mock this disease of mine. But be patient. This ulcer will follow its course. Cicero's dictum "Time wounds and time cures"[13] will be true of me, and against this pretend-Laura, as you call her, perhaps I shall have some benefit also from my pretend-Augustine. With all my serious reading and reflection I expect to become a wise old man before I am old in years.

But what limit is there to your facetiousness? Where will you stop? Here you are saying that you too were subjected to my powers of invention and were almost taken in, no, were taken in, and waited quite a while for me in Rome, since I gave the impression of wanting enormously to come and see you. Then at last, just as the sharper spectators see through the displays of traveling quack doctors at some point, your eyes opened, you saw the depths of my trickery, and the whole pantomime was laid bare. Good heavens, what is this? Your slanders make me out to be a magician. I'm beginning to see myself as Zoroaster,[14] who invented magic, or else one of his followers. So be it. Let me be Dardanus, Damigeron, Apollo, or any famous practitioner of the art.[15] Don't you think it no mean piece of conjuring to make someone a conjuror just by words alone?

That really is enough joking. I should like you to reply seriously. Let's leave aside the burning desire to see your face again that I have had to live with for more than three years, thinking all the time, "Look, tomorrow he'll be here, and the day after you'll go to see him." Let's forget the all too many worries of mine that I would not be happy to share with any living being but you. And let's say nothing of the pleasure of seeing your distinguished father, your noble-hearted brothers, your virtuous sisters, and the faces of other longed-for friends.[16] But can you not guess how much it would mean to me to see the walls and hills of the Eternal City and, as Virgil puts it, "the Tuscan Tiber and the Roman palaces"?[17] It is unbelievable how much I covet seeing that city that I have never seen, with the image (though a destitute one)[18] that it offers of ancient Rome. I blame my own sluggishness, of course,

[13] An adaptation of Cicero's *Tusculan Disputations* 3.24.58.

[14] Zoroaster, the Persian sage, is often cited as the inventor of the arcane arts.

[15] Dardanus and Damigeron are ancient magicians. Apollo, among his many other functions, was the god of fortune-tellers.

[16] For Stefano and Giovanni Colonna, see Introduction, section 5.

[17] Virgil, *Georgics* 1.499.

[18] Petrarch may be alluding to the abandonment of Rome by the papacy, which moved to Avignon in 1309, rather than to the ruins of the ancient city.

though perhaps it's been more necessity than sluggishness that's kept me away. I imagine Seneca writing to Lucilius from the very villa of Scipio Africanus, thinking it no mean privilege to have seen the place where such a great man spent his exile and where he left the bones he denied to his homeland.[19] Seneca was a Spaniard; think what my feelings as an Italian will be, not at the villa in Liternum nor at Scipio's tomb, but in the city of Rome, where he was born and brought up, where he triumphed equally gloriously as a victor and as a man convicted by the courts. And he was not alone; there lived countless others whose fame will endure forever. It is a city, I declare, whose like was never seen before nor shall be again. It was called a city of kings even by one of its enemies; we read that he said of its people that "Great is the good fortune of the Roman people, great and terrible their name."[20] And its unprecedented greatness and its incomparable imperial rule both in the present and future were sung by divinely inspired poets. But I shall not go on praising Rome here. It is too great a subject for cursory mention. But I did want to touch on it so that you could grasp how I do not disparage seeing this queen of cities, of which I have read an infinite amount, and of which I have written about at length myself and hope to write more, unless an early death cuts short the work I have embarked on.[21]

Imagine that none of this matters to me. Think, however, how sweet it is for a Christian to see the city that is most like heaven, that is fretted with the bones and bodies of the martyrs and bathed in the precious blood of those witnesses to the truth, to see the image of our Savior held in universal awe, and His footsteps imprinted in hard stone to be adored forever by the peoples of the earth![22] It is the place where it is plainer than the light of day that the words of Isaiah have been fulfilled to the letter: "The sons also of those who oppressed you shall come bending low to you; and all who despised you shall bow down at your feet."[23] How sweet it will be to visit the tombs of the saints and to walk in the halls of the Apostles, with higher thoughts for company and my anxieties for the present abandoned on the shore of Marseilles! All that being so, why do you call me a sluggard, when you know that my departure depends on the decisions of another? I had given

19 Seneca, originally from Cordoba in Spain, wrote in his *Letters to Lucilius* (86.1) how thrilled he was to visit Liternum (in Campania), where Scipio Africanus, the victor in the wars against Hannibal, had been exiled after falling into disfavor in Rome, and where he died, refusing permission for his body to be taken back to Rome.

20 Livy (*History of Rome* 38.46.4) attributes these words to Cineas, the emissary of Pyrrhus to Rome after the battle of Heraclea (280 BCE).

21 At this stage Petrarch had written no sustained work about ancient Rome but was about to start on his series of biographies of Roman heroes, *On Famous Men*.

22 The image is the Veronica, which is believed to preserve the image of the face of Jesus. A stone supposedly imprinted with His footstep was also preserved in Rome. A copy survives in the church of *Domine Quo Vadis*.

23 Isa. 60:14.

myself to you, a small gift perhaps but a gift in perpetuity. You decided that I should follow the orders of another, if a brother such as yours who is of one mind with yourself can really be called another.[24] I have nothing on my conscience. If there is a fault, yourself or your brother are the ones you need to pardon.

In the last part of your letter, perhaps nervous that I might take your really very polished witticisms amiss—the playfulest tap from a lion will scare off lesser beasts—you spread a drop of sweet-smelling balm on the spot you think you have stung, pressing me most engagingly to give you my love, or rather to reciprocate the love that you feel for me. What am I to say? Pain and joy are both obstacles to lengthy discourse. But however silent I might be, you do know this: I have not become so hardened that I need to have such a due and noble affection urged upon me. In fact if only I needed to be spurred on rather than reined back in love! The years of my youth would certainly have passed in greater tranquillity, and a more tranquil manhood would be following.[25] I beg you this one thing at least: do not pretend that I have been pretending. My best wishes.

Avignon, December 21[26]

[24] Giovanni Colonna. See Introduction, sections 1 and 5.

[25] Here and elsewhere Petrarch is following a scheme derived from Isidore of Seville: infancy (zero to seven years), boyhood (to fourteen), youth (*adolescentia,* to twenty-eight), manhood (*iuventa,* to fifty), maturity (to seventy), and old age (after seventy).

[26] Petrarch always uses the ancient Roman system to date his letters. The original has "XII Kalends of January."

2

To Giacomo Colonna (*Verse Letters* 1.6)

You'd like to hear what I am doing, what
my life is like, the state of my affairs.
I'll not suppress the truth or tell you tales.
I speak as to myself. Let empty glory
stay far away: I want nothing, content
with what I have. That's the first thing, to have
a pact with golden poverty, a guest
who's neither squalid nor so difficult.
If she so wills, may Fortune keep for me
this bit of land, the small house and dear books,
and keep all else herself. Or, if she wishes,
she can take everything, I'll not protest.
Those things are hers. I don't want some estate
or rich inheritance that curbs high aspirations,
shackles the spirit, and sows seeds of evil.
Just let her not touch the wealth that comes
from poetry, or my free time, that misses
none of the worries of extravagance.
I envy nothing, hate no one, despise
none but myself, though I scorned everyone
till now and set myself above the stars.
But human lives do change. And now I've learned
just what I am, unless my dreams deceive me.
What good is it to slake my thirst a little
at the Muses' spring, if a greater thirst
burns and rages always around my heart?
Or to lie basking deep in Helicon[1]
mocking the insane labors of the tribe,
if my own labor brings no peace or profit?
What's a clear face, if in the mind there's turmoil?
I feel my tongue could never give to God
due praise for all his gifts, I must admit,
and much should make me happy, did not this

[1] "Helicon"—the Greek mountain sacred to Apollo and the Muses, here standing for poetry itself.

vile obsession gnaw my ill-fated heart.
I see your cheeks already bathed in tears
of pity, if I've learned to know you well.
But since you, like your father,[2] wished to know
the full details, I'll let love drive my pen,
and think of disobedience as a crime.
I shall be frank. You may help with advice,
and voicing my distress gives me relief.
My soul was haunted by a marvelous woman,
known for her virtue and her noble birth.[3]
My poems sang of her and spread her fame.
She has come back, striking all sorts of terror
in me, and with no sign as yet of quitting.
It was not art, but just a simple beauty
and rare sweet form that first took hold of me.
I bore for ten years round my weary neck
a heavy chain, angered I should submit
for so long to this woman's yoke. Sapped by
concealed disease, I was transformed,
with flames she gently lit eating my bones.
I longed to die, and barely had the strength
to move my desiccated limbs. But then
a love for freedom seized this wretched lover
and started a rebellion in his heart.
I roused myself and struggled with the yoke.
But it is hard to drive a mistress out
after ten years and try a mighty foe
with shattered troops. Yet I attack and God
himself assists, helping untie the rope
around my neck and from that war emerge
the victor, while she, wounded, sends her forces
after her fleeing slave, and, though in pain,
attacks. Now she arrays sweet flashing eyes
equipped with covert fires and tender arrows.
How many times she felled me in my doubts
about my way! Again what could I do?
How counter her? She had still worse chains waiting.
I flee, and wander off round the whole world.
I risk Tuscan and Adriatic storms,
ready to trust this self torn from the yoke
to an unsteady boat. Tortured, hating life,

[2] Stefano Colonna, head of the family.

[3] The chronology and evolution of Petrarch's love for Laura that he sketches out here does not completely fit with the story that emerges from the *Canzoniere*.

how could I suffer worse by hastening death?
I travel west, and Pyrenean peaks
see me concealed in sunny greenery.[4]
And Ocean sees me, where the tired sun bathes
his steaming chariot in the western waves,
and, looking the mountain frozen by
Medusa's gaze, throws from the peaks long shadows
that hide the Moors beneath the hurrying night.[5]
And then I go alone toward the Pole,
to Boreas[6] and harsh languages, to regions
where the uncertain land is worn away
by shifting tides of murky British seas,
where icy ground rejects the friendly plough,
keeping Bacchus and Ceres from the hills,
and barely hosting barren tamarisks.[7]
What else was left but to pursue the sun's
burnt track into the snake lands and vast deserts,
to see the Ethiopians on the far equator
baring black backs when Leo blazes most,[8]
or seek the fold of the dark world in which
nature has held for centuries the secret
of the Nile's source?
Thus, far away, the waves
of pain and fear and rage slowly subsided.
My moist eyes soon could close in tranquil slumbers,
and now and then a smile gleamed on my face.
The image of the one I'd left now hovered
before me with less frequency and power.
But oh, what am I saying? Still, you force me.
I thought it safe to scorn the still fresh wounds
and stabs of insane passion, being deceived
by a light scarring over and the rare relief
from suffering. I struck camp to return

4 He refers to the summer of 1330, which he spent with Giacomo Colonna, Bishop of Lombez in southwest France, where he himself was granted a canonry a few years later.

5 These lines seem to refer to an otherwise undocumented visit by Petrarch to southern Spain, with views over to North Africa. Atlas was petrified by the gaze of Medusa and became the Moroccan mountain named after him.

6 "Boreas"—the north wind, standing for the North in general.

7 Petrarch visited northern France and the Flanders coast in 1333. He exaggerates, of course, the dearth of vineyards (Bacchus) and cornfields (Ceres). Compare the similar evocation of his travels in Poem 360 of the *Canzoniere*.

8 "Leo"—the constellation of Leo, associated with the hottest temperatures.

to certain death. Cursed fate pressed me to go,
and my own state of error drove me on.
I'd barely halted in my loved one's city[9]
before my vacuous heart felt the old burden,
and the disease came back in all its fury.
What shall I say? where start to tell the story
of my second misery? or find an art
of song that might express how often pain
drove me to pray for death, or take worse steps,[10]
how much I had to struggle once again
for freedom? I'll just say that, since at last
the final chains have fallen from my neck,
flight is the only weapon I have hopes for.
No sailor shudders at the rocks by night
as I do at her face, her words that fire my mind,
her golden hair and jeweled snow-white neck,
and shapely shoulders, and the eyes I'll love
even in death. Surely I must not now
anger my God a third time with vain vows
to hang my broken oar and soaking rags
at the holy door? Or that my wax image
will be placed kneeling in an ivory shrine?[11]
Brooding upon the troubles that beset me,
I spied a distant rock on a secluded shore,
which might give refuge to my wreck.[12] At once
I set sail. And now hidden in these hills,
I tearfully go over my past years.
But she pursues me still. Claiming her rights,
she stands before my waking eyes, and then,
threatening and scary, mocks my fitful sleep.
Often, astoundingly, through triple bolts,
deep in the night, she breaks into my room,
boldly demanding back her slave, while I
feel my limbs freeze and straightaway the blood
rush from my veins to guard the heart's redoubt.
And no doubt someone coming with a light
into the room would see my frightening pallor

[9] Avignon.

[10] I.e., he contemplated suicide.

[11] The first somewhat classical promise, metaphorically, is to hang up his oar and clothes outside a temple to indicate his gratitude for being saved from shipwreck. The second promise is more obviously Christian fashion; it is to have a small shrine made containing an image of himself giving a prayer of thanks to God.

[12] The "rock" is the house he acquired near the Fontaine de Vaucluse in 1336–1337.

and awful signs of terror in my soul.
I start awake in panic, drenched in tears,
and stagger out of bed. The pure white bride
of old Tithonus does not yet peep out
from the light-bringing heavens,[13] when secretly
I leave the dreadful confines of the house,
and seek woods and mountains, looking behind
and all around, lest she who spoiled my rest
should now come and waylay me as I walk.
It's barely credible, and would I could
break free from these delusions, but so often,
in trackless woods, when most I seemed alone,
the very bushes or the trunk of a lone oak
present the face I fear, or she's appeared
from a clear spring, or shone from under clouds
or in the empty air, or sprung alive
from solid stone, freezing me in my tracks.[14]
Love weaves these snares for me. The one hope left
is that from such great turmoil God almighty
might snatch my weary spirit free, and then
want me, whom he plucked from the enemy's jaws,[15]
to be safe in this hideaway at least.
    Enough of that. For you want more. So here
briefly are the main features of my life.
My dinner's light, flavored by hunger, work,
and abstinence that's lasted the whole day.
A peasant serves me, and for company
I've myself and my faithful dog. The place
has frightened off everyone, for the pleasures
that go with Cupid's darts stay well away,
preferring for the most part wealthy cities.
Here, back from exile, with me in secret,
live the Muses. Odd visitors come too,
drawn by the marvel of this famous spring.
Though I've lived in Vaucluse a year, I've had
visits from much-missed friends just once or twice.
Regard yields to the obstacles, though letters
come often, saying they speak just of me
during long winter nights before the fire,
and just of me in the cool shade in summer;

[13] Aurora, the ever-youthful dawn, married to the immortal but ever-aging Tithonus.

[14] Compare the similar apparitions in Poem 129 of the *Canzoniere*.

[15] "the enemy"—the devil.

I'm on their lips by day, again by night.
But meeting's disallowed. They're horrified
by thorn bushes and snow and what I eat;
the city teaches luxury too well.
Opting for the hard life, I'm left abandoned
by caring comrades and by faithful servants.
The few with love enough to come, console me
as if I were in jail, and rush away.
And country people wonder how I've dared
to scorn delights they think are best of all,
and do not know my joys, my other pleasures,
my secret friends who gather to me here
from every age and land, each an outstanding
writer, or genius, or warrior, or speaker.
They are not difficult, content to fill
one corner of my modest house, accepting
my bidding, ever helpful, never irked.
They go when told, and they return, when summoned.
I quiz some and then others, and in turn
they give copious replies in verse and prose.
Some reveal nature's secrets, others give
the best advice regarding life and death.
Some tell their ancestors' great deeds or else
their own, making the past live with their words.
Some drive out care with their lightheartedness,
their jokes bringing back smiles, while others teach
one to bear all, want nothing, know oneself.
They're masters in the arts of peace, of war,
of farming, legal pleading, navigation.
They lift you in adversity, deflate you
if fortune puffs you up, bid you remember
that things must end, days speed by, and life's fleeting.
For all these services the charge is small:
they ask an open door and lodging, since
Fortune's hostility has left them few
hostels in the world and few active friends.
Nervous when let in anywhere, they think
a hovel is a palace, as they wait
for the cold clouds to clear and summer
to bring the study of the Muses back.[16]
They don't need silken hangings covering
the stone and mortar, wafts of fancy food,

[16] I.e., the cultivation of poetry and all the forms of writing that we would call literature.

or din of servants in the echoing hall
loading the tables for impressive banquets.
A sober group, content with what they have,
sharing their riches with me, they console me
upon a bed of roses when I'm weary,
admit me to their table when in need,
and feed me sacred victuals and sweet nectar.
They're not just indoor friends, but eagerly
come with me through the glades and meadows
that are the haunts of Nymphs. Like me, they hate
the moaning populace and noisy cities.
We wander off and spend whole days alone,
pen in my right hand, paper in the left,
my heart filled with its various concerns.
And as we go, how many times we've fallen
unthinkingly into the lairs of beasts,
how often been distracted from grand thoughts
by a small bird and its untimely song.
Then I'm put out if someone comes along
the shady path, or softly greets me, when
my mind is elsewhere, bent on serious projects.
My pleasure is to drink the silence in
of the great wood, disturbed by any murmur,
unless a clear stream skips its sandy way,
or else my papers ruffle in the breeze,
which taps the poems to whisper easy music.
Often it's been my lengthening shadow that
has told the time and bid me turn for home.
And sometimes only night has forced me back:
then Hesperus or else Diana, rising
as Phoebus sank away, have shown the path
and signaled out for me the piercing thorns.[17]
That's how I am. That's how I live. If only
my major misery would fade, I'd be
a happy man, born under a glad star.

[17] Hesperus is the evening star, Diana the moon, and Phoebus the sun.

3

To Dionigi da Borgo San Sepolcro (*Familiares* 4.1)

The highest mountain in this region is rightly called Mount Ventoux, or the windy mountain. Today I climbed it, simply out of a desire to see a summit that is so famous. I had had the excursion in mind for many years. As you know, the destiny that shapes human affairs has meant that I have lived in this area since childhood, and the mountain, being visible far and wide from all around, has been almost always before my eyes. A compulsion finally to do what I had been daily thinking of doing overwhelmed me yesterday as I was reading over some Roman history in Livy and came across that passage in which King Philip of Macedon, the one who waged war with the Romans, climbs Mount Haemus in Thessaly, believing reports that from its summit two seas could be seen, the Adriatic and the Euxine.[1] I have been unable to ascertain whether that is so or not, since that mountain is remote and a lack of consensus between the relevant authorities leaves the issue in doubt. Not to go through them all, the geographer Pomponius Mela affirms the truth of the story without hesitation,[2] but Livy thinks it is false. For my part, if climbing Mount Haemus were as easily undertaken as climbing Mount Ventoux, I would not let the question remain open for long. However, to leave all that aside and come to our mountain here, I thought that a young private citizen could be excused for attempting something that an elderly monarch was not blamed for.

But when I turned my mind to possible companions, oddly enough, none of my friends seemed completely suitable. For even between people who are close, it is so rare for there to be a perfect harmony of purpose and feeling. One friend seemed sluggish, another overactive, one slow, another too quick, one gloomy, another overcheerful, one silly, another too cautious, and then the silences of this friend and the chirpiness of that were equally off-putting, as were weight and obesity in one and weakness and skinniness of another,

[1] Livy (*History of Rome*, 40.21–22) tells how Philip V of Macedon (238–179 BCE) climbed Mount Haemus (now Mount Balkan in Bulgaria) hoping to be able to see from the summit both the Aegean to the south and the Euxine (the Black Sea) to the east, partly to help him plan his campaigns against Rome. Livy thought that the expedition was futile and, as Petrarch says a few lines later, that Philip cannot possibly have seen so far.

[2] Pomponius Mela (1st c. CE), *Description of the World* 2.16.

not to mention the cold indifference and the fiery excitability of two others. However serious the flaws, they are bearable at home (charity suffers all and friendship refuses no burden), but they become more grievous on the move. So, being difficult to please but eager for honorable enjoyment, I carefully weighed up each of the possibilities from every angle, not wishing to damage friendships at all but quietly ruling out anyone whose character promised to spoil the proposed excursion. What do you think happened? I finally turned homeward for help and put the idea to my younger and only brother, whom you know well.[3] He could not have been happier and expressed his delight at being treated by me not just as a brother but also as a friend.

We set off on the day we agreed,[4] and toward evening reached Malaucène, a village at the base of the mountain on its north side. We stayed there one further day, and then today at last made the ascent with our two servants. It was not without problems, since the rocky mass of the mountain is very steep and almost unclimbable. But, as was well put by the poet, "unstinting labor conquers all."[5] Our progress was helped by the long hours of daylight and the mild air, as well as by our enthusiasm, physical strength, agility, and so on. Only the character of the terrain was against us.

In one of the dips in the mountainside we met with an elderly shepherd. He struggled hard to dissuade us from the climb, telling us that fifty years earlier, fired by the same youthful energy, he had climbed right to the top and had come back with nothing to show for it except remorse and weariness, his body and his clothes torn by rocks and briars. He had never heard of anyone else from thereabouts, before or after him, daring to make the attempt. But young people like ourselves lend little credence to admonitions, and his attempts to stop us only made us more eager. When the old man realized his efforts were in vain, he went ahead of us a little way among the crags and then pointed out the strenuous route we would face, with much more advice that he then kept on reiterating from behind when we took our leave. We left some clothing with him and some other things that might have impeded us, and set about the ascent just by ourselves, climbing vigorously.

But the usual thing happened; great exertion was quickly followed by tiredness, and we came to a halt at a bluff not very far away. Then we set off again, but more slowly. I took a way up with a more moderate gradient, while my brother followed a shorter route that led along the ridges directly to the higher reaches of the mountain. But I was softer and found myself veering downhill. When he called back to me and pointed to the straight path, I replied that I hoped to find an easier approach around the other side and didn't mind taking a longer route if it was less steep. I was really finding

[3] Gherardo was born probably in 1307 and had been a student with Petrarch in Bologna. See also Introduction, section 1.

[4] This seems to be at variance with the "yesterday" mentioned earlier.

[5] Virgil, *Georgics* 1.145–46.

excuses for my weakness, and so, with the others[6] already on the peaks, I wandered about down in the valleys without any better route up emerging, making my way longer and wearying myself with useless exertion.

In the end, flustered and irritated with myself over my complicated meanderings, I decided that I must make a direct ascent. I was in an anxious, tired state when I caught up with my brother, who was waiting for me, refreshed by a good rest. For a while we went along side by side. But we had barely left behind the crest where we had met up, when I went and forgot my earlier deviation, and lurched downward again. For a second time I wandered about hollows in the mountainside looking for an easier long way round and ended up in prolonged difficulties. I was keeping on postponing the bother of ascent, though human ingenuity cannot alter the nature of things, and it is impossible for something corporeal to make progress upward by going down. To put it briefly, my brother couldn't help laughing when to my indignation I had three or four misadventures of this sort in a short while.

Thoroughly discouraged, I sat down in one of the hollows and found my mind leaping rapidly from corporeal to incorporeal matters, addressing myself in something like these words: "Just think how what you have experienced so many times today climbing this mountain happens to you and many others trying to attain a happy life. But people find it hard to appreciate; while bodily movement is plain to see, movements of the spirit are invisible and hidden. The life we call happy is located on high, and narrow is the way, as they say, that leads to it.[7] Many high peaks obstruct our progress and we must step gloriously upward, climbing from one virtue to another. At the top is the final terminus, the conclusion to which our pilgrimage is directed. We all wish to reach it, but, as Ovid says, 'Wishing is too little; to win the prize, you must really desire it.'[8] Unless you are tricking yourself again as you often do, you have the desire, as well as the wish. What is holding you back then? Surely it can only be taking the easy path of lower earthly pleasures, which at first sight looks more straightforward. However, with so much straying, either your ascent to the summit and happiness will be all the more onerous on account of the ill-judged postponements, or else you will slump down devoid of energy in the valley of your own sinfulness. And if 'darkness and the shadow of death'[9] overtake you there—it is a horrifying thought—the consequence will be eternal night and perpetual torment."

It is incredible how much these reflections stirred me mentally and physically to get on with the remainder of the climb. I just wish I could complete the journey of the spirit that keeps me sighing day and night in the way I overcame all the difficulties and completed on foot today's physical journey.

[6] Presumably Gherardo and at least one of the two servants mentioned earlier.

[7] See Matt. 7:14.

[8] Ovid, *Letters from Pontus* 3.1.35.

[9] Compare Job 3:5 and 34:21–22.

I am not sure whether the leap achieved by the nimble immortal soul in the wavering blink of an eye without any spatial motion shouldn't be easier than working to the same end over time making necessary concessions to a body that must fade and die, and is weighed down by its bulky limbs.

The highest summit is called the "Filiolus" or "Little Son" by the rustics, why I do not know, unless it implies its opposite, as I guess sometimes is the case. For in reality it is more like the father of all the peaks nearby. On its very top is a small level area, and there at last we wearily rested. Since I have told you about how my anxieties progressed as I climbed, let me now tell you, father, about subsequent developments. I beg you, give one hour of your time to reading through an account of the events in one day in my life.

At first I was stirred, indeed almost dumbfounded, by the unusual quality of the air and the vast panorama opening before me. I looked back and saw the clouds below our feet. Athos and Olympus immediately became less incredible, when I perceived what I had heard and read about them occurring on a mountain that is much less well known. I turned my gaze toward Italy, where my thoughts are most often drawn. Though they were far away, I could see as well as if they were near at hand, the frozen, snowcapped Alps over which there once passed Rome's ferocious enemy, Hannibal, breaking the rocks down with vinegar, if reports are to be believed.[10] I sighed, I confess, as I looked toward the Italian skies that appeared before my imagination rather than my eyes and an inestimable longing overcame me to see you, my friend, and my country again. At the same time I reproached myself for such unmanly softness on both counts, even though I was not short of good excuses that I could have backed up with citations from the best authors.

Then I had another thought that shifted my attentions from place to time. "It is ten years today," I said to myself, "since you abandoned your early studies and left Bologna. O immortal God and his unchangeable wisdom, how many changes and what great ones have there been in you in the meantime! And that is to omit an endless number of things. For I have not yet reached the harbor in which I can safely recall the storms that are over. Perhaps the time will come when I can recount them all in the order in which they occurred, prefacing them with words from your saint, Augustine: 'I wish to recall the foulness of my past and the fleshly corruptions of my soul, not out of love for them, but in order to love you, my God.'[11] In me there is still much that is murky and dangerous. I do not love what I once loved. But I'm lying; I love, but more sparingly. That too is a lie: I love, but am ashamed and saddened to do so.

"And at last I have spoken the truth. That is really how it is. I love, but the object is something I should love not to love, that I want to hate. I love, but against my will, under constraint, miserably, tearfully. I am experiencing

[10] Hannibal is reported by Livy (*History of Rome* 21.36–37) to have broken down rocks blocking his route by pouring boiling vinegar over them.

[11] Augustine, *Confessions* 2.1.1.

in my wretched self the truth encapsulated in that line of the renowned poet: 'I shall hate if I can; and if I cannot, love in spite of myself.'[12] It is not yet three years since that vile perversion of the will that did have total control of me and reigned alone and unchallenged in every chamber of my heart, found a contrary side of my will rebelling and resisting its power.[13] Since then my thoughts have been a battlefield on which the two sides have been joined in a wearying struggle for control over the divided man I am, and the struggle still goes on unresolved."

I brooded over the past ten years in this way, and then turned my attention to the future. I put it to myself, "Let us suppose that your fleeting existence is prolonged for another two decades, and that you manage to continue with the kind of progress toward virtue that has emerged from the struggle between the old side and the new side of your will, and have distanced you gradually over the last two years from your former obsession. If that happens, might you not be able to be ready to meet death at the age of forty and dismiss with a tranquil mind the decline into old age that will be all that is left of life? You can't be sure, but you can at least hope for that."

I kept turning over these reflections and others in the same vein in my mind, father, gladdened by my progress, bemoaning my faults, and grieving for the instability inherent in all human behavior. I seemed somehow to forget where I was and why I had come there, until, at last, these worries, which would have been more appropriately considered somewhere else, ceased to occupy me.

I looked around to see what I had come to see, startled to realize that it was almost time to leave since the sun was sinking and the mountain's shadow was lengthening. I turned and looked toward the west. The heights of the Pyrenees, which constitute the border between the French lands and Spain, are not visible from Mount Ventoux, not because of any obstacle that I know of, but solely because of the weakness of mortal sight. But the mountains of the province of Lyons were clearly visible on the right, and so too on the left were the gulf of Marseilles and the sea around Aigues Mortes, though both were several days' journey away, while nearby we could see the Rhône just below us.

Gazing this way and that, intent at one moment on acquiring earthly knowledge, at another on raising my thoughts to higher things after the example of my body, I suddenly thought of looking into the book you gave to me out of the warmth of your heart containing the *Confessions* of Saint Augustine. I keep it with me as a memento both of the author and of the

[12] Ovid, *Amores* 3.11.35.

[13] Presumably Petrarch is here talking of his passion for Laura. It is impossible to integrate this claim of being partly cured with the sequence of events (such as it is) proposed in the *Canzoniere,* though one or two poems do say similar things (e.g., Poem 89 of the *Canzoniere,* which is not included in this collection, declares that the difficult process of becoming free from the delusions of love is underway).

giver, and am constantly consulting it. It's a small volume that barely fills your hand, but the sweetness it contains is infinite. I opened it, ready to read whatever presented itself, which I knew of course could only be something expressing pious thought and religious devotion. It was the tenth book that offered itself. My brother stood there eagerly waiting to hear words of Augustine issue from my lips. As God and he are my witnesses, the passage I first set eyes on was this: "And men go to admire mountain heights, and great waves of the sea, and wide courses of rivers, and the vast circle of the ocean and the revolving stars, and have no thought for themselves."[14] I was astounded, I admit. My brother was agog to hear more, but I asked him not to disturb me and closed the book, angry with myself for attending to earthly wonders when I should have learned even from pagan philosophers that it is only the spirit that is wonderful with a greatness that makes everything else pale into insignificance.

Then, happy to have seen enough of the mountain, I turned my inner eye upon myself, and from that moment no one heard a word from me until we reached the plain. Those words had given me a great deal to mull over in silence. I couldn't believe that they had come up by chance. What I had read I thought had been addressed to me and to no one else. I recalled what Augustine himself had once wondered about himself; he relates that the first passage that caught his eye during a reading of the book of the Apostle was this: "not in reveling and drunkenness, not in debauchery and licentiousness, not in quarreling and jealousy. But put on the Lord Jesus Christ, and make no provision for the flesh to gratify its desires."[15] The same thing had already happened to Antony when he heard the words of the Gospel, where it is written: "If you would be perfect, go, sell what you possess and give to the poor, and you will have treasure in heaven, and come, follow me."[16] "Just as if this part of the scripture were being read specially for him," writes his biographer Athanasius, "he pressed himself into the service of the Lord."[17] Just as Antony looked no further on hearing these words, just as Augustine looked no further after reading what he read, so I too limited myself to the few words I have quoted. I silently reflected how poor are the moral resources of mortal men, who neglect the noblest part of themselves, drifting from one distraction to another, lost in vapid entertainments for the eye, and looking in the outer world for what could have been found within. At the same time I marveled at the noble origins of the human soul, the problem being that it falls away of its own accord from its original state and goes

14 Augustine, *Confessions* 10.8.15.

15 Augustine's account of reading these words from Paul's Epistle to the Romans (Rom. 13:13) is in *Confessions* 8.12.29.

16 Petrarch adapts the words of Jesus in Matt. 19:21.

17 Athanasius, *Life of Antony* 2. Saint Antony (251–356) became a hermit in the Egyptian desert at the age of twenty. The story referred to, with the quotation from Matthew, is in the passage from Augustine mentioned in note 14.

astray, making a disgrace for itself out of what God gave it as a means to honor.[18]

How often that day, you may suppose, I turned around as we came down and looked back at the mountain peak! It seemed barely a foot or two high in comparison with the heights the human mind can reach if it is not mired in the filth of earth. And another thought also occupied my mind every step of the way: If I had not shrunk from so much sweat and labor to raise my body only a little nearer heaven, what cross, what jail, what torture should frighten the soul from coming closer to God and stamping down the swelling heights of pride and the mortality that is our fate? To which was added this: how many find themselves being diverted from this path either by fear of the duress involved or out of desire for softer options? Yes, it is a really happy man, if one exists anywhere, that I judge the poet was speaking of, when he wrote:

> Happy is he who was able to learn
> things' causes, and trod underfoot all fears,
> unyielding fate and greedy Acheron's roar.[19]

Oh, with what energy we have to work if we are to feel our feet trampling, not higher ground but the appetites stemming from earthly instincts.

In this state of inner turmoil, unaware of the rocky path we were on, I returned late at night to the rustic lodging I had left before dawn, the full moon having kept us welcome company during our descent. While the servants are occupied preparing our dinner, I have crept off into a secluded part of the building to dash off this hasty letter to you. If I postponed writing, there was a risk it would lose its urgency when I moved on somewhere else, perhaps in a different emotional state. Observe, my much loved father, how I wish to keep nothing hidden from your eyes and carefully set before you not just the general picture of my life but all the thoughts that pass through my mind. I beg you pray that they eventually stop wandering and vacillating and find rest at last, that after being futilely tossed this way and that they change course and steer toward the one goal that is good, true, sure, and fixed.

My best wishes to you.
April 26, Malaucène[20]

[18] Presumably, freedom of the will.

[19] Virgil, *Georgics* 2.490–92.

[20] Petrarch's original has "VI Kalends of May," in accordance with his habit of using the ancient Roman system of dating.

4

To Giovanni Boccaccio (*Seniles* 5.2)

"I have something to say to you,"[1] if I, a sinner, may use the words of our Savior. But what do you expect that "something" to be? And do you think it will be anything different from what I usually say? Prepare yourself to be patient and to hear about a disagreement between us. While I feel nothing is more in accord with me than your spirit, it often happens, remarkable to say, that I find your behavior and your decisions more at variance with me than anything else I can think of. I often ask myself how that comes about in your case, and also in the case of several other friends with whom I have the same experience. The only reason I can find for it is that Mother Nature made us alike, but that habit, which they call a second nature, made us unlike. If only we had had the chance to live close together, then surely this second nature would have made us share a single mind and heart, though divided, as it were, between two bodies.

Perhaps you think that I'm going to speak about something of great moment. That is not so at all. And could something that its own maker rates as trivial be anything but insignificant? Everyone takes a special pleasure in things they have made, so much so that barely anyone makes a fair assessment of their own compositions. Almost everyone is tricked by self-love and love of their possessions. You are unique among thousands in being led to make a false evaluation of a work of your own by hatred or contempt, not by love, unless I'm deceiving myself on this point by attributing to humility what is actually a result of pride.

And now let me tell you plainly what I'm driving at. You are certainly well acquainted with the kind of popular performers who make a living from other people's compositions, something which has become distressingly widespread around here. They are men of no great talent, but with very good memories, great application, and even greater temerity. They frequent the halls of kings and other powerful figures, with nothing they themselves have created to display but decked out with the verse of others. They put immense verve into delivering the finest compositions, specially vernacular ones, that they have managed to extract from one writer or another, hoping thereby to gain favor with the nobility, and hence money, clothes, and other gifts. They travel around, obtaining these tools of their trade from each other by begging or bartering, or else they extract them from the original

[1] Luke 7:40.

begetters, taking advantage, when they can, of the greed or need of the seller. Juvenal was no stranger to the latter situation when he wrote of the poet who "starves, unless he sells his virgin Agave to Paris."[2]

How many times do you think that I—like others, I believe—have had to suffer their annoying wheedling and pestering, even though nowadays it happens less frequently, either out of respect for my age and the new direction my studies have taken,[3] or because of my rejections? I often try to stop them getting into the habit of molesting me, turning them down sharply and not yielding to any pressure. But sometimes, especially when I know that the petitioner is a modest person and in need, I am driven by a kind of Christian concern to see what I can do to help him out with some product of my mind. After all the beneficiary gets a long-term gain, whereas for me the trouble only lasts a moment or two. There have been some who overcame me with their entreaties, got what they wanted and went off in their rags with not a thing to call their own, and then not long after came back dressed in silk, laden with money and possessions and thanked me for a gesture that helped them cast off the crushing burden of poverty. Sometimes I have been so moved that I have decided that it is a form of charity, and resolved to refuse none of these people, until the wearisomeness of it all has overwhelmed me again, and I have changed my mind.

But when I asked some of them why they always pressed me for these things and not others, and mentioned your name particularly, they replied that they had often done as I suggested, but to no effect. When I expressed my amazement that you, who are so generous with other things, should be so mean with the words you have written, they went on to say that you had made a complete bonfire of all the vernacular poems of yours that you still had. That did not diminish my amazement but rather added to it. When I asked them why you had done this, they all said they did not know and fell silent, except for one man, who said that he thought—I am not sure he didn't hear it from someone else—that all these poems had passed out of your hands when you were still in your twenties or thirties, or even earlier, and that you had intended to revise them with the stalwart creative maturity that comes with the grey hairs you have now. Both he and I thought that showed too much confidence that this all too uncertain life would be prolonged for quite some time, particularly since you have reached a time of life when caution is in order.[4] But I was even more amazed at this way of proceeding, whereby you burned what you wished to revise, so that there was actually nothing there to work on!

[2] Juvenal (*Satires* 7.87–88) writes of Statius that, in spite of his success as a poet, he will have to sell his unpublished *Agave* to the outrageously powerful actor Paris if he wants to avoid starvation.

[3] Petrarch often claimed that as he got older he had directed his studies away from poetry toward moral philosophy.

[4] Boccaccio was in his early fifties when this letter was composed.

The astonishment stayed with me for a long time. Then I finally came to this city,[5] where I met our mutual friend Donato[6] again. No one is as attached or as devoted to you as he is, and he and I frequently meet informally together. Just recently, in the course of one of our ordinary conversations, we happened to light on this topic, and I was told the facts, which I already knew, and also the cause, which I didn't know. He says that your one pleasure as a young man was vernacular writing, and that you gave most of your time and effort to it, until, in the course of your researches and readings, you landed on my own youthful vernacular productions. And then your own impulse to that sort of writing froze completely. Nor could you be satisfied simply by abstention. Your loathing of the poems you had released made you burn them all, not with any view to making different versions but with the aim of destroying them utterly. You deprived yourself and future generations of the fruits of your labors in this field for no other reason than that you judged them inferior to my own. It was an unworthy hatred and an undeserved bonfire.

I am still undecided, however, whether your action betokened self-deprecating humility or that pride that sets itself above others. You who can see into your own mind must judge what is the truth. I drift from one conjecture to another, as if, as usual, speaking to myself were like speaking to you. I applaud the fact that you should rank yourself below those to whom you are in reality superior. It is an error that I myself much prefer to that of the man who is actually inferior but thinks the opposite. I take to heart a passage about Lucan—that Cordoban writer with the sort of intensity in his genius and character that can lead both to great heights and to disaster—who saw that he was achieving highly positive results when still a rather inexperienced young man. Reflecting on his age and the progress of the works he had begun, he felt elated by his success and dared to compare himself with Virgil. At a recitation of part of his *Civil War* (the book that his early death prevented him from completing), he said in his introduction, "So how far have I to go to match the 'Gnat'?"[7] I don't know if this insolent outburst provoked any sort of response from one or other of his friends who were there, but such self-glorification filled me with indignation as soon as I read it for the first time. "My good fellow," I silently replied, "maybe nothing separates you from the 'Gnat,' but an immensity separates you from the *Aeneid!*" Why then should I not give more value to your humility in placing me before yourself in your judgment than to Lucan's empty boast of surpassing or equaling Virgil?

[5] Venice, where Petrarch lived from 1362 to 1368.

[6] Donato degli Albanzani (1328–1411) was a teacher of grammar and rhetoric, who shared Petrarch's and Boccaccio's enthusiasm for ancient literature and thought.

[7] Petrarch twists a story in the ancient biography of the poet Lucan (probably written by Suetonius), which has Lucan admitting that he cannot even equal what Virgil achieves in a playful early poem such as his "Culex" ("Gnat").

But there is something else here that I want to probe, something so deeply buried that it cannot be easily brought to light and put into words. However, I shall do my best. I do fear that this signal humility of yours may be really pride. Many people will find it strange, perhaps startling, to use the adjective "proud" of humility. If that formulation grates on the ears, I can put it differently: I am afraid that this great humility contains an admixture of pride. At dinners or meetings I have seen someone who is not given a place of sufficient honor rise to his feet and go looking for the lowest seat under a show of humility, though it is actually pride that motivates him. I have seen others leave, though in this case the pride is hardly concealed. When these things happen, the person who has not been allotted the first place, which can only fall to one person and no more, behaves as if he either deserves no place at all or only the lowest one, although the ranks of glory are graded, as are those of merit. In your case, not to claim the first place for yourself is humility, considering that there are some who have neither your creative intelligence nor your command of language, and who have the nerve to hope and aspire to the first place, in a way that often both amuses and exasperates us, given they also often have popular support. Let us hope that they do not damage the law courts any more than they do Parnassus![8]

However, consider whether for you not to be able to accept second or third place is not a mark of pride. I may find myself standing in front of you, when I would much rather be your equal, and that prime master of our vernacular eloquence[9] may also precede you. But is that so terrible for you to bear? Both of us are your fellow citizens, and put together we make a very tiny number. Think whether your attitude means being more proud than does pursuing absolute primacy. For to want to reach the furthest heights suggests greatness of spirit, but to be disgruntled by only coming close betrays a propensity to pride. I gather that the old fellow from Ravenna,[10] who is no mean judge of such things, is given always to assigning the third place to you whenever the topic comes up. If you have no regard for him, and if you find me an obstacle between you and the holder of first place, I really will not stand in your way; I willingly withdraw and yield the second place to you. If you turn that down, I'm not sure your behavior will be tolerable; if only the first shine with glory, then you are casting innumerable others into obscurity and allowing only a very few individuals to have the privilege of brightness. Often the second place is both safer and more profitable. If you are second, there is someone else who meets the first brunt of envy, who

[8] Petrarch is being ironic. The ambitious pen-pushers he has in mind are lawyers or notaries by profession. They can do no damage to true poetry (symbolized by Mount Parnassus). He hopes they won't similarly damage the law courts, but his rhetoric implies that they will.

[9] Dante.

[10] Perhaps the minor poet Menghino Mezzani (ca. 1295–1375/6), who had been a friend of Dante.

risks his own reputation by marking out a path for you, whose tracks you can study to see what to avoid and what to follow, who will provoke and energize you, whom you work to equal and desire to surpass, doing your utmost not to have him always there in front of you. For a creative mind of any nobility these are all incentives, and often lead to marvelous successes. The man who can put up with second place can certainly come quickly to deserve the first, whereas the man who finds it unbearable will begin not to merit even the place that he rejects. Certainly, if you think back, you will barely find any leader, philosopher, or poet of the first rank whose ambitions have not been goaded on in this way.

The first place, on the other hand, almost always leads to conceit in oneself, envy from others, and, in many cases, slothful complacency. Jealousy stimulates both the lover and the serious writer; without a rival love grows dull, without someone to compete with, so too does natural talent. A poor man who works hard is better than a rich layabout; it is a finer thing to show vigilant application and keep pressing on upward than to wallow in shameful torpor on the heights; and it is better and surer to strive actively forward than to put one's trust in inert celebrity.

So there you have good reasons, as I see it, for not turning down the chance of second place when it is offered. And if it were third place, or fourth? Would that bother you? Perhaps you have lost sight of what Annaeus Seneca said in response to Lucilius' preference for Fabianus Papirius.[11] Seneca put Cicero first instead and added, "It does not immediately follow that what is less than the greatest is trivial." He then cited Asinius Pollio, saying, "It is a great thing to come after these two." Lastly he added Livy, "And look," he said, "how many that man precedes who is beaten only by three others, and what is more by the three most eloquent orators of all." So you, my friend, be careful that something very similar is not said of you, though understand that, whatever place you yourself are assigned, anyone you see put before you, in my judgment, will certainly not be me.

Be sparing then with the flames and have pity on your poems. If you or others are convinced in your heart of hearts that, whether I like it or not, I should be ranked above you in this regard, is that something you should complain of, as if being second to me would bring discredit on yourself? You must accept that if that is how you feel, you have long been deceiving me and display neither the modesty of spirit nor the love for me for which I hoped. Those who truly love spontaneously put the people they love first, wanting to be surpassed by them and taking great pleasure when and if it happens. No dutiful father will deny that it is so, since nothing will give him greater pleasure than to be surpassed by his son. Leaving aside the question of sons, I hoped, and still do hope, that I could be no less dear to you than

[11] Seneca (*Letters to Lucilius* 100.7–9) argues that Lucilius is mistaken to put the obscure Fabianus Papirius before Cicero, or even before Asinius Pollio and Livy, but is ready to grant him fourth place.

you are yourself, and that you would hold my name dearer than your own. I recall that you once protested as much in a moment of friendly, unthreatening indignation. If you had really meant it, you should have been happy to see me leading you and not abandoned the race, but have pressed on with greater vigor to make sure that none of the other runners could break in between us and snatch your place from you. A friend who sits down with another friend, or walks at his side, does not ask how important a position he can have, but how close to him he can be. Nothing is sweeter than a deeply desired closeness, and between friends there is great love, but almost no question of priority; the first are last and the last first since all are but one together.

Thus far I've been putting the case against you. Now comes the defense of your action. One reason, revealed by your own confession, was conveyed to me by the mouth of our aforementioned friend.[12] I shall however strive to uncover a different cause, and one that shows a certain generosity of spirit. For the same action may be laudable or detestable, depending on the intentions of the perpetrator. Let me explain what I have in mind; when you destroyed your poems, you were not driven by overbearing pride—nothing is farther from your gentle nature—nor by envy of anyone else, nor by impatience with your lot. Otherwise you would have been making a criminal assault both on them and on yourself. It was a sense of splendidly high-minded outrage that made you decide to snatch the possibility of passing judgment on your genius from the times we live in, since these are futile, self-important, totally ignorant times, bent on corrupting everything and, what is more intolerable, totally cynical. Just as Virginius of old took his sword to his daughter,[13] so you burned your beautiful creations, the offspring of your mind and heart, and set them free from shameful abuse. Oh, what do you say? Have I somehow hit on the truth? I have teased out this conjecture, because I too, you know, from time to time, resolved to do the same thing with my vernacular compositions, few though they are. Perhaps I would have actually done so, if they had not already passed into the public domain and were quite beyond my own jurisdiction. Then at other times I was of the opposite mind, and thought of giving over all my time to literary activity in the vernacular, since both of the more elevated forms of Latin writing had been developed to such a degree by the geniuses of ancient writers,[14] that there was barely room for anything else to be added through my own

[12] Donato degli Albanzani (see note 6).

[13] Virginius killed his beautiful and innocent daughter Virginia rather than leave her in the hands of the decemvir Appius Claudius, who had abducted her. He thereby began a revolt that led to the restoration of Roman freedom (Livy, *History of Rome* 3.48).

[14] The two forms of writing ("styles," in the original) are prose and verse, the highest possibilities of which it was generally felt had been realized by Cicero and Virgil, respectively.

efforts or those of anyone else, whereas the vernacular was of recent formation and still fresh. Although in a primitive state, thanks to the frequent incursions of vandals and the rarity of the pioneer cultivators, it gave signs of being capable of great refinement or growth. What then, you ask? What with the attractions of hopes of this kind and the stimulus of youthful energy, I began a major work in the vernacular.[15] I laid the edifice's foundations and assembled the mortar, stone, and timber. But then, when I looked again at the present age (the very mother of pride and sloth), I became sharply aware of what force of genius there was in public performers, what grace in their delivery. You might say that they were not reciting the texts, so much as ripping them apart. I heard this happen once, then a second time, then again and again. As I thought about it more and more, I realized in the end that it was a waste of effort to build on a quagmire and quicksand, and that I and the fruits of my labor would be torn to pieces at the hands of a vulgar rabble. So, like someone hurrying along who runs into a snake in the middle of his path, I made a halt, thought again, and took another route, which I hope is both straighter and more lofty.[16] While those uncollected, short pieces that I composed in my youth in the vernacular should now, as I said, no longer be considered to belong to me but rather to that rabble, I shall take steps to ensure they cannot mangle my major works in the same way.[17]

Why, however, am I berating the untutored plebs, when there are more serious and more justifiable reasons for complaining about those who term themselves learned? As well as a host of absurdities, they add to ignorance the odious finishing touch of their extreme pride. Once they thought it a magnificent achievement to understand bits and pieces of great authors; today they try to shred their reputations. What an inglorious epoch you are, spurning your mother antiquity, the discoverer of all honorable arts, and daring to claim not just to be its equal, but to have overtaken it! I am not speaking here about those dregs of humanity, the vulgar herd, whose words and opinions deserve more to be laughed at than criticized. And I am not speaking either about the soldiers and generals who do not blush to opine that the art of war has been completed and perfected in their own time, when without a doubt it has withered away in their hands and totally collapsed. They go to war as if they were going to a wedding, dressed up, devoid of aggression, with wine and food and sex on their minds, treating flight as victory, and purposefully doing all they can not to strike their opponents but to find ways of surrendering, aiming not to frighten the enemy but to charm the common

[15] It is unclear what Petrarch is referring to, but it might be what became the *Triumphs* (see Introduction, section 3).

[16] The decision, that is, to compose his principal works in Latin.

[17] Petrarch may mean that he intends to safeguard his Latin writings by depositing edited manuscripts with friends or patrons, but it may be that he has manuscripts of the *Canzoniere* in mind, and that here for once he is acknowledging that he considers it a major work.

tarts they have in their train. They too have the excuse of ignorance and a complete lack of education.[18] And I say nothing about kings who behave as if kingship lay in gold and purple, in scepters and crowns, and think that equaling their great forebears in these is the same as equaling them in glory and virtue. Though set on their thrones only to rule (hence the term ruler or king),[19] they do not rule in reality but are themselves ruled, and what directs them is made plain by the facts; they are placed over their peoples, but are the subjects of their pleasures; they are kings of men, but slaves of sloth and sensuality. They too in a sense are excusable given their ignorance of antiquity, the dazzlement of good fortune in the present, and the vanity that always accompanies too much success.

But what, I ask, can excuse the educated who should not be ignorant of the ancients but who are enveloped in the same mental blindness? Let me tell you, my friend, that I say this with bitter anger. These days we see petty dialecticians emerge who are not only ignorant but out of their minds too.[20] They are like an array of black ants streaming out of their hiding holes in some rotten oak to devastate all the fields where wholesome learning grows. These people condemn Plato and Aristotle, and laugh at Socrates and Pythagoras. And, good God, what witless guides do they have for what they do! I do not wish to name those whom the facts themselves show to have made no valid name for themselves, though their enormous folly makes them well enough known. I do not want to bracket with the greatest those I have seen really keep company with midgets. Our educated writers leave the tried and trusted masters on one side, and glory in these figures and follow them. Perhaps they have learned something after death, but certainly in life they had no knowledge and no reputation of being knowledgeable. What shall I say of those others who pour scorn on Marcus Tullius Cicero, who is the shining sun of eloquence, who despise Varro and Seneca,[21] who recoil from the style of Livy and Sallust as if it were grating or coarse? These too rely on new and shameful guides. I was once present at an occasion when Virgil, the other sun of eloquence, was being run down. I was amazed and asked the crack-brained schoolman what he found in a man of such stature to deserve such denigration. He raised his eyes heavenward full of contempt, and—listen to what he replied—"He overdoes the conjunctions," he said. Go on then, Virgil, keep at it, really polish that poem that you brought down from heaven with the Muses' aid,[22] since it will fall into hands like these!

[18] Compare Poem 128 (lines 65–68) of the *Canzoniere*.

[19] The Latin plays on the connection between *rex* (king) and *regere* (to rule).

[20] Petrarch's primary targets are contemporary intellectuals working in the scholastic tradition of philosophy and logic and their 13th-century masters, though, as he goes on to say, he refuses to dignify any of the latter by naming them.

[21] Petrarch cites the major prose writers of ancient Rome, with Cicero, his favorite, at their head. The others are the polymath writer Varro, the philosopher and essayist Seneca, and the historians Livy and Sallust.

[22] The *Aeneid*.

And what shall I say about those other monstrous individuals, dressed in clerical garb, but profane in their attitudes and conduct, who call Ambrose, Augustine, and Jerome wordy rather than wise?[23] I don't know where these new theologians come from who are currently so critical of the doctors of the Church, will soon be equally critical of the Apostles and in the end will be rash enough to rail against Christ himself, unless He, who is the one really at issue, does not step forward and rein in these untamed animals. They have now got into the regular habit of giving a silent jerk of the head, or lashing out disrespectfully, whenever these holy and venerable names are mentioned. "Augustine," they say, "was full of ideas but knew little." And they have nothing more decent to say about the others.

One of them appeared in my library not long ago, not dressed as a cleric (but it is actually being Christian that is after all the highest form of religion), but still, I mean, one of those who practice philosophy in the modern manner,[24] thinking they have achieved nothing unless they can blather out something against Christ and Christ's divine teachings. When I brought to bear a passage in the sacred works of the Fathers, he foamed with rage, his ugly features made yet more ugly by his scorn and fury. "Keep for yourself those miserable doctors that you and the Church make so much of," he said. "I have someone to follow, and I know whom I have believed." "You have drawn on the words of the Apostle."[25] I said, "If only you would draw on his faith too!" "That Apostle of yours," he said, "scattered his words about like seed. And he was a madman." "You are going along well, philosopher," I said. "Your first point was made against him by other philosophers and the second by Festus, the governor of Syria.[26] And he was assuredly the sower of the most profitable word. That seed was cultivated by the saving ploughshare of his successors and watered by the holy blood of the martyrs. We can see what a harvest of faith it bore." He almost vomited and gave a laugh. "You," he said, "be a good Christian. I don't believe any of this lot. Paul and Augustine and all the rest you're preaching at me were windbags. If only you could stomach Averroës[27] so that you could see how much greater he is than your piffle-heads." I blazed up at this, I admit, and could barely keep my hands from his dirty, sacrilegious mouth. "This is going back to an old quarrel," I said, "between me and other heretics. But get out, and take your heresy with you and never return." So I seized him by the cloak and pushed him from my house in a more aggressive way than is my habit, though it fitted well enough with his character.

[23] Saints Ambrose (339–397), Augustine (354–430), and Jerome (ca. 341–420) were all major influences for the development of Christian thought.

[24] It was normal for philosophy to be taught and studied by clerics.

[25] The last phrase of Petrarch's opponent is from Paul's Second Epistle to Timothy (2 Tim. 1:12).

[26] See Acts 17:18 and 26:24.

[27] Averroës (Ibn Roschd), the 12th-century Arab thinker whose writings (in Latin translation) were influential in Christian Europe from the middle of the 13th century.

Thousands of incidents like this occur. It is not just the majesty of Christianity and the reverence due to Christ himself (whom angels flock to adore but miserable little men insult), which is powerless against them. Terror of punishment can do nothing, nor can the armed might of the inquisitors. The threat of prison and the stake cannot curb their unruly ignorance or their heretical presumption.

These are the times we have landed in, my friend, this is the age in which we live and are now growing old, these are the judges we find ourselves among. It is something I often complain and rage about. These people are void of knowledge and morality, but full of their false opinion of themselves. They are not satisfied with having lost the books of the ancients but have to go on competing against their geniuses and their ashes. They rejoice in their own ignorance, as if it were of no importance that they know nothing, giving free play to their bloated, blubbery minds, and imposing newfangled authors and bizarre fashions of thought on the uneducated populace. If you used fire to snatch your work from the hands of judges, or rather tyrants, like these, since there was no one else to stand up for you, then it was an action I cannot disapprove of, and I applaud your motives. I myself almost wish that I had done the same thing to all my writings when I had the chance, as I did do to many of them. There is no hope of more reasonable judges emerging, and these we have are becoming more and more out of control and more numerous every day. They are now not just filling the schools but packing the roads and squares of cities far and wide. I have reached the point of angrily reproaching myself for railing against the vengeance taken on us in recent years and weeping over a world drained of inhabitants.[28] There may have been worthy men, I admit, but no age, I think, has been more full of human vice. All in all, I believe, that if I had been magistrate and in this frame of mind, I would have let the daughter of Appius Caecus go free.[29]

And now goodbye. This, and no more, is what I wanted to say to you at the present time.

Venice, August 28[30]

[28] Petrarch has in mind the various plagues that had ravaged Europe, especially the Black Death of 1348.

[29] According to Aulus Gellius (*Attic Nights* 10.6), the daughter of the Roman censor Appius Caecus was severely fined for making arrogant and disparaging comments about a crowd that jostled her as she was returning from the public games.

[30] In the original, "Fifth Kalends of September," following Petrarch's practice of using the ancient Roman system of dating.

5

To Posterity

Perhaps you will have heard something about me, although it is uncertain whether my poor and obscure name will travel far through time and space. And then perhaps you will want to know what kind of man I was and what happened to the books I wrote, especially those whose reputation has reached you, or of which you have heard some vague report. On the first point, no doubt, there will be various opinions. For almost everyone is driven by their own whims, not the truth, and there is no moderation when it comes to praise or blame.

I was, however, one of your race, a mere mortal man, of neither particularly high nor particularly low origins, although from an ancient family, as Augustus Caesar puts it speaking of himself.[1] In character I was neither vicious nor immodest, except in so far as I was infected by bad behavior in others. Youth deceived me and manhood corrupted me, but age corrected me. Thus I learned from experience the truth of something that I had read much earlier, that is, that youth and pleasure are vanities. Or rather I was given the lesson by the Creator of all times and ages, who sometimes allows wretched mortals to swell up with baseless pride and to go astray solely in order that they may sooner or later become mindful of their sins and come to know themselves. As a young man, I was not especially strong physically but very agile. I do not boast of being exceptionally good-looking, but in my greener years I had a certain appeal. I had a healthy complexion that was neither too pale nor too dark, and quick eyes. My sight was very sharp for a long time, although it became unexpectedly much weaker in my sixties when I had to resort reluctantly to the aid of a lens. My body was always very sound, until the coming of old age beset me with the usual array of ills.

I was a stern despiser of wealth, not because I did not want riches, but because I hated the efforts and worries that are their inseparable companions. I had neither the means for splendid feasts, nor the bother that comes with them, but I lived more happily on a modest diet of plain dishes than all the successors of Apicius[2] with their exquisite repasts. I always found so-called banquets distasteful, considering them excuses for gluttony and inimical to modesty and decency. I thought it was profitless and wearisome to

[1] Suetonius, *The Caesars,* Augustus 2.

[2] Apicius (1st c. CE) was famous as a gourmet and chef. A later collection of Roman recipes is ascribed to him.

invite others for such a purpose and also to accept invitations myself. However, I found the company of my friends such a pleasure that I could think of nothing more satisfying than their visits and never willingly took food without company. I disliked luxury particularly, not merely because it is a bad thing in itself and contrary to humility of spirit, but because it creates difficulties and disturbances. In my youth I was troubled by love of the fiercest kind, although it was a single, honorable love, and I would have been troubled by it for longer if its already cooling fires had not been extinguished by a cruel but beneficent death.[3] I would like to be able to say that I was quite free from physical lust, but I would be lying. I can say with certainty, however, that even when the fervor of youth and my own temperament carried me away, in my heart I always deplored lust as something contemptible. Then, as my fortieth year approached, when I was still quite susceptible, and quite vigorous too, not only did I put aside the obscene act itself but also all memory of it; it was as if I had never looked upon a woman. I count this one of my prime sources of happiness, and thank God who freed me, still hale and flourishing, from a servitude I felt to be so vile and loathsome.

But, to turn to other things, I was aware of pride in others but not in myself. Though I was of slight importance, I always judged myself to be of less. My anger hurt me often enough, others never. I can boast fearlessly—for I know I speak the truth—that I was quickly incensed, but forgot offenses just as quickly, while remembering kindnesses done to me. I eagerly sought out honorable friendships and cherished them faithfully. A torment reserved for age, however, is to have to shed tears with increasing frequency for close friends who have died. I was fortunate, even enviably so, in my familiarity with princes and kings and in my friendships with men of noble rank. But in spite of deep attachments I kept away from many of them. So deeply rooted in me was my love of liberty that I strenuously rejected any who found the word itself unpalatable.[4] The greatest monarchs of my age[5] loved and honored me. I do not know why and guess it was up to them. But sometimes it was not a case of my looking for their company as much as they wanting mine. I was not incommoded by their eminence, but rather derived many advantages from it.

[3] The word Petrarch uses is *adolescentia,* which denotes the ages fourteen to twenty-seven. Laura died in 1348, that is, when he was thirty-four and well into *iuventa* (first manhood), which ran from twenty-eight to fifty. As often with Petrarch, the various dates and time indications he gives do not quite tally with each other. Presumably he wished here both to acknowledge his love for Laura and to relegate it to an earlier phase of his life.

[4] He is presumably defending himself against those who criticized him for accepting the patronage of the Visconti rulers of Milan.

[5] He is probably alluding particularly to Robert of Anjou, king of Naples, and the emperor Charles IV, king of Bohemia.

I had a balanced rather than a penetrating intelligence, one that was fitted for all forms of virtuous, healthy study, but was especially drawn to moral philosophy and poetry. In the course of time I left the latter alone and took great pleasure in the Holy Scriptures, finding a hidden sweetness in them that I had once despised, and treating poetic writing as purely ornamental. Among my many activities I devoted myself particularly to the study of antiquity, since I always disliked the age in which I lived. If love of those dear to me had not pulled me in a different direction, I would have preferred to have been born in any other age and to forget this one, striving always to penetrate other times at least in spirit. So I took pleasure in the historians. When I was disturbed by disagreement between them, I dealt with the problem by following the version of the facts that seemed most probable, or was put forward by the most authoritative writers. My formal speech, some people said, was clear and forceful, although to me it seemed weak and muddled. But really, in ordinary conversation with friends and acquaintances I never aimed at eloquence and am amazed that Augustus Caesar made such a point of it.[6] However, when the topic, the occasion, or the audience seemed to require something more, I did try to raise my tone. How effectively I do not know, and leave judgment to those who were present. For myself, so long as I lived righteously, I set little store by how I spoke. That glory is mere wind that seeks renown only through the glitter of words.

My parents were honorable. Originally from Florence, they were middle-ranking but, to tell the truth, verging on the impoverished. Since they had been driven from their home city, I was born in exile, in Arezzo in the year of our Lord 1304, around dawn on Monday, July 20.

Chance and choice have divided my lifetime so far as follows.[7] I spent not quite the whole of my first year in Arezzo where nature first thrust me into the light of day. My mother's exile having been revoked, the next six were spent at Incisa, about fourteen miles upriver from Florence, on a farm belonging to my father. My eighth year was spent in Pisa, and the ninth and subsequent years in Transalpine Gaul on the left bank of the Rhône in the city of Avignon, where the Roman pontiff has long kept the Church of Christ in disgraceful exile, although it seemed a few years ago that Urban V had restored it to its rightful home.[8] But plainly it all went conspicuously wrong, and, what I find even harder to bear, it did so during his lifetime. It was as if he regretted his good deed. If he had lived a little longer, he would certainly have learned what I thought of his leaving Rome. The pen was already in my hand when he suddenly abandoned both his bid for glory and his very life. What a wretch! What a happy death he could have died before

[6] He has in mind Suetonius, *The Caesars,* Augustus 87.

[7] For more information than Petrarch gives here about his life and career, see Introduction, section 1.

[8] The papal court moved to Avignon in 1309. Pope Urban V moved it back to Rome in 1367, only to return to Avignon in 1370, where he died that December.

the altar of St. Peter and in his proper residence! If his successors had stayed in the papal seat, he would have achieved something of real value. If they had left, his own virtues would have shone out all the more and their guilt would have been correspondingly more evident. But this complaint is taking too much space and is not appropriate here. So there, on the bank of the windswept river,[9] I spent a boyhood that was guided by my parents, and then an entire youth that was guided by frivolous pleasures.

Not that there were not lengthy absences. I lived a full four years of this time in Carpentras, a small town not far to the east of Avignon. In these two places I learned what little grammar, dialectic, and rhetoric I could learn at that age, or what can be learned in schools. You can guess how little that means, dearest reader.

I then went to study law at Montpellier, where I spent another four years. From there I went on to Bologna, where I stayed another three, studying the whole body of civil law.[10] I was a young man who would have gone far, in the opinion of many, if I had persisted. But I abandoned my legal studies completely as soon as the watchful eye of my father was removed. It was not that I rejected the authority of the law, which is indubitably great, and rich in that ancient Roman lore that I love, but human wickedness uses the law to perverted ends. I hated the thought of learning something that I did not want to use dishonestly and that I would find it hard to use honestly. If I had tried to do so, my uprightness would have been put down to naiveté. And so at the age of twenty-two I returned home, by which I mean my place of exile in Avignon, where I had lived since childhood. For habit has almost as much force as nature. I began to be known there and my company to be sought by men of importance. I now confess that I do not know why this happened and am amazed that it did, though at the time I was not at all surprised, thinking, as one does at that age, that I deserved any honors paid to me. I was particularly sought out by members of the famous and noble Colonna family, who frequented the papal court at the time, or, to be more accurate, gave it luster.[11] I was summoned by them to enter their service, and held in an esteem that I am not sure I deserve now, and which I certainly did not deserve then. Giacomo Colonna, a man of incomparable distinction, whose like I have never seen nor will see in the future, was then Bishop of Lombez. I was taken by him to Gascony and spent a summer in the foothills of the Pyrenees that was almost divine, thanks to the delightful company of the master of the house and of the friends we shared. I sigh whenever I think back to it. On my return I entered the service of his brother, Cardinal Giovanni Colonna, in which I remained for many years. But he was not so much

[9] The Rhône.

[10] Petrarch studied in Montpellier from 1316 to 1320 and effectively spent six years, not three, at Bologna (1320 to 1326).

[11] For Giacomo and Giovanni Colonna, see Introduction, sections 1 and 5.

a master as a father to me, or rather a very dear brother, and I felt as much at ease as if I were in my own house.

At that time I was full of the restless curiosity of youth, which set me off on travels through France and Germany. Though other reasons were found to justify my departure to my superiors, the real reason was my ardent desire to see as much as I could. My first expedition was to Paris, where I enjoyed separating what was true from what was invention in all the stories told about that city. When I returned I set out for Rome, which I had passionately wanted to see since I was a boy. There I paid my respects to Stefano Colonna, the princely head of his family and a man comparable to the best of the ancient Romans, and was welcomed by him as if there were no difference between me and his sons. The love and affection shown toward me by that outstanding man remained constant right to the end of his life, and is still alive within me, as it will be until I die.[12] Back once again in Avignon, I found the place intolerable. I have a natural aversion to all cities, and Avignon was particularly loathsome. I looked for a refuge as one looks for a port in a storm. I found a little valley, but a solitary and attractive one, called Vaucluse, the closed valley, about fifteen miles from Avignon. The source of the river Sorgue is there, and it is the finest spring in the world. Captivated by the charm of the place, I moved to it with my books, just after the end of my thirty-fourth year.[13]

It would take a long time to tell all that I did there over a period of many years. Suffice it to say that almost every one of my paltry works was completed or begun or conceived there—and they were so numerous that I am still laboring away at them even at the age I have reached now. My mind was like my body, with more agility than strength, and I found many projects that I formulated with ease difficult to carry through and abandoned them. The very appearance of the place suggested the idea of embarking on my woodland work, the *Bucolic Poem,*[14] and the two books of the *Life of Solitude,*[15] which I dedicated to Philippe de Cabassoles. He has always been a remarkable man, but at that time he was the modest Bishop of Cavaillon, not the great Cardinal Bishop of Sabina that he is now.[16] He is the only one of my old friends who is still alive, and has always loved me like a brother, rather than in the Episcopal way in which Ambrose loved Augustine.[17]

[12] Stefano Colonna died sometime between 1348 and 1350.

[13] The move to Vaucluse took place, therefore, in 1337, though he may have acquired the house the previous year.

[14] *Bucolicum carmen.*

[15] *De vita solitaria.*

[16] Philippe de Cabassoles had become a close friend to Petrarch soon after the poet first established himself in Vaucluse, which fell within the diocese of Cavaillon. He was about the same age as Petrarch. He was Cardinal Bishop of Sabina near Rome from 1370 until his death in 1372.

[17] See Augustine, *Confessions* 5.13.

It was while wandering in those mountains one Friday of Holy Week, that the idea came over me with great force of writing a poetic work in the epic manner about the first Scipio Africanus,[18] whose wonderful name had been dear to me since my early years. I took the title from the subject and called it the *Africa*. Either through its good fortune or my own, it won its way into many hearts before it was actually known. I began it with great vigor, but allowed myself to be distracted by other works and broke off.

I was staying in my valley when, by some amazing coincidence, I received two letters on one and the same day. One was from the Senate in the city of Rome and the other from the chancellery of the University of Paris. They contained competing invitations to me to come and be crowned poet laureate in Rome and Paris. Being young still, I reveled in the glory of it all, and judged myself as deserving of the honor as men of such stature judged me to be, giving more weight to others' assessments than to my real merits. For a short while I hesitated which invitation to accept. I wrote to Cardinal Giovanni Colonna asking his advice, and, since he was very nearby, I received a reply to the letter I sent the previous evening before nine o'clock the following morning. Taking his advice, I decided that the authority of the city of Rome had exclusive precedence. I still have the two letters, one seeking advice, the other agreeing to what he suggested.[19] So off I went. I judged my works very indulgently as younger writers do, but I shrank from trusting my own judgment, or even that of those who had invited me, though they certainly would not have invited me if they had not considered me worthy of the honor they had offered. I decided, therefore, to head first for Naples. I presented myself before King Robert,[20] a great philosopher and a great monarch, as illustrious in the realm of letters as in the rule of his country, and the one king of our time to be a friend both to learning and to manly virtue. I wanted him to examine me and pronounce his verdict on me. I am now amazed to think how positively he assessed me and how acceptable he found me, and I think that you, reader, will be just as amazed to learn what happened. It gave him remarkable pleasure to learn why I had come. He recognized my youthful trust in him and perhaps also that the honor I was asking from him could not but redound to his own glory, since I had selected him as the one adequate judge among mortal men. To waste no more words, we had countless exchanges on a variety of topics, and then I showed him my *Africa*, which filled him with such delight that he asked me, as if he were asking a great favor, to dedicate it to him. This I could not refuse, nor did I want to. Then he finally told me a day on which he would deal with the matter for which I had come. He kept me with him from noon to dusk. But

[18] The victor over Hannibal and Carthage in the First Punic War. The Good Friday on which Petrarch claimed to have the first inspiration for the *Africa* was that of 1338 or perhaps 1339.

[19] *Familiares* (*Letters on Familiar Matters*) 4.4 and 4.5.

[20] Robert of Anjou (1275–1343) was king of Naples from 1309. He patronized Giotto and Boccaccio as well as Petrarch.

our discussions ranged ever wider and the time seemed too short, and so he did the same thing on the next two days. After having probed the depths of my ignorance over this three-day period, at the end of the third day he pronounced me worthy of the laurel crown. He offered to crown me in Naples and pressed me repeatedly to agree, but my love for Rome did not yield to the insistence even of so great a king, however much it demanded my respect. And so, seeing that my resolve was inflexible, the king supplied me with letters for the Roman Senate and pronouncements for the Roman Senate, expressing his judgment on me in highly favorable terms.

The king's verdict accorded with what many others thought, including, first and foremost, myself. Today I think that he, I, and all those others who unanimously agreed with us were mistaken, and that the king was swayed more by his affection for me and by his wish to encourage a young man than by a concern for the truth. In the end I went to Rome, and, however unworthy I was, I relied on a verdict of such authority. Buoyed up by it, I received the laurel crown, to an ecstatic reception from those Romans who were able to be present at the ceremony, despite the fact that in reality I was still an unskilled rhetorician.[21] There are letters of mine in verse and prose on all this.[22] My laurels did not bring me wisdom but rather a great deal of envy from others. This too is a lengthier story than there is room for here.

I then left Rome and went to Parma. There I spent a short time with the Da Correggio brothers,[23] who were very generous and upright toward me but in conflict with each other, subjecting the city to a regime without parallel in its previous history, the like of which, I hope, it will never suffer again in this present age.[24] I was mindful of the honor I had received and concerned that it should not be seen as having been bestowed on an unworthy recipient. One day when I happened to be walking up a hill on the far side of the river Enza in territory belonging to the city of Reggio, I reached a wood called Selvapiana. I was struck by the beauty of the spot and, pen in hand, took up the interrupted *Africa*. The inspiration that seemed to have been lost was reawakened. That day I wrote a little and then something more on each of the days that followed. Finally I returned to Parma, found a quiet house off the main thoroughfares—which I later bought and still own—and with a fervor that still astounds me, brought the work to a conclusion in quite a short space of time.[25] I then left Parma and returned to my transalpine solitude.[26]

[21] Petrarch was crowned on April 8, 1341. He left Rome at the end of the month.

[22] *Familiares* (*Letters on Familiar Matters*) 4.7 and 4.8, and *Verse Letters* 2.10.

[23] The quarrelsome Da Correggio brothers took control of Parma days before Petrarch entered the city on May 23, 1341.

[24] That is, in the last age of the world then considered to be underway.

[25] In fact, the poem was never completed.

[26] There is now a gap Petrarch's account, no mention being made of events in his life from 1342 to 1347.

My reputation had long won me the favor of Jacopo da Carrara the Younger,[27] a man of real excellence, who I think, or rather am certain, had no equal among the lords of his time. For years I had been subjected to letters and communications from him, even when I was beyond the Alps and wherever I was in Italy, seeking to establish a friendship with me. Though I hoped for nothing from anyone privileged by fortune, I finally decided to go and see what a great man whom I did not know was so insistent about. So, somewhat tardily, after spending periods in Parma and Verona, and having been treated everywhere—thanks be to God—with much greater consideration than I deserved, I arrived in Padua. My reception by that man who has left such a luminous memory behind him, did not merely show human warmth, but resembled the reception blessed souls must be given in heaven. He was overjoyed and displayed unimaginable affection and concern, so much so that I cannot find adequate words to describe his behavior and will add nothing more. His many acts of kindness to me included (when he learned that I had been a member of the clergy since my youth) arranging for me to become a canon in Padua, so as to bind me more closely both to himself and to his city. All told, if he had lived longer, it would have meant the end of all my wanderings and journeyings. But, alas, there is nothing lasting for mortal men, and any sweetness that befalls has a bitter end. God granted him to me and his city and the world for less than two years, and then took him away. It is not my love for him that deceives me, but neither I nor his city nor the world were worthy of him. He was succeeded by his son,[28] an outstanding man of great practical wisdom, who followed his father in always holding me dear and honoring me. But I had lost one who was much closer to me, not least in years, and I returned to France.[29] I did not know how to stay still, and was driven less by the desire to see again places I had seen a thousand times than to attempt, as sick people do, to cure my ills by changing location.[30]

[27] Jacopo was ruler of Padua from 1345 until his assassination in 1350.

[28] Francesco da Carrara, expansionist ruler of Padua from 1355 until his death as a prisoner of the Visconti in 1392.

[29] Petrarch arrived back in Vaucluse in the summer of 1351. It was to be his last stay there. He moved definitively to Italy in 1353.

[30] The letter is incomplete and undated.

Index of Italian First Lines of Poems from the *Canzoniere*

Index of English First Lines of Poems from the *Canzoniere*